ASP.NET
Database Programming
Weekend Crash Course™

Jason Butler and Tony Caudill

Hungry Minds™

Cleveland, OH • Indianapolis, IN • New York, NY

ASP.NET Database Programming Weekend Crash Course™
Published by
Hungry Minds, Inc.
909 Third Avenue
New York, NY 10022
www.hungryminds.com

Library of Congress Catalog Card No.: 2001089343
ISBN: 0-7645-4830-1
Printed in the United States of America
10 9 8 7 6 5 4 3 2 1
1B/SZ/RR/QR/IN
Distributed in the United States by Hungry Minds, Inc.
Distributed by CDG Books Canada Inc. for Canada; by Transworld Publishers Limited in the United Kingdom; by IDG Norge Books for Norway; by IDG Sweden Books for Sweden; by IDG Books Australia Publishing Corporation Pty. Ltd. for Australia and New Zealand; by TransQuest Publishers Pte Ltd. for Singapore, Malaysia, Thailand, Indonesia, and Hong Kong; by Gotop Information Inc. for Taiwan; by ICG Muse, Inc. for Japan; by Intersoft for South Africa; by Eyrolles for France; by International Thomson Publishing for Germany, Austria, and Switzerland; by Distribuidora Cuspide for Argentina; by LR International for Brazil; by Galileo Libros for Chile; by Ediciones ZETA S.C.R. Ltda. for Peru; by WS Computer Publishing Corporation, Inc., for the Philippines; by Contemporanea de Ediciones for Venezuela; by Express Computer Distributors for the Caribbean and West Indies; by Micronesia Media Distributor, Inc. for Micronesia; by Chips Computadoras S.A. de C.V. for Mexico; by Editorial Norma de Panama S.A. for Panama; by American Bookshops for Finland.

For general information on Hungry Minds' products and services please contact our Customer Care department within the U.S. at 800-762-2974, outside the U.S. at 317-572-3993 or fax 317-572-4002.

For sales inquiries and reseller information, including discounts, premium and bulk quantity sales, and foreign-language translations, please contact our Customer Care department at 800-434-3422, fax 317-572-4002 or write to Hungry Minds, Inc., Attn: Customer Care Department, 10475 Crosspoint Boulevard, Indianapolis, IN 46256.

For information on licensing foreign or domestic rights, please contact our Sub-Rights Customer Care department at 212-884-5000.

For information on using Hungry Minds' products and services in the classroom or for ordering examination copies, please contact our Educational Sales department at 800-434-2086 or fax 317-572-4005.

For press review copies, author interviews, or other publicity information, please contact our Public Relations department at 317-572-3168 or fax 317-572-4168.

For authorization to photocopy items for corporate, personal, or educational use, please contact Copyright Clearance Center, 222 Rosewood Drive, Danvers, MA 01923, or fax 978-750-4470.

About the Authors

Jason Butler is a Principal Consultant with PricewaterhouseCoopers LLP. Jason has built numerous Microsoft-centric Web applications for Fortune 500 companies. When not writing code, he religiously works out at a gym near his home in northern Virginia. Jason is also a devoted Hootie & The Blowfish fan.

Tony Caudill is a Principal Consultant at PricewaterhouseCoopers LLP. Tony has written and deployed custom Microsoft Solutions for twenty Fortune 500 Companies to support the integration of SAP, Siebel, and other ERP/CRM applications. When not managing system implementation projects, he avidly pursues surfing in southern California at his favorite beaches and tackles skiing at Big Bear.

Dedications

I would like to dedicate this book to my family and friends who have provided me with tremendous support and happiness throughout my life. To my mother, Marian, for inspiring me to be that best person that I possibly can. To Donna, without whose support, encouragement, and patience this book would never have been completed. To my father, Al, for always providing much needed advice and support. And to my stepfather, Steve, for being who you didn't have to be. I would also like to send my prayers to all of the families impacted by the tragic events of September 11, 2001.

- Jason

I would like to dedicate this book to my family and friends, who have supported me and given me tremendous joy over the past year: Marie and Bradley Caudill. I also would like to offer my prayers for the families impacted by the tremendous tragedies of September 11 and my support for the policemen, firefighters, and communities of New York and Washington. And to the US military leadership, such as my father, Sy, and his wife Sue, who like so many soldiers before them will face a long, challenging, and difficult road to building a foundation for us all in our search for peace.

-Tony

Credits

Acquisitions Editor
Sharon Cox

Project Editor
Sharon Nash

Development Editor
Michael Koch

Technical Editors
Todd Meister
Peter MacIntyre

Copy Editor
Maarten Reilingh

Editorial Assistant
Cordelia Heaney

Editorial Manager
Mary Beth Wakefield

Senior Vice President, Technical Publishing
Richard Swadley

Vice President and Publisher
Joseph B. Wikert

Project Coordinator
Maridee Ennis

Graphics and Production Specialists
Sean Decker
Joyce Haughey
Gabriele McCann
Kristin McMullan
Jill Piscitelli
Betty Schulte
Erin Zeltner

Quality Control Technician
John Bitter
Susan Moritz
Angel Perez
Carl Pierce
Sossity R. Smith

Proofreading and Indexing
TECHBOOKS Production Services

Preface

ASP.NET Database Programming Weekend Crash Course™ introduces the reader to ASP.NET database programming in one weekend: 30 sessions of a half hour each, for 15 hours stretching from Friday afternoon to Sunday evening. At the end of each section of the book, you'll get a chance to test your knowledge before continuing. Good luck!

Who Should Read This Book

This book is for people who want to learn to write ASP.NET applications in order to access and manipulate data in a Web environment. This book assumes that you have a basic understanding of Web development, including experience with Visual Basic or Visual Basic Scripting in developing ASP-based applications. The book's focus is on ASP.NET and ADO.NET as a suite of components used in data-driven Web application development. It includes a CD-ROM with ASP.NET editor software and sample code mentioned in the text.

Organization and Presentation

We've organized the book into 30 sessions, each requiring approximately 30 minutes. We divide the sessions as follows:

- **Friday evening.** Sessions 1 through 4. Reading time: 2 hours.
- **Saturday morning.** Sessions 5 through 10. Reading time: 3 hours
- **Saturday afternoon.** Sessions 11 through 16. Reading time: 3 hours.
- **Saturday evening.** Sessions 17 through 20. Reading time: 2 hours.
- **Sunday morning.** Sessions 21 through 26. Reading time: 3 hours.
- **Sunday afternoon.** Sessions 27 through 30. Reading time: 2 hours.

At the end of each session, we present questions designed to check your progress. The text is sprinkled with icons designed to catch your attention.

**30 Min.
To Go**

The "minutes to go" icons mark your progress in the session.

The Tip icons offer suggestions on style and mention shortcuts that can save programming effort.

The Note icons highlight incidental or technical information that clarifies and expands upon the discussion.

The CD-ROM icon refers to material furnished on the book's CD. Use it to find electronic versions of programs and software elements mentioned in the text.

Contacting the Authors

We can't guarantee we will solve all of your ASP.NET database programming problems in this book, but we promise to take a look at your questions and see if we can help. If you get stuck, you can contact us at the following e-mail address:

    tony_and_jason@hotmail.com

Acknowledgments

Tony: First, I would like to acknowledge my wife, Marie, who has been extremely patient and has provided tremendous support throughout the course of this project. A lot of new life changes and accomplishments are hitting us this year, including our first child, Brad, and of course the publication of this book. I'd like to thank Jason Butler, my co-author, for making this opportunity available and being a solid source of support in its development.

Jason: I would like to dedicate this book to two people: my mother, who has always inspired me to be the best person I can, and Donna, without whose patience, support, and encouragement this book would never have been completed.

There are also a few people whom I would like to thank for their support throughout this project. First, I would like to thank the PwC-eArmyU team, especially Chrystyna, Chris, FJ, Mark, Volodya, PV, Julie, Travis, and Michael. They truly are some of the finest people with whom I have had the privilege to work. I would also like to thank my fathers, Steve and Al, for their unwavering support.

Last but not least, I would like to thank Tony Caudill, my co-author, for being a great friend and mentor.

Tony and Jason: We would both like to thank PricewaterhouseCoopers LLP and Hungry Minds for providing the financial and motivational support to accomplish this task while supporting an extensive consulting practice.

Health and Peace . . .

Contents at a Glance

Contents

Introduction

With the release of the .NET Framework, Microsoft is taking the most significant risk in its history. Microsoft has spent billions of dollars, representing over 80 percent of its R&D budget, on designing and constructing this fundamental shift in its development tools in order to build a framework for the future of application development. Microsoft has effectively realized its vision of Windows in every PC and a PC on every desktop. Its current problem is that the desktop represents only a portion of the new Internet universe. With the huge shift brought on by the Internet and its pervasiveness into everything from watches to cell phones to cars, Microsoft must now shift its view of the future from a PC-centric orientation to a service-centric orientation.

So what is the future? From Microsoft's point of view, the future is delivering software as a service. Instead of purchasing a shrink-wrapped installable solution, you will instead rent, borrow, or purchase application logic across a distributed network. Software will of course still be sold on store shelves. However, most, if not all of the business logic and power of these applications will reside across a set of distributed applications using open Internet-based standards such as XML and HTTP. This framework will open extensive new possibilities for you in the process of designing, constructing, delivering, licensing, and collecting fees for your software.

Why Microsoft .NET?

Why would you as a developer invest in learning and understanding this new foundation of products and services? Those of you who are practicing solution developers already probably have a code base of Windows- and Internet-based applications written in Visual Basic, ASP, C++, or a combination of all three. If you have to address Windows API calls from C++ and Visual Basic and then integrate those calls as a COM component called by an ASP page, you will be amazed at how the .NET Framework–based classes provide a common approach and object model to accessing Windows services and resources. You will be further impressed at how the choice of development languages is no longer dependent upon power, flexibility, or support of OOP best practices. Now all languages compile to a Microsoft Intermediate Language (MSIL) and execute against a Common Language Runtime (CLR).

To those familiar with Java, this will seem very interesting. Because there is an intermediate language, Microsoft needs only to provide support for the CLR on multiple platforms in order to provide full cross-platform portability. While at the time of this writing there were no major announcements in this area, it is anticipated that ports to Linux and other operating systems is a key way Microsoft will be able to recoup its investment. In fact, Microsoft has a migration kit, the Java User Migration Path or JUMP, which contains a set of tools that will enable Java developers to take advantage of the .NET platform. The stated goal of these tools is to provide a path for Visual J++ and other Java developers to preserve their existing Java language projects and migrate those projects to the .NET platform. Once you begin experimenting with C# you will clearly see how realistic it is for this type of approach to affect the Java community.

The Microsoft .NET Architecture

The Microsoft .NET Architecture is split into three essential areas:

- **The .NET platform,** which includes the .NET infrastructure and tools to build and operate a new generation of Web services and applications. The core of the .NET platform is the .NET Framework, which includes C#, VB .NET, ASP.NET, and ADO.NET.
- **.NET products and services,** which include Microsoft Windows, MSN.NET, personal subscription services, Microsoft Office .NET, Microsoft Visual Studio .NET, and Microsoft bCentral for .NET.
- **Third-party .NET services,** which are services created by a vast range of partners and developers who now have the opportunity to produce corporate and vertical services built on the .NET platform.

The .NET platform contains all of the building blocks for creating .NET products and services and integrating third-party .NET solutions. Microsoft is using components of the .NET platform to extend the platform itself and to build additional .NET products. For example, as a developer you will be very impressed or possibly amazed that the entire ASP.NET platform is actually built on C#, which is a new .NET language! Additionally, large portions of the Visual Studio .NET code base are built on a combination of C++, C#, and VB .NET.

One of the most common themes heard throughout the development community concerns the stability of the .NET products and services. Compared with prior shifts in technology, such as when Microsoft moved from a 16-bit architecture to a 32-bit architecture or from DOS to Windows, this round is much more bearable.

.NET servers and applications

Microsoft's .NET servers can be split into two primary categories: core services platforms and specialized services. The core services platforms form the underpinnings of a traditional Microsoft-centric application, including Windows 2000, SQL Server 2000, and Exchange 2000. These applications are .NET in that they robustly support XML plumbing at the core of their applications and provide the foundation for building distributed applications. The second category of servers provides specialized services. The BizTalk Server 2000, for instance, leverages a higher-level language called XLANG that enables you to define process flows, transaction flows, and contracts. XLANG also allows very deep integration across heterogeneous environments. These specialized servers are designed to accelerate the integration and aggregation of Web services.

Next-generation Web Services

Microsoft's core piece of the .NET solution is Web services. Web services are small, specific, reusable chunks of application logic that can be easily shared across the Internet using open standards such as XML and HTTP. Solution providers, application developers, and end users will be able to rent, lease, or purchase the use of these solutions as needed and integrate them to solve specific problems. Examples of Web services include calendars, notifications, currency conversions, and user authentication and identity services.

Microsoft's first entry into this space is the use of the Microsoft Passport User Identity Service, which provides a single authentication mechanism for any Web site or application. A user can register with the Passport service and then be seamlessly validated from any participant Passport site without the need for an additional login procedure. This service can be embedded for use as an authentication mechanism by any Web-connected application.

You can look at Web services in the same way you would look at outsourcing portions of a business. Why would you ever create a delivery infrastructure when you can use FedEx? Why process your own paychecks, when companies like ADP can handle all of the mechanics for you? Web services enable you to outsource the generic portions of application development that today are commonly developed over and over each time a new application is built. Some people have compared it to building with Legos. From a relatively generic set of components, in a very short period you can build a complex, robust product that is great fun to use!

We hope this brief introduction provides you a foundation for jumping into our book on ASP.NET and gives you a perspective on how it is but one small yet important component of the overall .NET solution.

ASP.NET
Database Programming
Weekend Crash Course™

☑ **Friday**

☐ Saturday

☐ Sunday

Part I — Friday Evening

PART

I

Friday Evening

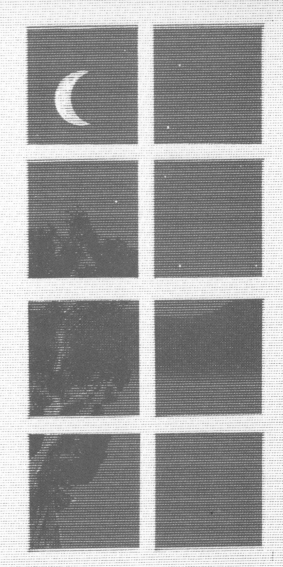

Introducing ASP.NET

Session Checklist

✔ Reviewing the history of ASP

✔ Learning about the .NET vision

✔ Understanding the differences between ASP and ASP.NET

30 Min. To Go

I n this session we will introduce the Microsoft .NET Framework and ASP.NET. We will address the evolution of Microsoft's Active Server Platform and discuss how .NET improves upon Microsoft current Active Server offerings, including Active Server Pages. First, however, let's examine how the Internet works . . .

Internet Standards

Before, we dive into the evolution of ASP, we should review some basic Web client/server fundamentals. At the highest level, communication in a Web-based environment occurs between two entities: (1) a Web client (most commonly a Web browser such as Internet Explorer or Netscape Navigator), which is an application that requests files from a Web server, and (2) a Web server, which is a software application, usually residing on a server, that handles client requests.

It's easy to deduce that a *server* is a computer that *serves* something. In a Web environment, a server "serves" HTTP responses. A server generally has more processing power than a personal computer (PC) in order to handle a large number of simultaneous client requests. A *Web server* is a server that is capable of handling Web, or HTTP, requests. In the Microsoft world, this Web server is one part of Internet Information Services (IIS).

Web browsers and servers communicate using a protocol called Transmission Control Protocol/Internet Protocol (TCP/IP). A *protocol* is simply a set of rules and procedures that define how two entities communicate. TCP/IP is actually composed of two parts, TCP and IP. TCP, often referred to as a *transport protocol*, wraps data in a digital envelope, called a *packet,* and ensures that the data is received in the same state in which it was sent. IP, a *network protocol,* is responsible for routing packets over a network, like the Internet. In addition to TCP/IP, Web clients and servers use a higher-level protocol, called HyperText Transfer Protocol (HTTP). To clarify, let us use the analogy of sending a letter through the mail. The letter is analogous to HTTP. When writing a letter, you'll probably write it in a language that the receiver understands, right? So, if you were a Web browser or server you would write your letter in HTTP rather than English. The envelope, which contains a mail-to and return address, is analogous to TCP and your friendly mail carrier is analogous to IP. The mail carrier ensures that your letter is delivered to the correct street address, in the correct city, in the correct state. Likewise, IP ensures that your TCP packet is delivered to the correct IP address.

HTTP is a *request-response type* protocol that specifies that a client will open a connection to a server and then send a request using a very specific format. The server will then respond and close the connection. HTTP has the ability to transfer Web pages, graphics, and any other type of media that is used by a Web application. Effectively HTTP is a set of messages that a Web browser and server send back and forth in order to exchange information. The simplest HTTP message is GET, to which a server replies by sending the requested document. In addition to GET requests, clients can also send POST requests. POST requests are used most commonly with HTML forms and other operations that require the client to transmit a block of data to the server.

That is basically how the Internet works. Now let's see how we have arrived at ASP.NET.

The Evolution of ASP

Although it may seem as though Microsoft's Active Server Pages (ASP) technology has been around forever, it is actually a relatively new technology, introduced in 1996. Prior to ASP, developers were able to create active Web sites on a Microsoft platform using the Common Gateway Interface (CGI) and Internet Server Application Programming Interface (ISAPI), each of which played a part in the evolution of ASP.

CGI was the first widely accepted technique of delivering dynamic Web content. CGI is effectively a method of extending the functionality of a Web server to enable it to dynamically generate HTTP responses using a program typically written in C or a scripting language such as Perl. This allowed page content to be personalized for the user and constructed from information stored in a database. Although powerful, CGI did have several shortcomings. For each HTTP request that a CGI application receives, a new process is created. After the request has been handled, the process is killed. Repeatedly creating and killing processes proved be a tremendous burden for even the most capable of Web servers.

Along came Microsoft's Active Server platform, which addressed the technical limitations of CGI programming. The Active Server platform was, and really still is, a set of tools that developers can utilize to write Web applications. Microsoft's Active Server platform didn't however originally include Active Server Pages, ASP. Developers were forced to write ISAPI extensions or filters.

ISAPI extensions and CGI are very similar with one major exception. Unlike CGI applications that are generally implemented as executables (EXEs) on the Windows platform, ISAPI extensions are implemented as Dynamic Link Libraries (DLLs), which means they are loaded into memory only once, on first demand, and then stay resident in the same process as IIS.

Therefore, ISAPI extensions do not suffer the same performance problems as CGI applications. Additionally, ISAPI extensions are multithreaded, which means that they can manage concurrent requests without degrading system performance.

Like ISAPI extensions, ISAPI filters are multithreaded, implemented as DLLs, and run in the same memory space as IIS. However, ISAPI filters are not invoked by client requests. Instead, ISAPI filters do exactly as their name implies — they filter or intercept and optionally process HTTP requests. ISAPI filters are actually quite useful in many situations, particularly web server logging and security. However, because ISAPI filters act on every HTTP request, they should be used sparingly to avoid severe performance problems.

As useful and powerful as ISAPI extensions and filters are, they can be difficult for novice programmers to develop. ISAPI DLLs must written in C++; and, even though Visual C++ does provide a wizard to assist with the task, this proved to be quite a barrier. Recognizing this issue, Microsoft released several short-lived Active Platform development products that were actually based on ISAPI. These included dbWeb and Internet Database Connector (IDC), which evolved into ASP.

In 1996, Microsoft released Active Server Pages and as they say "the rest is history." ASP allows developers to execute code inline within a Web page. Although, ASP technology is still a relatively new way to create dynamic Web sites, during its short life span, it has evolved to become one of the foremost dynamic Web site development products. This is probably due to the ease with which complex pages and applications can be created, combined with the ability to use custom components and existing Microsoft and third party commercial components through the Component Object Model (COM/COM+) architecture.

Since 1996, there have been several versions of ASP. In 1998, Microsoft introduced ASP 2.0 as part of the Windows NT 4.0 Option Pack. With ASP 2.0 and IIS 4.0, an ASP application and its associated components could be created in a memory space separate from the Web servers space to improve fault tolerance. In 2000, with the much anticipated release of Windows 2000 (and IIS 5.0), Microsoft unveiled ASP 3.0. To us, differences between the capabilities of ASP 2.0 and 3.0 appeared to be quite limited. However, running on Windows 2000, ASP's performance was greatly improved.

While ASP is powerful and incredibly simple to use, it does have the following drawbacks:

- **ASP code can get complicated very quickly.** ASP code tends to be unstructured and gets really messy. Tons of server-side code intermixes with client-side script code and HTML. After awhile it becomes difficult to figure out what is going on. If you have a few free hours to blow, try reading someone else's ASP code and you'll see what we mean. It can be a truly painful experience.

- **To do anything in ASP you have to write code.** ASP has no actual component model. Developers tend to start at the top of a page and zip right down to the bottom, executing database queries, running business logic, and generating HTML along the way.

- **Code is mixed with presentation.** This causes problems when developers and designers work together. Supporting internationalization and multiple client types is difficult.

- **The combination of ASP and IIS isn't always the most reliable of platforms.** Sorry, Mr. Gates! However, in Microsoft's defense, this instability isn't necessarily — or even probably — a platform issue. Microsoft, by making the Active Platform so open, gave developers the ability to create applications that could quite easily bring

IIS to its knees. Developing an ASP application is one thing, developing a good, efficient, reliable ASP application is another. Anyway, ASP fault tolerance could have been a little better.

- **Deploying an ASP application that utilizes COM can be difficult.** COM objects must be registered and are locked by the operating system when being used. As a result, managing a production application, especially in a Web farm, or a Web application that utilizes more than one Web server, proved to be quite challenging.

The Benefits of ASP.NET

Microsoft, realizing that ASP does possess some significant shortcomings, developed ASP.NET. ASP.NET is a set of components that provide developers with a framework with which to implement complex functionality. Two of the major improvements of ASP.NET over traditional ASP are scalability and availability. ASP.NET is scalable in that it provides state services that can be utilized to manage session variables across multiple Web servers in a server farm. Additionally, ASP.NET possesses a high performance process model that can detect application failures and recover from them.

Along with improved availability and scalability, ASP.NET provides the following additional benefits:

- **Simplified development:** ASP.NET offers a very rich object model that developers can use to reduce the amount of code they need to write.

- **Language independence:** ASP pages must be written with scripting. In other words, ASP pages must be written in a language that is interpreted rather than compiled. ASP.NET allows compiled languages to be used, providing better performance and cross-language compatibility.

- **Simplified deployment:** With .NET components, deployment is as easy as copying a component assembly to its desired location.

- **Cross-client capability:** One of the foremost problems facing developers today is writing code that can be rendered correctly on multiple client types. For example, writing one script that will render correctly in Internet Explorer 5.5 and Netscape Navigator 4.7, and on a PDA and a mobile phone is very difficult, if not impossible, and time consuming. ASP.NET provides rich server-side components that can automatically produce output specifically targeted at each type of client.

- **Web services:** ASP.NET provides features that allow ASP.NET developers to effortlessly create Web services that can be consumed by any client that understands HTTP and XML, the de facto language for inter-device communication.

- **Performance:** ASP.NET pages are compiled whereas ASP pages are interpreted. When an ASP.NET page is first requested, it is compiled and cached, or saved in memory, by the .NET Common Language Runtime (CLR). This cached copy can then be re-used for each subsequent request for the page. Performance is thereby improved because after the first request, the code can run from a much faster compiled version.

Probably one of the most intriguing features of ASP.NET is its integration with the .NET CLR. The CLR executes the code written for the .NET platform. The .NET compilers target the

.NET runtime and generate intermediate language (IL) binary code (kind of like Java and byte code). The code generated by .NET compilers cannot be run directly on the processor because the generated code is not in machine language. During runtime, the .NET compilers convert this intermediate code to native machine code and that machine code is eventually run on the processor. Additionally, the .NET compilers also produce metadata that describes the code. The .NET runtime loads metadata information for performing different tasks like resolving method calls, loading different dependent modules, marshaling data from one component to another, and so on. Since the .NET runtime produces binary code that is later compiled, effectively any language that is CLR compliant and can generate IL code can be used to write ASP.NET applications and components.

 Code written using the .NET Common Language Runtime, is said to be *managed code.* **Code that does not use this infrastructure is referred to as** *unmanaged code.*

.NET offers many programmatic improvements and features, one of which is a new version of ActiveX Data Objects (ADO) called, not surprisingly, ADO.NET. ADO.NET provides a suite of data handling and binding facilities. The Web is an inherently disconnected environment: a Web application connects to a datasource, manipulates the data, reconnects to the data-source, and updates the data. ADO.NET has been designed to work in a disconnected fashion, which increases data sharing. Additionally, ADO.NET treats data in a very loose, multidimensional, object-oriented way through a strongly typed object model. With ADO, all data is represented in two dimensions, rows and columns. With ADO.NET these n-dimensional data representations of data are called *datasets*. Iterating through, updating, and deleting related tables in a dataset is exceptionally simple.

What Is .NET?

10 Min.
To Go

With .NET, Microsoft is formalizing a vision of an Internet made up of an infinite number of interoperable Web applications or services, which will operate in concert to form a global exchange network. The .NET Framework is really a strategy to tie disparate platforms and devices together, moving data around in a far more efficient manner than it is currently.

.NET is Microsoft's platform for Web Services. Web Services allow applications to communicate and share data over the Internet, regardless of operating system or programming language. The Microsoft .NET platform includes a comprehensive family of products, built on Internet standards such as XML and HTTP, that provide facilities for developing, managing, using, and experiencing XML Web services. There are five areas where Microsoft is building the .NET platform: .NET Experiences, Clients, Services, Servers, and Tools.

.NET Experiences

.NET Experiences are XML Web services that enable you to access information across the Internet and from standalone applications. Microsoft will deliver .NET Experiences for individuals and for businesses. Some of the products that Microsoft is transitioning into .NET Experiences are the Microsoft Network (MSN) and bCentral.

.NET Clients

.NET Clients are PCs, laptops, workstations, phones, handheld computers, Tablet PCs, game consoles, and other smart devices. All of these devices will have the ability to consume Web Services. .NET Clients use software that supports Web Services, and enable you to access your data regardless of location or type. The .NET client software Microsoft will offer includes Windows CE, Window 2000, and Windows XP. These applications will power PCs, laptops, workstations, smart phones, handheld computers, and Tablet PCs.

.NET Services

In addition to developers creating XML Web services, Microsoft is creating a core set of services that perform routine tasks and act as the backbone for developers to build upon. The first set of Web Services being built, codenamed "HailStorm," is user-centric services focused on users, rather than devices, networks, or applications. "HailStorm" is based upon the Microsoft Passport user authentication system. With "HailStorm," users receive relevant information, as they need it, delivered to the devices they're using, and based on their established preferences.

.NET Servers

The .NET Servers, including the Windows 2000 server family, make up Microsoft .NET's server infrastructure for developing, deploying, and managing Web Services. Designed with performance in mind, the .NET Servers will provide enterprises with the resources required to integrate their systems, applications, and partners via Web Services. The .NET Enterprise Servers are

- SQL Server 2000 to store, retrieve, and analyze relational data.
- Application Center 2000 to deploy and manage highly available and scalable Web applications.
- BizTalk Server 2000 to build XML-based business processes across applications and organizations.
- Commerce Server 2000 for quickly building scalable e-commerce solutions.
- Content Management Server 2001 to manage content for dynamic e-business Web sites.
- Exchange Server 2000 to enable messaging and collaboration.
- Host Integration Server 2000 for integrating data and applications on legacy systems.
- Internet Security and Acceleration Server 2000 for establishing secure, fast Internet connectivity.
- Mobile Information 2001 Server to enable application support for mobile devices.
- SharePoint Portal Server 2001 to publish business information.

.NET Tools

Visual Studio .NET and the Microsoft .NET Framework supply a complete solution for developers to build, deploy, and manage Web Services. The .NET Tools maximize the performance, reliability, and security of Web Services.

Visual Studio .NET is the next generation of Microsoft's multi-language development environment. Visual Studio .NET will help developers quickly build Web Services and applications (including ASP.NET applications) using their language of choice. Visual Studio .NET advances the high-productivity programming languages Visual Basic, which includes new object-oriented programming features; Visual C++, which advances Windows development and enables you to build .NET applications; and C# (pronounced C sharp).

The .NET Framework is a high-productivity, standards-based, multi-language application execution environment that handles the essential "house keeping" chores and eases deployment and management. It provides an application execution environment that manages memory, addresses, versioning issues, and improves the reliability, scalability, and security of applications. The .NET Framework consists of several parts, including the Common Language Runtime and ASP.NET.

Done!

REVIEW

ASP is relatively new Web development technology. Although it is very powerful and simple to use, it does has some flaws. With ASP.NET, Microsoft has introduced a new Web development platform that addresses many, if not all, of ASP's shortcomings. ASP.NET offers many programmatic improvements including a new data access technology called ADO.NET. ADO.NET is designed to work on the Web, which is inherently disconnected. ASP.NET and ADO.NET are part of larger framework, generically referred to as the .NET Framework. The .NET Framework is a set of products and services designed to facilitate the development of interoperable Web applications based on open standards such as SOAP, XML, and HTTP.

QUIZ YOURSELF

1. What is the function of TCP/IP? (See "Internet Standards.")
2. What are two problems when developing ASP applications? (See "The Evolution of ASP.")
3. What are two improvements provided by ASP.NET over ASP? (See "The Benefits of ASP.NET.")

Setting Up .NET

Session Checklist

✔ Requirements for ASP.NET and ADO.NET

✔ Installing ASP.NET and ADO.NET

✔ Testing the installation

**30 Min.
To Go**

Before getting too deep into .NET you need to make sure that you have the minimal requirements for the .NET Framework and have successfully installed the software so that you can walk through the samples in this book. This session will cover the minimal and recommend configurations and give you some pointers for installing and testing the .NET Framework.

Installation Requirements

Before you get started with .NET you should first evaluate the minimum system requirements for the .NET Framework. These include but are not limited to the following:

- Windows 98, Windows ME, Windows NT 4.0, Windows 2000, and Windows XP
- Internet Explorer 5.01 or higher
- Microsoft Data Access Components (MDAC) 2.6 Required, MDAC 2.7 Recommended
- IIS 4.0, IIS 5.0 or higher

While the .NET Framework SDK can be installed on the platforms listed above, for developers building ASP.NET solutions, and for you, the reader of this book, there are fewer options. As a server-based component, ASP.NET takes advantage of certain security, threading, and transaction-based functionality that is not compatible with Windows NT 4.0, Windows ME, or Windows 98. Table 2-1 provides an installation matrix covering the mix of solutions recommended by the authors for deploying and developing ASP.NET solutions.

Table 2-1 *Recommended Configurations for ASP.NET*

Operating System	Web Server	Database	Web Browser	MDAC	Develop / Deploy
Windows 2000 Professional or XP Professional	IIS 5.1	SQL Server 2000 Developer	Internet Explorer 5.5	MDAC 2.7	Develop
Windows 2000 Server, Advanced Server, Data Center	IIS 5.1	SQL Server 2000 Standard or Enterprise	Internet Explorer 5.5	MDAC 2.7	Develop and Deploy

For more information on Windows 2000, including demonstration versions and purchasing a license visit http://www.microsoft.com/windows2000/.

Furthermore, in order to run many of the examples in this book you will need to have access to one of the following versions of SQL Server 2000:

- SQL Server 2000 Developer Edition
- SQL Server 2000 Standard Edition
- SQL Server 2000 Enterprise Edition

SQL Server Developer Edition is the only version of those listed above that you will be able to install with Windows 2000 Professional. If you are running Windows 2000 Server, Advanced Server or Data Center, then you can choose the Standard or Enterprise versions of SQL Server. Please note that while we recommend that you utilize SQL Server 2000 as your choice for a database platform, you can also use SQL Server 7.0 for the vast majority of examples in the book.

The .NET Framework includes the option to install the SQL Server 2000 Desktop Edition (MSDE), however this version of SQL Server does not include its own user interface or tools, instead users interact with MSDE 2000 through the application in which it is embedded. MSDE 2000 is packaged with the .NET Framework, but will not be suitable for running all of the scenarios needed for this book.

For more information on SQL Server 2000 editions, downloading demo versions of the product, or purchasing a license, please go to http://www.microsoft.com/sql/techinfo/planning/SQLResKChooseEd.asp

20 Min.
To Go

Table 2-2 provides a consolidated list of locations for you to download core components of the .NET Framework, including operating systems, databases, and data access components.

Table 2-2 *Download Sites for Core .NET Application Components*

Component	Download Site
Windows 2000	http://www.microsoft.com/windows2000/
Windows 2000 SQL Server	http://www.microsoft.com/sql/default.asp
Microsoft Explorer 5.5	http://www.microsoft.com/windows/ie/default.htm
Microsoft Data Access Components (MDAC) 2.6	http://www.microsoft.com/data/download.htm
Microsoft Data Access Components (MDAC) 2.7	http://www.microsoft.com/downloads/release.asp?ReleaseID=30134
.NET Framework setup files	http://msdn.microsoft.com/net/
Visual Studio .NET	http://msdn.microsoft.com/vstudio/

Installing ASP.NET and ADO.NET

In order to get started with ASP.NET development there are two approaches you can take:

- Install Visual Studio .NET
- Install the .NET Framework SDK Standard or Premium versions

If you choose to install Visual Studio .NET, then there is no need to install the .NET Framework SDK, however you should still install MDAC 2.7, as it contains new and useful functionality for data access. In the following section we will cover the installation of the freely available .NET Framework SDK, which is all that is required to run the samples contained in this book.

Installing the .NET Framework SDK

After installing your selected operating system, Web browser, and database system, go to the MSDN download section at http://www.asp.net to get the setup files you will need to get started. Alternatively you can visit http://www.microsoft.com/net, http://msdn.microsoft.com/downloads/default.asp, or http://www.gotdotnet.com.

When selecting which files to download, you should be aware that ASP.NET comes in two versions:

- Standard, which is what is installed when you install the standard .NET Framework SDK
- Premium, which provides advanced features specific to ASP.NET development such as Output Caching, Web Farm Session State, Code Access Hosting, and support for 4 CPU's and above

For the purposes of running all of the examples in this book, we recommend that you download and install the Premium version.

Installation is fairly easy and consists of a single executable file. There are typically two key issues that arise during the installation process.

- You may be asked to update the Microsoft Windows Installer Components, if this occurs be sure to allow this update to occur to prevent installation issues.
- You may receive a warning message indicating that Microsoft Data Access Components 2.7 is not installed on your system. If you have followed our recommend installation scenarios illustrated earlier you should not receive this alert. If you have not installed MDAC 2.7, all is not lost you can select the ignore button and continue with the installation. However we recommend that you install MDAC 2.7 prior to beginning development.

All of the ADO.NET components and ASP.NET components are installed automatically when you run the setup routines for the .NET Framework SDK. Once the setup routines have completed, you should plan on activating the samples that are included with the .NET Framework. The setup page can be located on your PC typically at `C:\Program Files\ Microsoft.Net\FrameworkSDK\Samples\startsamples.htm`.

To activate the samples, you will need to follow the steps as outlined on the SDK Samples page. Here are the steps and common issues related to setting up the samples:

1. Select the Install the .NET Framework Samples Database hyperlink and when prompted choose Run this program from its current location. If you receive any security warnings, select Yes to allow the installation to continue. This setup will check to see if you have MSDE installed, if not it will install it, and then it will proceed to install the sample databases.

2. Select the Complete the Installation hyperlink and when prompted choose Run this program from its current location. Again, if you receive any security warnings, select Yes to allow the installation to continue. This will complete the installation of the setup files.

3. To begin reviewing the samples, navigate to the Start ⇨ Programs ⇨ Microsoft .NET Framework SDK Menu and select the Samples and QuickStart Tutorials item. Then select the hyperlink labeled, Start the ASP.NET QuickStart Tutorial. This will present you with the screen shown in Figure 2-1.

4. Run the setup programs included on the CD with this book to install the sample databases and application files used throughout this book.

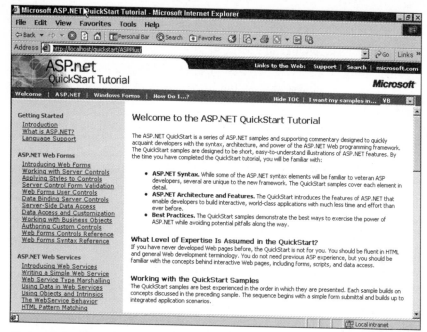

Figure 2-1   *The ASP.NET QuickStart Tutorial Page*

Testing Your Installation

**10 Min.
To Go**

To test your installation, you can simply begin walking through the default sample applications by running the QuickStart Tutorials discussed in the previous section. These tutorials are broken down into the categories shown in Table 2-3:

Table 2-3   *QuickStart Tutorials*

In This Category	You'll Find . . .
Getting Started	An introduction to ASP.NET and a summary overview of each of the core languages. We highly recommend that you review the discussion on language support here to familiarize yourself with Visual Basic .NET and C#.
ASP.NET Web Forms	A discussion of the fundamentals of designing pages, using server controls, accessing databases and building business objects with ASP.NET. This should be your next stop in the tour of tutorials.
ASP.NET Web Services	A few good examples to familiarize yourself with the concepts of creating and using Web Services.

Continued

Table 2-3 *Continued*

In This Category	You'll Find . . .
ASP.NET Web Applications	A cursory overview of what an ASP.NET application is, how to handle state within the application and how the global.aspx file is used.
Cache Services	A good overview of how all of the new caching features are handled including, output, fragment and data caching.
Configuration	Details about the machine.config and the Web.config files, which are critical in supporting major aspects of how your application operates from security and state maintenance to localization.
Deployment	A high-level overview on the benefits of the .NET Framework for deploying applications.
Security	A good summary of the multiple methods available to support authentication and authorization for your application and Web services.
Localization	Information on how to handle date/time, encoding and other format-related issues when targeting multiple languages. You'll also find a high-level overview of using resource files to support language localization.
Tracing	An discussion of how the new tracing functionality can help you keep your sanity when debugging applications.
Debugging	The basics of the new visual debugger and how to turn debugging on for testing.
Performance	A high-level overview of the positive and negatives related to the in-process and out-of-process state maintenance.
ASP to ASP.NET Migration	The key differences in ASP and ASP.NET. This is a great starting point for those of you familiar with developing for ASP.
Sample Applications	Consists of several excellent sample applications, including a Personalized Portal, an E-Commerce Application, A Class Browser Application, and the best example of all the IBuySpy.com application which covers many of the most crucial elements you will need to understand such as user logins, shopping baskets, the use of n-tier development best practices, and the use of Web services. An absolute must review!

You will likely face challenges if you have previously installed beta versions of the .NET Framework SDK. If you have installed beta versions, plan to reinstall the operating system prior to installing the production version. Even though the beta versions were fairly stable, anytime you try and simply install production bits over beta bits you are likely to create problems.

Support for .NET

There are a tremendous number of newsgroups and knowledge base articles available on-line to support your development efforts. In order to help you identify some of the more popular support groups available on-line that are specific to ASP.NET and ADO.NET, please refer to Table 2-4.

Table 2-4 *Support Resources for ASP.NET and ADO.NET*

Name	Type of Support	URL
MSDN Online Newsgroups	Newsgroup	http://msdn.microsoft.com/newsgroups/
ASP.NET Homepage	Web Site	http://www.asp.net/
Cold Rooster Consulting	Web Site	http://www.coldrooster.com/default.asp
ASPNG Discussion Lists	Discussion List	http://www.aspng.com/aspng/index.aspx
IBuySpy Homepage	Web Site	http://www.ibuyspy.com/
GotDotNet	Web Site	http://www.gotdotnet.com

Done!

REVIEW

You should now be on your way to developing! If you run into issues, be sure to check http://msdn.microsoft.com and http://support.microsoft.com for additional troubleshooting tips.

QUIZ YOURSELF

1. What are the minimal requirements for installing the .NET Framework? (See "Installation Requirements.")

2. Can you successfully use the .NET Framework on Windows 95? (See "Installation Requirements.")

3. List two on-line resources that provide support on ASP.NET or ADO.NET? (See "Support for .NET.")

Designing a Database

Understanding database design concepts

Learning to normalize database tables

Learning the basics of Structured Query Language

**30 Min.
To Go**

The key to developing an *active* Web site is data. Data is basically unstructured information such as a name, address, or user preference (a favorite color, for example). When you think about it, as Information Technologists, all we do is move data from one place to another and present it in different formats. There are many different types of data, including numbers, strings, and dates. For example, the number 30 might represent age, the string "Jason Butler" might present a name, and 1/1/2000 might represent a date.

A dynamicWeb site starts with a *database*. This is where information — that is, a collection of related data elements — is stored, modified, and transmitted. There are many databases on the market, including Microsoft Access, SQL Server, and Oracle. The type of database you choose as the *back end* (or database that supports an application) for your site ultimately depends on the size and security requirements of your company, as well as your budget.

There are two types of data: (1) relational and (2) non-relational. The difference between the two is how the data is organized. This session focuses on relational data. Relational data is stored in a Relational Database Management System (RDBMS). The information in relational databases is often presented in tables. Tables are created by grouping related data in columns and rows. When necessary, tables are related back to each other by the RDBMS.

Designing a Database

We believe that the best way to learn is by doing — so, let's start building a database. We will be using SQL Server 7.0, but you can use anything you like. The important thing to take away from this session is not only how to build a SQL Server database, but rather how to

**20 Min.
To Go**

design *and* build a database. Use the RDBMS with which you are most comfortable. If you are a novice, try using Microsoft Access. Access is generally not the RDBMS of choice as the back end for a high traffic Web site, but it's a good program to start with.

In the remainder of this session, we will show you how to build a music catalog database — band names, band members, albums, and so on. For this purpose, you need to know what information, or *data elements*, your database will store. For example, you may want to gather the following information about a band:

1. Band Title
2. Music Type Title (the type of music a band plays, for example, Rock & Roll)
3. Record Company Title
4. Albums
5. Band Members

Next, you need to determine the *data type* for each element. The data type specifies the kind of information (numeric, character, and so on) and how much space that information takes up in a particular column. Though each RDBMS handles data types differently, you are likely to encounter at least three — characters, integers, and dates — as described in Table 3-1.

Table 3-1   *RDBMS Data Type Categories*

Data Type	SQL Server Data Type	Comments
Character	char(n), varchar	Stores character information such as a contact's first name.
Integer	int, smallint, tinyint	Stores integer values such as a contact's age. Integers can also be used to store foreign key values. We'll get to that later.
Date	datetime, smalldatetime	Store dates and times such as time stamp information.

Next, you have to decide which data type to assign to each band item. At the same time, you need to determine which elements are optional and which are required (see Table 3-2) and how much space each element will occupy in the database. For example, you can reasonably assume that a band's name won't exceed fifty characters in length. So you specify in the database design that the column should not accept data elements that are longer than 50 characters in length. Data types represent the kind of data that can be stored in a particular column. For example, if you want to store a band's name, you will store character data. If you want to store the number of members in the band, you would store the data as a number or integer. Each RDMS supports different data types. SQL Server, for instance, provides VARCHAR and CHAR among other data types to store character data, and INT and FLOAT among others to store numeric data.

Refer to your RDMS's documentation for supported data types.

Table 3-2 *Optional and Required DB Elements*

Contact Element	Data Type	Size	Optional/Required
Band Title	VARCHAR	50	Required
Music Type Title	VARCHAR	25	Required
Record Company Title	VARCHAR	25	Required
Band Members	VARCHAR	200	Required
Albums	VARCHAR	500	Optional

Table 3-2 does not present an optimal table definition. It is merely a starting point from which to begin discussion. Database normalization techniques will be explored later in this session.

Armed with this information, you can now create your table. Follow a standard naming convention when creating table and column names. For example, you may choose to always name your tables using the following convention:

```
t_[plural object descriptor]
```

Since the table you are creating will contain a record, or row, for each band, choose t_bands as the table name. Use the following convention to name columns:

```
[singular object descriptor]_[column descriptor]
```

You don't need to follow our naming convention, but we highly recommend that you use some sort of object naming convention — it will save you time later.

Figure 3-1 shows the design of your t_bands table.

t_bands						
Column Name	Datatype	Length	Precision	Scale	Allow Nulls	
band_id	int	4	10	0		
band_title	varchar	50	0	0		
band_music_type_title	varchar	25	0	0		
band_record_company	varchar	25	0	0		
band_members	varchar	200	0	0		
band_albums	varchar	500	0	0	☑	

Figure 3-1   *t_bands table*

You'll notice that we have created a field for each of the data elements we defined earlier. The first field, band_id is our unique identifier. Without going into SQL Server details, we created the unique identifier by selecting the column's identity field.

Your RDBMS should be structured to create a unique identifier for each record. For example, the first band could be assigned a unique identifier of 1, the second, 2, and so on. In Oracle, this is called a sequence, in SQL Server it is referred to as an identity. You should generally make this unique identifier the table's *primary key*. A primary key is a field or group of fields that uniquely identifies a record.

Take great care when defining a table's primary key. If there's even the slightest possibility of having duplicate information in a primary key or of your requirements changing in such a way that your primary key is no longer valid, use something else or a sequence number. Good candidates for primary keys might be social security numbers or e-mail addresses, but you can never be too careful. That's why it's a good idea to use sequences as primary keys; the RDBMS ensures that this field will be unique.

OK, now let's talk *constraints*. A constraint is a mechanism for enforcing the integrity of the data in your table. There are several types of constraints. Among these are primary key constraints, foreign key constraints, unique constraints, and check constraints. *Check constraints* ensure that the data entered in a column follows a set of rules. A *unique constraint* ensures that the data inserted into a column, or group of columns, is not duplicated in the table. A *foreign key* references the primary key of another table and ensures the data in the foreign key column is present in the referenced table.

The implementation of constraints differs drastically by RDBMS, so instead of actually going through the process of creating a constraint in SQL Server, you need to consider where constraints might be useful in your t_bands table. Because band titles are generally unique, it's a good idea to place a unique constraint on the band_title column.

Normalization of Data

**10 Min.
To Go**

Now let's take a moment to review and validate the design of the t_bands table. Generally, to validate the design of our table, it's a good idea to ensure that it is normalized. *Normalization* is the process of organizing data into related tables. By normalizing your data, you are effectively attempting to eliminate redundant data in your database. Several rules have been established for the normalization of data. These rules are referred to as *normalization forms*. The first three normalization forms are:

- **First Normal Form (FNF):** This rule states that a column cannot contain multiple values. If you further inspect t_bands for FNF compliance, you should come to the conclusion that the albums and members fields, band_albums and band_members, should be broken down into smaller, discrete elements. The band_members and band_albums columns are currently defined such that if a band has multiple members or have released multiple albums, then band_members and band_albums columns will contain multiple values.

- **Second Normal Form (SNF):** This rule states that every non-key column must depend on the entire key, not just the primary key. Because you are using band_id as your primary key, you are in good shape with respect to SNF.

- **Third Normal Form (TNF):** This rule is very similar to the SNF rule and states that all nonkey columns must not depend on any other nonkey columns. A table must also comply with SNF to be in TNF. OK, you pass this test too!

There are three other normalization rules that aren't covered here. Generally, if your tables are in Third Normal Form, they probably conform to the other rules.

To fully optimize your tables, you should take some additional measures. It's a good idea to break your t_bands table into several tables and link them to t_bands via foreign keys. Also, you should create a t_music_types table that holds all the possible music types. The t_bands table should have a foreign key to the primary key of the t_music_types table. This is generally good practice for two reasons: (1) it ensures that your band's music type falls into the music type domain and (2) it is easier to maintain. For example, if you change your mind and want to refer to "R&B" as "Rhythm & Blues," you won't have to change every instance of "R&B" in the band_music_type_title column — you only need to change the music type title in the t_music_types table. You could also do the same thing for the band_record_company_title and contact_business_state fields.

At this point, your database contains three tables: (1) t_bands, (2) t_music_types, and (3) t_record_companies. Figure 3-2 shows a diagram of our new database design:

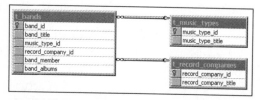

Figure 3-2   *Database design showing relationship of three tables*

In the diagram in Figure 3-2, t_bands is linked to t_music_types via a foreign key to music_type_id and linked to t_record_companies via a foreign key to record_company_id. This new relationship between the tables is called *one-to-many*. In a one-to-many relationship, each entry in the contact type table may be referenced by one or many contacts.

You now have three tables and have met your current requirements. However, what about bands and albums? Currently, you are storing all of the band's albums and members in a single column, band_albums and band_members, respectively. Currently, if you wanted to retrieve a list of a band's members or albums, you would need to retrieve the data in the band_members or band_albums column and parse it. This is not the optimal approach. The best approach for this situation is to further normalize your database by creating two new tables. The first is a table to store all albums (for example, t_albums) and a second that stores all band members (for example, t_band_members). The tables t_albums and t_band_members will have foreign keys to the t_bands table. Figure 3-3 shows the new database diagram.

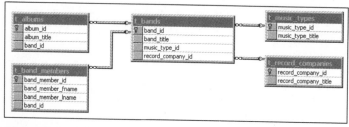

Figure 3-3   *Diagram of expanded table design*

You could certainly modify your table design further. But at some point you need to start considering performance. Performance can be adversely impacted if, on a regular basis, you need to join multiple tables with a lot of data. We recommend that you keep the number of tables in your database to a minimum while following the normalization rules as closely as possible. You will soon learn that database design is as much art as it is science.

Security Considerations

Probably the most overlooked aspect of database design is security, when it should be a major consideration. By not securing your database and thereby your data, you are asking for trouble. Not all data is intended for everyone's eyes, and not everyone should have the ability to manipulate your data and definitely not your database's structure. The majority of your database users will only need and should only be granted read (or select) access. When designing your database, you should establish a list of policies and users for your database. A database user is anyone who needs access to any part of your database. The highest level of user is the database administrator who will have access to all database objects and data. Other users will only have access to certain objects and data. The average end user will only have access to certain objects, but should never have the ability to alter your database structure. It never ceases to amaze us how many organizations have one "global" user that has complete control of the database. This is typically a bad scenario, not because people are intentionally malicious, but because they are people and no one is perfect. The impact of a simple mistake can take hours and even days to reverse, if reversal is possible at all. Policies are basically rules that define which actions a user can perform on your database. Most RDMSs enable you to assign a separate set of policies, or rights, for each object in your database. User rights generally fall into one of six different categories:

- SELECT enables the user to view data.
- INSERT enables the user to create new data.
- UPDATE enables the user to modify existing data.
- DELETE enables the user to delete data.
- EXECUTE enables the user to execute a stored procedure.
- ALTER enables the user to alter database structure.

We will discuss stored procedures in Session 4, "Building a Database."

Each user in a database should have a unique user name and password combination. This will enable your RDMS to enforce the security policies you have established for the user.

Done!

REVIEW

In order to have a truly active Web site, you need to have some sort of data store from which to retrieve personalized information. In most cases, this "data store" is a relational database management system (RDBMS) such as SQL Server, Oracle, or Microsoft Access. A database can consist of many types of objects such as tables and constraints. Designing the structure of your tables (and other objects) and their interactions is just as much art as it is science. However, the database normalization rules provide good guidelines to help you along your way.

QUIZ YOURSELF

1. What is the importance of the primary key in table design? (See "Designing a Database.")
2. What is the difference between a primary key and a foreign key? (See "Designing a Database.")
3. What is the purpose of normalization? (See "Normalization of Data.")

SESSION

4

Building a Database

**30 Min.
To Go**

In the previous session, we explained how to design and build a database. In this session, you'll build the Music database using SQL Server. (If you're going to build the database as you go through this session, use either SQL Server 7.0 or 2000.)

When working with SQL Server, you can create a database and its related objects in one of two ways. Probably the easiest method is to use Enterprise Manager. Enterprise Manager provides a user interface that enables you to graphically create a database, tables, constraints, and so on. If you installed SQL Server on your local machine, Enterprise Manager should be located in the SQL Server program group on the Start menu.

The second method of creating a database with SQL Server is to execute Transact-SQL (T-SQL) commands against your SQL Server. Although writing T-SQL commands is a little more difficult than using Enterprise Manager, you have greater control of the objects you create and can save time.

Which method you use is a matter of personal preference. Throughout this session, we demonstrate creating database objects with both methods.

Creating a Database

The first step in building a database with SQL Server is to actually create the database. That's right. SQL Server is a piece of software that runs on a computer, or server. Once the SQL Server software is installed you can create a database (or databases) with the SQL Server software that is then managed by that SQL Server software. Many people refer to SQL Server as a database, which it is, sort of. SQL Server is actually an application, a Relational Database Management System (RDBMS), which can contain multiple databases.

We will be using SQL Server 7.0 to create the database in this session. If you are using SQL Server 2000, the steps will be slightly different.

OK, let's create the Music database. You'll start by creating the database using Enterprise Manager and perform the following steps:

1. Expand the SQL Server Group item, if it isn't already expanded, in the Enterprise Manager tree. Once expanded you should see a list of SQL Servers that are registered with Enterprise Manager.

2. Right-click the SQL Server in which you want to create the Music database.

3. Select New ⇨ Database. Figure 4-1 illustrates steps 1, 2, and 3.

4. You see the Database Properties dialog box, shown in Figure 4-1. On the General tab, enter **Music** in the Name field. The Database Properties dialog box allows you to control other features of your database such as file growth, maximum database size, transaction log files, and so on. For the sake of brevity, accept the defaults.

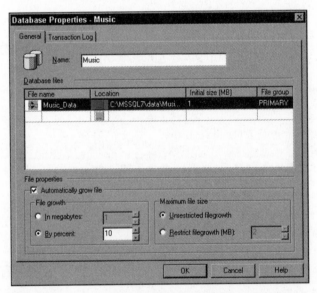

Figure 4-1 *Specifying database properties with Enterprise Manager*

That's it. You have created a SQL Server database using Enterprise Manager. If you want to create a database with T-SQL, follow these steps:

1. Select Start ⇨ Programs ⇨ Microsoft SQL Server ⇨ Query Analyzer to open SQL Server's Query Analyzer.

2. You see the Connect to SQL Server dialog box. Select the SQL Server on which you would like to create the Music database from the SQL Server drop-down box. Select the Use SQL Server authentication radio button. Now enter the appropriate authentication information in the Login Name and Password fields as shown in Figure 4-2.

Figure 4-2 *Query Analyzer logon*

3. In the Query Analyzer window, enter the following T-SQL statement:

```
USE master
GO
CREATE DATABASE Music ON PRIMARY
( NAME = MusicData,
  FILENAME =  'C:\MSSQL7\data\MusicData.mdf'
)
```

In the previous script, you may need to alter the FILENAME **string so that it reflects a valid path on your computer.**

In step 3, you essentially created a database named Music and specified that the data should be stored in the MusicData.mdf file located, in this example, in the C:\MSSQL7\data directory. The CREATE DATABASE statement accepts many other parameters, such as MAXSIZE, FILEGROWTH, SIZE, and so on. However, again, for the sake of brevity, you used the SQL Server defaults.

Once you have entered the previous SQL statement in the Query Analyzer window, hit the F5 button, which will execute the SQL script.

That's it. You have now created a database using T-SQL and Query Analyzer.

Creating SQL Server Tables

Now that you have a database, Music, you can add tables to it. If you recall from the previous session, the Music database contains several tables including t_bands, t_band_members, t_albums, and so on. Figure 4-3 shows the schema for the Music database.

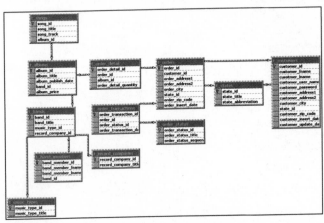

Figure 4-3   Schema for the Music database

You are not going to create every table in the Music database, but hopefully, based on the tables you do create, you will be able to build the remaining tables. So, go create the t_bands table:

1. In Enterprise Manager, right-click on the Music database node and select New ⇨ Table.

2. You see the Choose Name dialog box as shown in Figure 4-4. Enter **t_bands** in the "Enter a name for the table:" textbox and click OK. The table design grid is now ready for you to enter column information.

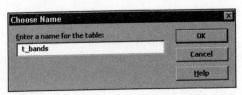

Figure 4-4   Specifying a table's name

3. In the design grid, enter **band_id** in the Column Name field of the first row as shown in Figure 4-5. In the Datatype column, select int to signify that the band_id field will contain integer type data. On the same row, deselect the Allow Nulls checkbox and select the Identity checkbox. Click the Set Primary Key button (it looks like a key) on the SQL Server toolbar to make the band_id column the primary key for the t_bands table.

4. Create the **band_title**, **music_type_id**, and **record_company_id** columns, using Figure 4-5 as a guide.

5. Right-click the t_bands table design grid as shown in Figure 4-5. You see the Properties dialog box.

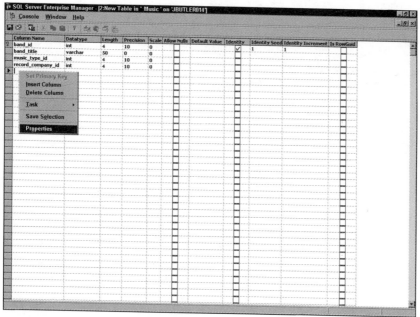

Figure 4-5 *Creating table columns*

6. Select the Indexes/Keys tab and click the New button to create a new index on the band_title column.

7. Select band_title from the Column name drop-down box and enter **IX_band_title** in the Index name text box.

8. Select the Create UNIQUE checkbox and the Index option button, and click the Close button (as shown in Figure 4-6).

9. Save and close the t_bands design grid.

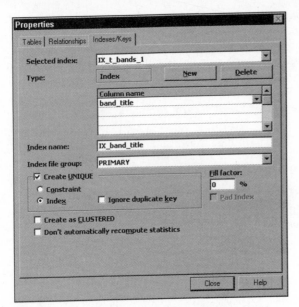

Figure 4-6   *Creating a unique constraint*

To create the t_bands table using T-SQL, execute the following commands in Query Analyzer:

```
USE Music
GO
CREATE TABLE [dbo].[t_bands] (
    [band_id] [int] IDENTITY (1, 1) NOT NULL ,
    [band_title] [varchar] (100) NOT NULL ,
    [music_type_id] [int] NOT NULL ,
    [record_company_id] [int] NOT NULL
) ON [PRIMARY]
GO
ALTER TABLE [dbo].[t_bands] WITH NOCHECK ADD
    CONSTRAINT [PK_t_bands] PRIMARY KEY  NONCLUSTERED
    (
        [band_id]
    ) ON [PRIMARY] ,
    CONSTRAINT [IX_bands_title] UNIQUE  NONCLUSTERED
    (
        [band_title]
    ) ON [PRIMARY]
GO
```

The second command, or the first command after USE Music, creates the t_bands table using the CREATE TABLE statement. The third command, ALTER TABLE, creates two constraints on the t_bands table. The first constraint, named PK_t_bands, is placed on the band_id field. The PK_t_bands constraint is the primary key for the t_bands table. The second constraint, named IX_bands_title, is placed on the band_title column and ensures that the band title is unique.

Now create t_albums as shown in Figure 4-7.

Figure 4-7   *t_albums table*

Next you need to create a few constraints on the t_albums table by following these steps:

1. Open the Properties dialog box for the t_albums table and select the Indexes/ Keys tab.

2. Create a constraint named **IX_band_albums** based on two columns, album_title and band_id. Make this constraint unique by selecting the "Create UNIQUE" check-box. This constraint ensures that a band doesn't have albums duplicated in the table. In this example, of course, you could assume that a band will never release two albums with the same name. At this point, you should start to realize that constraints are basically used to enforce business rules on our tables.

3. Close the Properties dialog box by selecting the "Close" button.

4. Expand the Music database node so you can see a complete listing of all database objects (that is, Diagrams, Tables, View, Stored Procedures, and so on).

5. Right-click the Diagrams node and select "New Database Diagram."

6. Work your way through the Create Database Diagram Wizard. Make sure that you add the t_albums and t_bands tables to the diagram. It is through this database diagram that you are going to create a foreign key. Specifically, you are going to create a foreign key to the t_bands table to ensure that all entries in the band_id column of the t_albums table have a corresponding band_id in the t_bands table. (This is simply a business rule. You can't have an album pop out of thin air. It has to be recorded by a band.)

7. Once the diagram has been created and the two tables mentioned in step 6 are on the diagram, drag the band_id entry in the t_albums table and drop it on t_bands.

At this point, you see the Create Relationship dialog box shown in Figure 4-8. On the Create Relationship dialog box, ensure that the primary key table is t_bands and the primary key column is band_id. Also ensure that the foreign key table is t_albums and the foreign key column is band_id. Click OK.

That's it. You have created the t_albums table using Enterprise Manager. Listing 4-1 shows the T-SQL script you could execute to create the t_albums table and its associated constraints.

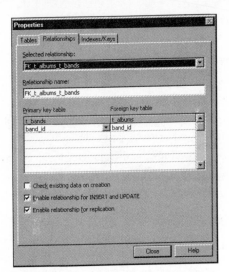

Figure 4-8   *Creating a relation between t_bands and t_albums*

Listing 4-1   *An example of a T-SQL script*

```
CREATE TABLE [dbo].[t_albums] (
    [album_id] [int] IDENTITY (1, 1) NOT NULL ,
    [album_title] [varchar] (255) NOT NULL ,
    [album_publish_date] [datetime] NOT NULL ,
    [band_id] [int] NOT NULL ,
    [album_price] [smallmoney] NOT NULL
) ON [PRIMARY]
GO
ALTER TABLE [dbo].[t_albums] WITH NOCHECK ADD
    CONSTRAINT [DF_t_albums_album_publish_date] DEFAULT (getdate()) FOR
[album_publish_date],
    CONSTRAINT [DF_t_albums_album_price] DEFAULT (0.00) FOR [album_price],
    CONSTRAINT [PK_t_albums] PRIMARY KEY  NONCLUSTERED
    (
        [album_id]
    )  ON [PRIMARY] ,
    CONSTRAINT [IX_band_albums] UNIQUE  NONCLUSTERED
    (
        [album_title],
        [band_id]
    )  ON [PRIMARY]
GO
ALTER TABLE [dbo].[t_albums] ADD
    CONSTRAINT [FK_t_albums_t_bands] FOREIGN KEY
    (
        [band_id]
    ) REFERENCES [dbo].[t_bands] (
```

```
        [band_id]
    )
GO
```

Everything here should look familiar. These commands are very similar to those used to create the t_bands table. The only difference is the last command that creates the foreign key to the band_id column in the t_bands table.

That's it for tables. Now try creating the rest of the database on your own. If you run into problems, feel free to use the T-SQL statements that are included on the CD.

Next, we take a quick look at the views, stored procedures, and triggers for SQL Server database objects.

Creating a View

**10 Min.
To Go**

A view is essentially a SQL Server object that specifies exactly how a user will see that data in a database. It is a stored query. Views are useful for enforcing security (that is, granting use access to views, but not tables) and simplifying the user interface to the database by creating views for the most frequently used queries.

You can create views with Enterprise Manager or T-SQL with Query Analyzer. For the remainder of this session, we focus solely on Query Analyzer for the sake of brevity. Generally, if you can create an object using Query Analyzer, using the Enterprise Manager is a cinch.

So, to create a view you use the CREATE VIEW statements as shown in the following example:

```
CREATE VIEW [owner.]view_name
AS select_statement
```

In this line, view_name is the name of the view and select_statement is the SQL SELECT statement used to return view results.

Suppose you wanted a view that would return the names of all the bands in the t_bands table. The CREATE VIEW statement would look like this:

```
USE Music
GO
CREATE VIEW all_bands
AS
SELECT band_title, band_id FROM t_bands
```

This is a pretty simple example, but a good starting point. To utilize the view, all you need to do is call it from a SQL statement, like SELECT:

```
SELECT * FROM all_bands ORDER BY band_title
```

Creating a Stored Procedure

Stored procedures are precompiled T-SQL statements stored in a SQL Server database. Because stored procedures are precompiled, they offer better performance than other types

of queries, including views. Additionally, you can pass parameters to and from stored procedures. To create a stored procedure, you use the CREATE PRODCURE statement, which has
the following syntax:

```
CREATE PROCEDURE procedure_name
[{@parameter_name data_type} [VARYING] [= default] [OUTPUT]]
[, ...n]
AS
sql_statement
```

If you wanted to create a simple stored procedure that returns all the albums in your
database, ordered alphabetically, you would execute the following statement:

```
CREATE PROCEDURE pr_albums
AS
SELECT album_title FROM t_albums ORDER BY album_title
```

**If you would like to test a stored procedure, simply go into SQL Server's
Query Analyzer tool and (1) type the word EXEC (short for execute) followed
by the name of the stored procedures and (2) hit the F5 button.**

This statement creates a stored procedure named pr_albums that returns a list of all the
albums in the t_albums table ordered alphabetically. Chances are that if the t_albums table
gets fairly large, you wouldn't want to return all the rows in the table. You might want to
return all the albums for a specified band. The following stored procedure, pr_albums2,
returns a list of a specified band's albums, ordered alphabetically:

```
CREATE PROCEDURE pr_albums2
    @iBandID INT
AS
    SELECT album_title
    FROM t_albums
    WHERE band_id = @iBandID
    ORDER BY album_title
```

This stored procedure accepts a parameter, @iBandID. You then include @iBandID in the
SQL statement to return only those rows, or albums titles, whose band_id value is equal to
@iBandID.

Creating a Trigger

A trigger is a special kind of stored procedure that is automatically invoked when the data
it is designed to protect is modified. Triggers help to ensure the integrity of data by pro-
hibiting unauthorized or inconsistent changes. For example, with a trigger you could ensure
that a band could not be deleted from the t_bands table if that band has an album or
albums in the t_t_albums table.

Triggers do not have parameters and cannot be explicitly invoked. They are only fired when you try to insert, update, or delete data from a table. The T-SQL syntax for a trigger is:

```
CREATE TRIGGER trigger_name
ON table_name
FOR {INSERT | UPDATE | DELETE}
AS sql_statement
```

Now try to enforce the business rule mentioned earlier. You want to make sure that a band is not deleted if it has an entry in the t_albums table.

Oh, if you haven't created the t_bands **and** t_albums **tables yet, please do so now. If you don't, you won't be able to create a trigger that references the** t_albums **table.**

Based on the requirements, it would appear that the trigger should be invoked, or fired, whenever a band is being deleted from the t_bands table, right? The syntax for this trigger is:

```
CREATE TRIGGER trg_DeleteBand
ON t_bands
FOR DELETE
AS
    IF EXISTS(SELECT album_id FROM t_albums, deleted WHERE t_albums.band_id =
deleted.band_id)
    BEGIN
        RAISERROR(Band has albums!',16,1)
    END
```

All you are doing is creating a trigger named trg_DeleteBand on the t_bands table. The trigger will be fired whenever a band is being deleted. In order for the band to be deleted, no records can exist in the t_albums table for that band. To validate that no records exist in the t_albums table, you use the IF EXISTS statement, which checks to see if there are any records that match a specified criterion. In your case, the specified criterion is a SQL statement.

Done!

REVIEW

In this session, you learned how to create tables, views, stored procedures, and triggers with SQL Server. Tables contain the data in a SQL Server database. A view is essentially a SQL Server object that specifies exactly how a user will see that data in a database. Views are useful for enforcing security and simplifying the user interface to the database (by creating views for the most frequently used queries). Stored procedures and triggers are used to enforce data integrity in a database.

Quiz Yourself

1. What are two methods of creating SQL Server objects? (See session introduction.)
2. What is the function of a view? (See "Creating a View.")
3. What three actions can fire a trigger? (See "Creating a Trigger.")

PART

I

Friday Evening
Part Review

The following set of questions is designed to provide you with feedback on how well you understood the topics covered during this part of the book. Please refer to Appendix A for the answers to each question.

1. Which of the following is not a component of Windows 2000 Internet Information Services?

   a. Gopher Server

   b. FTP Server

   c. SMTP Server

   d. NNTP Server

2. A Web server's primary responsibility is to manage TCP/IP traffic.
   True/False

3. TCP/IP and XML are the two primary protocols for Internet client/server communications.
   True/False

4. Which of the following was the first widely accepted technique for developing dynamic Web sites?

   a. Active Server Pages (ASP)

   b. ISAPI Filters

   c. ISAPI Extensions

   d. Common Gateway Interface (CGI)

5. Windows 3.1 is a supported platform for .NET.

   True/False

6. *Fill in the blank:* _____ is the lowest version of IIS that supports ASP.NET.

7. Should you install the .NET SDK over beta versions?

   Yes/No

8. Do you need to remove Visual Studio 6.0 prior to installing the SDK?

   Yes/No

9. In general terms, a database can be thought of as a collection of related data.

   True/False

10. Which of the following is not a Relational Database Management System (RDBMS)?

    a. Microsoft SQL Server 2000

    b. Oracle 8i

    c. Microsoft Excel

    d. IBM DB2

11. Data can be categorized as either relational or non-relational.

    True/False

12. Database tables are composed of stored procedures and columns.

    True/False

13. Which of the following terms refers to a field or group of fields that uniquely identify a record?

    a. Foreign Key

    b. Trigger

    c. Primary Key

    d. Stored Procedure

14. Enterprise Manager is used to create and manage SQL Server databases.

    True/False

15. Which of the following languages are used to create SQL Server databases?

    a. PL/SQL

    b. T-SQL

    c. Visual Basic

    d. C++

16. SQL Server is a piece of hardware that can contain multiple databases. True/False

17. The T-SQL statement used to create a new database is `CREATE INSTANCE`. True/False

☑ Friday

☑ **Saturday**

☐ Sunday

PART

II

Saturday Morning

Using SQL: A Primer

✔ Understanding the usefulness of SQL

✔ Writing SELECT, INSERT, UPDATE, and DELETE SQL commands

**30 Min.
To Go**

After you have built a database, whether it be SQL Server or Oracle or Access, a time will come when you need to do something with it, more than likely retrieve and modify data. When dealing with data in a database, it turns out that there are four actions you will most frequently perform: *create*, *retrieve*, *update*, and *delete*. Collectively these activities are referred to as CRUD. If someone, probably a manager, asks you for a CRUD diagram they are simply asking for a diagram representing what commands or actions you execute against the data store.

In order to execute CRUD commands against a relational database, you need to use Structured Query Language or SQL (pronounced *sequel*). SQL, as a querying language, is composed of a series of statements and clauses, which, when combined, perform different actions. In this session, we will address the most common SQL commands, INSERT, DELETE, UPDATE, and SELECT, and their related clauses. In order to demonstrate the use of SQL, you will execute commands against the Music database discussed in the previous session. So, if you haven't already done so, please create the Music database.

INSERT Statements

Now that you've designed and constructed a database, it's time to use it or have someone else use it. To make a database useful, it needs to contain some data. The SQL command to add data to a database is INSERT. The basic INSERT statement adds one row at a time to a table. Variations of the basic INSERT statement enable you to add multiple rows by selecting data from another table or by executing a stored procedure. In all of these cases, you must know something about the structure of the table into which you are inserting data. The following information is useful:

- The number of columns in the table
- The data type of each column
- The names of the columns
- Constraints and column properties

Following is the syntax for a basic INSERT statement:

```
INSERT INTO tablename [(columnname, ...)] VALUES (constant, ...)
```

where `tablename` represents the name of the table into which you want to insert data, `columnname` represents the name of the column into which you insert a specific piece of data, and `constant` represents the data you want to insert.

For example, if you wanted to add a music type to the t_music_type table in the Music database, you would write the following statement:

```
INSERT INTO t_music_types (music_type_title) VALUES ('Rock and Roll')
```

In plain English, this translates into, "insert a record into the t_music_types table and set the music_type_title field equal to the string Rock and Roll."

If you'll recall, the t_music_types table contains two columns: (1) music_type_id and (2) music_type_title. However, the previous INSERT statement only inserts data into the music_type_title column. That's because the music_type_id column is an IDENTITY column, which means that whenever a new row is added to the table, a unique identity value is automatically inserted into the music_type_column column. When executing an INSERT command, you must provide a field name/expression pair for each column that has not been assigned a default value and does not allow NULL values.

Let's try another insert statement:

```
INSERT INTO t_record_companies (record_company_title) VALUES
('Atlantic Records')
```

Now write an INSERT statement that's a little more involved. You're going to add a band to the t_bands table, which changes the number of columns of the t_bands table to four, two of which are foreign keys. The music_type_id column is a foreign key to the t_music_type_id field in the t_music_types table, and the record_company_id column is a foreign key to the record_company_id field in the t_record_companies table. This means that you must insert values into these two columns that have corresponding values in their foreign key column. Assume that in the t_record_companies table, "Atlantic Records" has a record_company_id value of 1. Assume the same thing for "Rock and Roll" in the t_music_types table. So the insert statement for the t_bands table should look like this:

```
INSERT INTO t_bands (band_title, music_type_id, record_company_id) VALUES
('Hootie & The Blowfish',1,1)
```

Notice that you enclosed the band_title value, but not the music_type_id and record_company_id values, in single quotes. This is why you need to know the data types

of the columns into which you are inserting data. If the column into which you are inserting is of a numeric data type, you do not enclose the value in single quotes, however if you
are inserting character data, you need to enclose the value in single quotes. Try running
this statement:

```
INSERT INTO t_bands (band_title, music_type_id, record_company_id) VALUES
('Toad The Wet Sprocket','1','1')
```

You should get an error when executing this command because you are attempting to
insert character data into columns that expect numeric data. Here's the correct INSERT
statement:

```
INSERT INTO t_bands (band_title, music_type_id, record_company_id) VALUES
('Toad The Wet Sprocket',1,1)
```

DELETE Statements

**20 Min.
To Go**

The DELETE command removes a row or multiple rows from a table. Following is the syntax
for a basic DELETE statement:

```
DELETE FROM tablename [WHERE where expression]
```

Executing a DELETE statement that does not contain a WHERE clause removes all the
records from a table. This is generally not what you want to do, so be careful when executing DELETE statements. Here's an example:

```
DELETE FROM t_albums
```

This previous statement will delete *all* records from the t_albums table.

The WHERE clause is used to narrow the scope of our DELETE statement by specifying criteria that identify the records to delete. Here's an example:

```
DELETE FROM t_albums WHERE band_id = 1
```

Assuming Hootie & The Blowfish have a band_id of 1 in the t_bands table, all of Hootie's
albums will be removed from the t_albums table.

The WHERE clause can consist of one expression as demonstrated with the previous
DELETE statement or a series of expressions separated by Boolean operators. The Boolean
operators most commonly used are AND, OR, and NOT. When using these operators together,
precedence rules determine the order in which they're evaluated. When the WHERE clause
consists of statements enclosed in parentheses, the expressions in parentheses are examine
first. After the expressions in parentheses are evaluated, the following rules apply:

- NOT is evaluated before AND. NOT can only occur after AND. OR NOT isn't allowed.
- AND is evaluated before OR.

Let's try it out . . .

```
DELETE FROM t_bands WHERE band_title = 'Hootie & The Blowfish' AND
record_company_id = 100
```

The previous statement will delete all rows from the t_bands table *where* the value in the band_title column is equal to Hootie & The Blowfish *and* the value in the record_company_id field is 100. Based on the data we inserted earlier, no record should be deleted from the t_bands table. There is a record that where band_title equals Hootie & The Blowfish, but that record has record_company_id value of 1. Let's try an OR . . .

```
DELETE FROM t_bands WHERE band_title = 'Toad The Wet Sprocket OR
record_company_id = 100
```

This statement will delete all rows from t_bands table *where* the value in the band_title column is equal to Toad The Wet Sprocket *or* the value in the record_company_id field is 100. So based on our sample data, one row should be deleted from the t_bands table because there is one row that contains Toad The Wet Sprocket in the band_title column, but no rows contain a record_company_id value of 100.

A WHERE clause can also contain something called a predicate. A *predicate* is a expression that makes a factual assertion about a column value. Some common examples of predicates are CONTAINS, LIKE, and NULL. CONTAINS returns true if the value in the specified table contains a specified value. LIKE returns true if the specified column's data matches a specified string pattern.

A string pattern can contain wildcard characters such as the percent sign (%), which matches one or more characters, and the underscore (_), which matches one character.

NULL determines whether a column contains data. Let's try it out:

```
DELETE FROM t_bands WHERE CONTAINS (band_title,'Toad')
```

This statement means, "delete all rows from t_bands where band_title contains Toad." Let's try another:

```
DELETE FROM t_bands WHERE band_title LIKE 'Toad%'
```

In SQL Server, the % is referred to as a wildcard character. The % wildcard character matches any string of zero or more characters. So placing % in our previous delete statement instructed SQL Server to delete all records in the t_bands table where the value in the band_title column begins with "Toad."

UPDATE Statements

The UPDATE statement enables you to change the data within existing rows. Following is the syntax for a simple UPDATE statement:

```
UPDATE  tablename SET columnname = contstant [AND columnname =
constant ...] [WHERE where-expression]
```

The good news about this statement is that the WHERE clause works the same here as it does with the DELETE statement. It simply more clearly identifies the rows that need to be updated.

Here's a sample UPDATE statement:

```
UPDATE t_bands SET band_title = 'Hootie and The Blowfish' WHERE band_id = 1
```

This statement says, "change the value in the band_title field to "Hootie and The Blowfish" in all rows where the value in the band_id field is 1." It's that simple.

SELECT Statements

10 Min.
To Go

The SELECT statement is an important one. You probably use this statement more than any other SQL statement. As you might have guessed, the SELECT statement is used to retrieve data from a table or group of tables. The syntax for a SELECT statement is far too complicated to show here. Instead, here's a demonstration, using the Music database, of some ways that you can use a SELECT statement. Now get started.

If you want to return all rows from a single table, let's say t_bands, you use the following command:

```
SELECT * FROM t_bands
```

In this statement, the * returns all columns. So what if you only want to return just a few rows based on certain criteria? Well, you would use a WHERE clause. To demonstrate this, execute the following INSERT statements:

```
INSERT INTO t_band_members (band_member_fname, band_member_lname, band_id)
VALUES
('Darius','Rucker',1)
INSERT INTO t_band_members (band_member_fname, band_member_lname, band_id)
VALUES
('Mark','Bryan',1)
INSERT INTO t_band_members (band_member_fname, band_member_lname, band_id)
VALUES
('Dean','Felber',1)
INSERT INTO t_band_members (band_member_fname, band_member_lname, band_id)
VALUES
('Jim','Sonefeld',1)
```

Now you can execute a command to return all the members of Hootie & The Blowfish as follows:

```
SELECT * FROM t_band_members WHERE band_id = 1
```

Generally, using * is not good practice because it returns all the columns in a table, which is not generally the desired result. For performance reasons it is a good idea to only request the columns you need. So what if you don't want to return all the columns in a row? In that case, you would simply explicitly define which columns to return. The following statement returns only two columns from the t_band_members table:

```
SELECT band_member_fname, band_member_lname FROM t_band_members WHERE
band_id = 1
```

You can also order the rows returned using an ORDER clause. The ORDER clause allows you to specify the columns you want to use to order the rows that are returned by a SELECT statement.

```
SELECT band_member_fname, band_member_lname FROM t_band_members WHERE
band_id = 1
ORDER BY band_member_lname, band_member_fname
```

In the previous statement, the results of the SELECT statement will first be ordered by band_member_lname and then by band_member_fname. So if you had two band members with the same last name, they would then be ordered by first name. Although, based on the data we have inserted thus far in the session, sorting by last and first name will yield the same results as sorting only by last name since all band members have different last names.

When you execute a SELECT statement, the column names are generally included. Sometimes that's not appropriate. Luckily, SQL allows you to get around this problem. You can use an AS clause to rename the columns returned from the SELECT statement as shown in the following example:

```
SELECT band_member_fname AS "Last Name", band_member_lname AS "First Name"
FROM
t_band_members WHERE band_id = 1 ORDER BY band_member_lname,
band_member_fname
```

Notice that the derived column names are enclosed in quotes. This is because the derived names contain spaces. If the derived names do not contain spaces — for example, "LName" — you do not need to use quotes.

OK, we're getting close to the end. The last type of SELECT statement involves returning data from more than one table. There are many ways to do this. Here's a simple example:

```
SELECT band_member_fname AS "Last Name", band_member_lname AS "First
Name",
band_title AS "Band Title" FROM t_band_members, t_bands WHERE
t_band_members.band_id
= t_bands.band_id ORDER BY band_title, _member_lname, band_member_fname
```

This statement returns data from two tables, t_bands and t_band_members. The FROM clause lists the tables from which you want to return data. With the statement, you are returning three columns from the two tables. The columns you want to return are listed after the SELECT statement. If, by chance, you have two columns with the same name in tables from which you are selecting, you need to preface the column names with the table name. For example, the following code is a rewrite of the previous SELECT statement that explicitly declares from which table you are selecting the columns:

```
SELECT t_band_members.band_member_fname AS "Last Name",
t_band_members.band_member_lname AS "First Name", t_bands.band_title AS
"Band Title"
FROM t_band_members, t_bands WHERE t_band_members.band_id =
t_bands.band_id ORDER BY
t_bands.band_title, t_band_members.band_member_lname,
t_band_members.band_member_fname
```

So, how are the tables joined when selecting data from two or more tables? Look at the WHERE clauses in the two previous SELECT statements. The WHERE clause links the tables on the band_id in each table. So all the rows in each table that have the same band_id value are displayed. Try taking out the WHERE clause and executing the SQL statement.

Done!

REVIEW

SQL is the language used to retrieve and manipulate data in a database. SQL is effectively a language composed of statements and clauses used in concert to create, retrieve, update, and delete data. From our experience, the INSERT, DELETE, UPDATE, and SELECT statements are the most commonly used SQL statements.

QUIZ YOURSELF

1. What is SQL? (See session introduction.)
2. What SQL statement is used to retrieve data from a database table? (See "SELECT Statements.")
3. How do you return data from more than one table with a SELECT command? (See "SELECT Statements.")

XML: A Primer

Session Checklist

✔ Understanding the basics and promise of XML

✔ Learning to create a simple XML document

**30 Min.
To Go**

Y ou have probably heard a great deal about eXtensible Markup Language (XML) over the past few years. XML is on its way to becoming the de facto language for communications between devices, Web browsers, computers, servers, and applications. In time, any two applications will be able to exchange information without ever having been designed to talk to each other.

In many ways, XML is just another file format — one more way to store information. However, XML as a file format is just the beginning. XML promises to liberate information from proprietary file formats and make it possible for information to move among multiple programs on different types of computers without facing the battery of conversion programs and lost information that is currently necessary. XML promises to dramatically increase both the efficiency and flexibility of the ways in which you handle information. In doing so, XML will have an impact on the way in which you use computers; it will change the way you look at applications.

Fundamentally, XML makes it easy to store information in a hierarchical format, providing a consistent, easy-to-parse syntax and a set of tools for building rules describing the structure used to contain information. The XML format can represent both simple and complex information, and allows developers to create their own vocabularies for describing that information. XML documents can describe both themselves and their content.

The XML Design Specs

When you think of an "application," you tend to think of a Web application — or a desktop application like Word or Excel. However, the creators of XML were a little less nearsighted when they developed the XML specification. They saw XML as a way of sharing data among many different kinds of applications. For this reason, the creators of XML established the following design commandments for the XML specification:

1. XML shall be straightforwardly usable over the Internet.

    This does not mean that XML should only be used over the Internet, but rather that it should be lightweight and easily usable over the Internet.

2. XML shall support a wide variety of applications.

    The idea here is that XML should not be application specific. It can be used over the Internet or in a traditional client/server application. There is no specific technology behind XML, so any technology should be able to use it.

3. It shall be easy to write programs that process XML documents.

    Unable to gain wide acceptance for various reasons, many technologies come and go. A major barrier to wide acceptance is a high level of difficulty or complexity. The designers of XML wanted to ensure that it would gain rapid acceptance by making it easy for programmers to write XML parsers.

4. XML documents should be human-legible and reasonably clear.

    Because XML is text-based and follows a strict but simple formatting methodology, it is extremely easy for a human to get a true sense of what a document means. XML is designed to describe the structure of its contents.

5. XML documents shall be easy to create.

    XML documents can be created in a simple text-editor. Now that's easy!

There are other XML guidelines, but since this only is an introduction to XML, these will do for now. The important thing to remember is that XML is simply a file format that can be used for two or more entities to exchange information.

XML documents are *hierarchical:* they have a single (*root*) element, which may contain other elements, which may in turn contain other elements, and so on. Documents typically look like a tree structure with branches growing out from the center and finally terminating at some point with content. Elements are often described as having parent and child relationships, in which the parent contains the child element.

20 Min.
To Go

The Structure of XML Documents

XML documents must be properly structured and follow strict syntax rules in order to work correctly. If a document is lacking in either if these areas, the document can't be parsed. There are two types of structures in every XML document: logical and physical. The logical structure is the framework for the document and the physical structure is the actual data.

An XML document may consist of three logical parts: a prolog (optional), a document element, and an epilog (optional). The prolog is used to instruct the parser how to interpret the document element. The purpose of the epilog is to provide information pertaining to the preceding data. Listing 6-1 shows the basic structure of an XML document.

Listing 6-1 *Basic structure of an XML document*

```
<?xml version="1.0" ?>
<!-- Above is the prolog -->

<!-- The lines below are contained within the document element: BANDS -->
<BANDS>
  <BAND TYPE="ROCK">
    <NAME>Hootie And The Blowfish</NAME>
    <MEMBERS>
      <MEMBER>
        <FIRST_NAME>Darius</FIRST_NAME>
        <LAST_NAME>Rucker</LAST_NAME>
      </MEMBER>
      <MEMBER>
        <FIRST_NAME>Dean</FIRST_NAME>
        <LAST_NAME>Felber</LAST_NAME>
      </MEMBER>
      <MEMBER>
        <FIRST_NAME>Mark</FIRST_NAME>
        <LAST_NAME>Bryan</LAST_NAME>
      </MEMBER>
      <MEMBER>
        <FIRST_NAME>Jim</FIRST_NAME>
        <LAST_NAME>Sonefeld</LAST_NAME>
      </MEMBER>
    </MEMBERS>
    <LABEL>Atlantic Recording Corporation</LABEL>
  </BAND>
</BANDS>
<!-- epilog goes here -->
```

The prolog is made up of two parts: the XML declaration and an optional Document Type Declaration (DTD). The XML declaration identifies the document as XML and lets the parser know that it complies with the XML specification. Although the prolog, and thereby the XML declaration, is optional, we recommend that you include them in all your XML documents. Here is an example of a simple XML declaration:

```
<?xml version="1.0" ?>
```

The XML declaration can also contain more than just the version attribute. Some of the more important ones are the encoding and standalone attributes.

The document type declaration establishes the grammar rules for the document or it points to a document where these rules can be found. The DTD is optional, but, if included, must appear after the XML declaration.

XML documents can also reference a Schema rather than a DTD. Schemas perform essentially the same function as DTDs, but can describe more complex data types and are actually XML documents themselves. When possible, we recommend using a Schema rather than a DTD as Schemas are quickly becoming the de-facto standard for describing XML documents.

An XML document is referred to as well formed when it conforms to all XML syntax rules. A valid XML document follows the structural rules defined in a Document Type Definition or Schema.

All the data in an XML document is contained within the document element (in this example, <BANDS>). You can't have more than one document element in the same document, but the document element can contain as many child elements as necessary.

XML Syntax

**10 Min.
To Go**

The contents of an XML document are constructed using a very strict syntax that must conform to the following rules:

- Tags are case sensitive.
- All tags must be closed.
- Attribute values must be enclosed in quotes.

 XML elements can have attributes that allow you to add information to an element that it does not contain. For example, in Listing 6-1, the BAND **element has a** TYPE **attribute with a value of** "ROCK".

XML tags are very similar to HTML tags. The less-than (<) and greater-than (>) symbols are used to delimit tags and the forward slash (/) is used to indicate closing tags.

Elements are building blocks of an XML document. Every element in an XML document, with the exception of the document element, is a child element. Child elements can contain one of four content types:

- Element content
- Character content
- Mixed content
- Empty

In our example, the <BAND> and <MEMBERS> elements contain element content. All others contain character content.

All elements in an XML document are nested, which gives the document a hierarchical tree appearance. If you'll notice in the <BANDS> example, all of elements' sub-elements are indented. The rules for nesting are strictly enforced.

XML elements can also have attributes. For example:

```
<BAND TYPE="ROCK">
```

In the previous example, the <BAND> element has an attribute named TYPE that is used to indicate what kind of music the band plays. Notice that the attribute value is enclosed in quotes, which are required. You can create attributes to help describe your elements. You could have also used another child element called `<TYPE>` rather than using an attribute. Either way is fine. It's really a matter of preference.

XML and the .NET Framework

The important thing to remember about XML is that it is simply a way of describing data so that any application that knows the structure of the document can use it. Why do you need to know about XML when dealing with ASP.NET? Well, much of the .NET Framework revolves around the concept of universal data and application access. In fact, pretty much everything in the .NET world revolves around the premise of universal access.

Probably two of the most evident examples of XML usage in ASP.NET are the config.web and global.asax files. Without going into too much detail about these files, they store application and configuration data. Here is an example of a config.web file:

```
<configuration>
  <sessionstate timeout="120"/>
  <assemblies>
    <add assembly="mscorlib"/>
    <add assembly="System.Web"/>
    <add assembly="System.Data"/>
  </assemblies>
  <appsettings>
    <add key="DSN" value="Server=127.0.0.1;Database=hootie; UID=sa"/>
  </appsettings>
</configuration>
```

From your knowledge of XML, you can see that the document element for the config.web file is `<configuration>`. The document element contains several child elements including `<sessionstate>`, `<assemblies>`, and `<appsettings>`. The `<sessionstate>` element has an attribute named timeout that has a value of 120. The `<sessionstate>` element is empty, which means that it does not contain any character data. When an element is empty is must be closed with the `/>` or `</ELEMENT>` syntax. The same could have been accomplished by writing:

```
<sessionstate timeout="120"></sessionstate>
```

XML is also used in ASP.NET with Web Services. A Web Service's results are always returned in XML format. Suppose you created a Web Service named Math that has a method named Add that sums two numbers. If you invoke the Web Service and call the Add function by passing 2 and 6 as the parameters you might get the following result:

```
<?xml version="1.0" ?>
<int xmlns="http://tempuri.org/">8</int>
```

You'll notice that the result is returned in XML format. The XML document contains a prolog and a document element. That's it.

This brief introduction of XML and how it is used by the .NET Framework will help you understand some of the concepts introduced later in the book. For further information about XML, we recommend visiting the World Wide Web Consortium's (W3C) XML Web site at www.w3c.com.

.NET Web Services, like the global.asax and config.web files, are based heavily on XML. All Web Services responses are serialized as XML. We'll talk more about Web Services in Session 28.

Done!

REVIEW

"XML is the future . . ." If you've heard that once, you've heard it a million times. You may be sick of hearing it, but you accept it because it's probably true. Simply put, the purpose of XML is to describe data so it can easily be exchanged. The nice thing about XML is that it's easy to learn as its syntax is very similar to its cousin HTML.

QUIZ YOURSELF

1. What is the purpose of XML? (See session introduction.)
2. How many root elements are in an XML document? (See "The XML Design Specs.")
3. What are the three logical parts of an XML document? (See "The Structure of XML Documents.")

Developing ASP.NET Pages

Session Checklist

Handling ASP.NET events

Using page directives and namespaces

Choosing a language

**30 Min.
To Go**

In this session, we are going to walk you through writing an ASP.NET page. Writing and ASP.NET page is a little more complicated than writing an ASP page, but once you get the hang of it, you'll end up writing a lot less code. ASP.NET pages are event-oriented rather than procedural. This means that instead of starting at the top of a page and writing code that is executed as the page is interpreted, you write event-handling code. An event can be pretty much any type of action, for example, a user submitting a form, a page loading, or clicking a button, and so on.

ASP.NET Events

When an ASP.NET page is loaded, a structured series of events is fired in a set order. You write code that responds to these events rather than interspersing it with HTML as the general practice with ASP. Figure 7-1 shows the ASP.NET event order.

As you can see, the first event to be fired when a page is loaded is the Page_Load event and the last to be fired is the Page_Unload event. The Page_Load event is fired every time a page is loaded. In between the Page_Load and the Page_Unload events, control events are fired. A control event is an event that is wired to a control of some sort. ASP.NET provides many types of controls including HTML controls, Web controls, user controls, validation controls, and so on. Don't concern yourself with the differences between controls right now (they're discussed in greater detail in Session 8, "Using HTML Controls", and Session 9, "Using Web Controls".), just be aware that they can all respond to events, like being clicked.

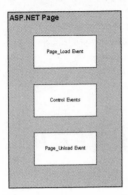

Figure 7-1 *ASP.NET page events*

In order to write code for these events, you need to include them in a code declaration block. In ASP.NET, a code declaration block looks like this:

```
<SCRIPT [LANGUAGE="codeLangauge"] RUNAT="SERVER" [SRC="externalfilename"]>
    ' Event Handling Code
</SCRIPT>
```

The LANGUAGE attribute in the <SCRIPT> element specifies the language used in the code block. The value can be any .NET language like VB or C#. The RUNAT="SERVER" attribute/value pair specifies that the script block should be executed on the server-side rather than the client-side. The SRC attribute enables you to specify an external file where the code is located.

So, based on what we know at this point, an ASP.NET page should look like this:

```
<SCRIPT LANGUAGE="VB" RUNAT="server">
    Sub Page_Load(Source As Object, E As EventArgs)
        ' Page_Load Code
    End Sub
    Sub Control_Click(Source As Object, E As EventArgs)
        'Control_Click Code
    End Sub
    Sub Page_Unload(Source As Object, E As EventArgs)
        ' Page_Unload
    End Sub
</SCRIPT>
<html>
<head>
<title>ASP.NET Page</title>
</head>
<body>
</body>
</html>
```

ASP.NET files have an .aspx extension. The .aspx extension simply tells IIS that an ASP.NET page is being requested and should be handled accordingly. All code in this session should be written in files with an .aspx extension.

**20 Min.
To Go**

In ASP.NET, a page is an object, which means it has properties, events and methods. The Page object has one *very* important property: isPostBack. The isPostBack property returns a Boolean value indicating whether the page is being loaded in response to a client post back. This is important because in many cases you will be initializing controls when a page is loaded. Since ASP.NET manages control state between requests, you probably don't want to initialize a control if the page is responding to a post back. Right? Listing 7-1 shows an example of using the isPostBack property:

Listing 7-1 *An isPostBack property example*

```
<SCRIPT LANGUAGE="VB" RUNAT="server">
    Sub Page_Load(Source As Object, E As EventArgs)
        ' Page_Load Code
        lblTest.Text = Page.isPostBack
    End Sub
    Sub Control_Click(Source As Object, E As EventArgs)
        'Control_Click Code
    End Sub
    Sub Page_Unload(Source As Object, E As EventArgs)
        ' Page_Unload
    End Sub
</SCRIPT>
<html>
<head>
<title>ASP.NET Page</title>
</head>
<body>
<form ID="frmTest" RUNAT="SERVER">
<asp:Label ID="lblTest" RUNAT="SERVER"/>
</BR>
<asp:Button ID="btnSubmit" TEXT="Submit" RUNAT="SERVER"/>
</form>
</body>
</html>
```

As shown in Listing 7-1, we added a snippet of code to the Page_Load event that checks if the page is being posted back using the isPostBack property. Something that may look a little foreign are the server-side control declarations a little further down the page. We declared three server controls including a Form HTML control, a Label Web control and a Button Web control. You'll notice that each of these declarations contains a "RUNAT=SERVER" attribute/value pair. This simply means that the control is rendered on the server and its events are handled on the server side rather than the client side. We'll talk more about controls in later sessions.

The Page class contains many useful properties and methods. Refer to your .NET documentation for a complete treatment of the Page class.

OK, try running the previous example. When the page is first loaded the word "False" appears above the Submit button. If you click the Submit button, the form is posted and the page is loaded again. The word "True" now appears above the Submit button. That is because the page is being loaded in response to a post back to the server.

Now, try adding some code to the `Control_Click` event handler and wiring the Submit button to fire the `Control_Click` event handler as shown in Listing 7-2.

Listing 7-2   *Using the Control_Click event handler*

```
<SCRIPT LANGUAGE="VB" RUNAT="server">
    Sub Page_Load(Source As Object, E As EventArgs)
        ' Page_Load Code
        lblTest.Text = Page.isPostBack
    End Sub
    Sub Control_Click(Sender As Object, E As EventArgs)
        'Control_Click Code
        Response.Write("The Submit button was clicked!")
    End Sub
    Sub Page_Unload(Source As Object, E As EventArgs)
        ' Page_Unload
    End Sub
</SCRIPT>
<html>
<head>
<title>ASP.NET Page</title>
</head>
<body>
<form ID="frmTest" RUNAT="SERVER">
<asp:Label ID="lblTest" RUNAT="SERVER"/>
</br>
<asp:Button ID="btnSubmit" onClick="Control_Click" TEXT="Submit"
RUNAT="SERVER"/>
</form>
</body>
</html>
```

Take a look at the Button Web control declaration. You'll notice that we added the `onClick="Control_Click"` attribute/value pair. This declaration wires the `btnSubmit` button to fire the `Control_Click` event handling routine.

Now take a look at the `Control_Click` event handling method. When fired, by the btnSubmit Web control, the phrase "The Submit button was clicked!" will be written to the page response. Try running the page to see what happens.

Page Directives

*10 Min.
To Go*

ASP.NET pages can optionally contain directives that specify settings to be used by the page compiler. Page directives can be located anywhere within an .aspx file. Additionally each directive can contain multiple attribute/value pairs specific to the directive. The syntax for a page directive is:

```
<%@ directive attribute="value"  [attribute="value" . . .]%>
```

Table 7-1 lists the directives that are supported by ASP.NET pages.

Table 7-1 *ASP.NET Page Directives*

Directive	Description
@Page	The @Page directive defines page-specific attributes used by the ASP.NET page parser and compiler. An example of a @Page attribute is Language, which specifies the default language for the page.
@Control	The @Control directive defines control-specific attributes used by the ASP.NET page parser and compiler. An example of a @Control attribute is Description, which provides a text description of the control.
@Import	The @Import directive explicitly imports a namespace into a page. The only attribute supported by the @Import directive is Namespace, which indicates the name of namespace to import. (More on namespaces later.)
@Register	The @Register directive associates aliases with namespaces and class names for concise notation in custom server control syntax. For more information on the @Register directive, see Session 10.
@Assembly	An assembly is a unit of reusable code compiled into a .dll file. The @Assembly directive links an assembly against the current page, making all of the assembly's classes and interfaces available for use on the page. The only attribute supported by the @Assembly directive is Assemblyname, which indicates the name of the assembly to link. Assemblies that reside in an application \bin directory are automatically linked to pages within the application, therefore, they do not need to be linked using the @Assembly directive.
@OutputCache	The @OutputCache directive controls the output caching policy for the page. An example of a @OutputCache attribute is Duration, which specifies the time (in seconds) that the output cache for the page will be maintained.

Listing 7-3 shows an example of an ASP.NET page with page directives.

Listing 7-3 *An ASP.NET page with page directives*

```
<%@ Page Language="VB" Description="ASP.NET Page" %>
<%@ Import Namespace="System.Net" %>
<SCRIPT LANGUAGE="VB" RUNAT="server">
   Sub Page_Load(Source As Object, E As EventArgs)
       ' Page_Load Code
       lblTest.Text = Page.isPostBack
   End Sub
```

Continued

Listing 7-3 *Continued*

```
    Sub Control_Click(Sender As Object, E As EventArgs)
        'Control_Click Code
        Response.Write("The Submit button was clicked!")
    End Sub
    Sub Page_Unload(Source As Object, E As EventArgs)
        ' Page_Unload
    End Sub
</SCRIPT>
<html>
<head>
<title>ASP.NET Page</title>
</head>
<body>
<form ID="frmTest" RUNAT="SERVER">
<asp:Label ID="lblTest" RUNAT="SERVER"/>
</br>
<asp:Button ID="btnSubmit" onClick="Control_Click" TEXT="Submit"
RUNAT="SERVER"/>
</form>
</body>
</html>
```

Our ASP.NET page now contains three directives: @Page, @Import, and @OutputCache.

Namespaces

As we have mentioned several times in this book, ASP.NET, and actually the .NET Framework, is a hierarchy of classes providing basic services. In order to gain access to these classes or services, you need to import their namespace into the ASP.NET page.

Table 7-2 lists several of the namespaces that are automatically imported into all pages.

Table 7-2 *Namespaces That Are Automatically Imported*

Namespace	Description
System	Contains fundamental classes and base classes that define commonly-used value and reference data types, events and event handlers, interfaces, attributes, and processing exceptions.
System.Collections	Contains interfaces and classes that define various collections of objects, such as lists, queues, arrays, hash tables, and dictionaries.
System.IO	Provides access to the File and Directory objects, which enable you to add, move, change, create, or delete folders (directories) and files on the Web server.

Namespace	Description
System.Web	Includes the HTTPRequest class that provides extensive information about the current HTTP request, the HTTPResponse class that manages HTTP output to the client, and the HTTPServerUtility object that provides access to server-side utilities and processes. System.Web also includes classes for cookie manipulation, file transfer, exception information, and output cache control.
System.Web.UI	Contains the ASP.NET control classes.
System.Web.UI.HtmlControls	Contains the HTML server controls.
System.Web.UI.WebControls	Contains the Web controls.

 For a list of all of the namespaces imported into ASP.NET pages by default, refer to your ASP.NET documentation.

Table 7-3 explains some other commonly used namespaces.

Table 7-3 *Other Commonly Used Namespaces*

Namespace	Description
System.Data	Provides access to general data access services.
System.Data.OleDb	Provides access to OLEDB -specific data access services.
System.Data.SQLClient	Provides access to SQL Server data access services.
SystemXML	Provides access to the services for manipulating XML.

So, for example, if you wanted to write a page that would be used to access a SQL Server database, you would include the following @Import page directives in your ASP.NET page:

```
<%@ Import Namespace="System.Data" %>
<%@ Import Namespace="System.Data.SqlClient" %>
```

Choosing a Language

In this session, we have used Visual Basic.NET to write the ASP.NET pages. One of the most attractive features about the .NET Framework is that it is language neutral. This means that any language that provides a .NET compiler can be used to write ASP.NET pages. The number of languages supported is continuously growing. More than likely, at some point, your favorite language will be supported. And since *all* code is compiled into intermediate language (IL) code, there is no performance penalty or gain for using one language rather than another.

So, when choosing a language, pick the language with which you are most comfortable. We are guessing that VB.NET and C# will gain the widest acceptance, so, if you're looking for support, those might be the best choices.

Done!

REVIEW

ASP.NET provides an event-oriented programming model. When an ASP.NET page is loaded, a structured series of events are fired in a set order. You can write code that responds to these events rather than interspersing it with HTML, as you had to do if you programmed in ASP. ASP.NET pages can also be managed and controlled through the use of page directives, which specify optional settings to be used by the page compiler. One of these page directives is Import, which provides ASP.NET page access to .NET services.

QUIZ YOURSELF

1. What is a page directive? (See "Page Directives.")
2. Which namespaces are used for data access? (See "Namespaces.")
3. What event is fired every time a page is loaded? (See "ASP.NET Events.")

Using HTML Controls

Session Checklist

✔ Understanding the usefulness of HTML controls

✔ Learning to utilize server-side event handling

✔ Implementing HTML controls to maintain state

**30 Min.
To Go**

In today's distributed computing environment, one of the biggest issues developers face is writing code that can effectively run on numerous browser types and versions, and maintaining state between server requests. Writing an Internet application can be very tedious when attempting to write code that can run simultaneously on different browsers, operating systems, and other devices. If you've ever tried writing an application that takes full advantage of the feature set of Internet Explorer 5.0 while still being compatible with Netscape 3.0, you know what we're talking about.

Many developers take the "lowest-common-denominator" approach to solving this problem. This means they write applications that utilize the feature set of older browser versions (for example, Netscape 3.0) and have all other clients, regardless of capability, execute the same code. Naturally, this approach has drawbacks of its own. For example, in this particular case, more round-trips to the server are required, resulting in performance degradation.

Using newer browser versions, state maintenance is less of a headache than with older browsers. For example, with IE 5 and DHTML, HTML form validation can be done on the fly by the client browser so fewer round trips to the server are required than when the same application is run on, for example, Netscape 3.0. All of these extra trips to the server dramatically increase server load and decrease application performance.

Yet another solution to the multiple browsers problem is writing different code for different browsers. This is generally accomplished by using a third-party component (or writing your own) that determines the type of client browser that is making the request and executing the server-side code written for the requesting browser type. This too is a valid approach to solving the problem, but also requires the maintenance of a lot of code. If requirements change while an application is being developed or produced, then code needs to be changed in multiple locations. That is neither fun nor easy!

Microsoft has effectively solved the problem of state maintenance and multiple client support by providing HTML controls and Web controls. In this session, we will discuss HTML controls.

Introducing HTML Controls

HTML controls look exactly like HTML elements with the exception that they have a runat="server" attribute/value pair in the opening tag of the HTML element. HTML controls offer many benefits, including:

- **Event sets.** They provide a set of events for which developers can write server-side or client-side events to handle.
- **Automatic management of the values of the form's controls.** If the form makes a round trip to the server, HTML controls are automatically populated with the values they had when the form was submitted to the server.
- **Interaction with validation controls.** This feature enables developers to verify that a user has entered correct appropriate information into the control.
- **Pass-through of custom attributes.** Developers can add any attributes needed to the HTML control, and the Web Forms framework will read them and render them without any change in functionality.

The following sections show you how to use HTML controls and how exactly they can be utilized to solve multiple client and state maintenance problems.

Using HTML controls

Before we start slinging code, there are several things to remember when using HTML controls:

- All HTML controls that post back events must be nested within an HTML control form.
- All HTML controls must be well formed and must not overlap. Unless otherwise noted, elements must be closed, either with an ending slash within the tag, or with a closing tag.

To illustrate how HTML controls work, we will first write a small application using ASP 3.0 and then re-create the same application using ASP.NET. We'll then compare the two, and you'll see how much time and effort HTML controls can save. Listing 8-1 shows the code for an ASP page that generates an HTML form.

Listing 8-1 *An ASP HTML form*

```
<html>
<body>
<%
Dim sName
```

```
sName = Trim(Request.Form("cmbPeople"))
If sName <> "" Then
  Response.Write(sName)
End If
%>
<form name="frmPeople" method="post">
People<BR>
<select name="cmbPeople">
  <option></option>
  <option>Bill Gates</option>
  <option>Larry Ellison</option>
  <option>Steve Case</option>
</select>
<input type="submit" value="Submit">
</form>
</body>
</html>
```

What we have effectively done here is create an ASP page with an HTML form that redirects to itself for processing. After the form is submitted, the HTML select element loses its state, that is, it no longer displays the value you selected prior to submitting the form.

Listing 8-2 shows another ASP page (see file C08-02.asp on the CD-ROM) that actually maintains the select element's state.

**20 Min.
To Go**

Listing 8-2   *An ASP page that maintains state*

```
<html>
<body>
<%
Dim sName
sName = Trim(Request.Form("cmbPeople"))
If sName <> "" Then
  Response.Write(sName)
End If
%>
<form name="frmPeople" method="post">
People<BR>
<select name="cmbPeople">
  <option></option>
  <option<% If sName = "Bill Gates" Then Response.Write(" selected")
%>>Bill Gates</option>
  <option<% If sName = "Larry Ellison" Then Response.Write(" selected")
%>>Larry Ellison</option>
  <option<% If sName = "Steve Case" Then Response.Write(" selected")
%>>Steve Case</option>
</select>
<input type="submit" value="Submit">
</form>
</body>
</html>
```

When you reload the page, the value selected is maintained in the select element. You'll notice that an If...Then statement was added to each option element to check if the option value is equivalent to the value submitted. If it is, the option element is marked as SELECTED. This may not seem like that big of a deal, but as your forms get more and more complex, the process of writing the code to maintain state for each element can be very tedious and monotonous. Additionally, this code is very prone to errors. For example, if we had inadvertently written:

```
<OPTION<% If sName = "Bill Gats" Then Response.Write(" SELECTED") %>>Bill
Gates</OPTION> (error in Gates intentional)
```

we would receive unexpected results. So, code like this definitely requires thorough testing.

The following sample code is a listing of the HTML source generated by our ASP page. We'll compare this source with the HTML source generated by the ASP.NET page we'll write in few seconds:

```
<html>
<body>
Bill Gates
<form name="frmPeople" method="post">
People<BR>
<select name="cmbPeople">
  <option></option>
  <option selected>Bill Gates</option>
  <option>Larry Ellison</option>
  <option>Steve Case</option>
</select>
<input type="submit" value="Submit">
</form>
</body>
</html>
```

In order to maintain state, you have to use an HTML control. To turn an HTML element into an HTML control, use the following model:

```
<HTML Tag [id="Optional Name"] [attribute="value" . . .]
runat="server">[</HTML Tag>]
```

Listing 8-3 shows a sample ASP.NET page (see file C08-03.aspx on the CD-ROM) that utilizes HTML controls.

Listing 8-3   *An ASP.NET page that utilizes HTML controls*

```
<html>
<body>
<%
Dim sName
sName = Trim(Request.Form("cmbPeople"))
If sName <> "" Then
  Response.Write(sName)
End If
```

```
%>
<form id="frmPeople" method="post" runat="server">
People<BR>
<select id="cmbPeople" runat="server">
  <option></option>
  <option>Bill Gates</option>
  <option>Larry Ellison</option>
  <option>Steve Case</option>
</select>
<input type="submit" value="Submit">
</form>
</body>
</html>
```

Notice that this page is nearly identical to people.asp with a few minor exceptions — we changed all the name attributes to identify attributes and added the runat="server" attribute/value pair to the HTML form and select elements. When you run this page, the select element's state will be maintained without the developer having to write an additional line of code.

Here is a listing of the HTML source generated by our sample code:

```
<html>
<body>
Bill Gates<form name="frmPeople" method="post" action="people.aspx"
id="frmPeople">
<input type="hidden" name="__VIEWSTATE"
value="YTB6LTE2NTY1NTY1MF9fX3g=54b44516" />

People<BR>
<select name="cmbPeople" id="cmbPeople">
    <option value=""></option>
    <option selected value="Bill Gates">Bill Gates</option>
    <option value="Larry Ellison">Larry Ellison</option>
    <option value="Steve Case">Steve Case</option>
</select>
<input type="submit" value="Submit">
</form>
</body>
</html>
```

This HTML source looks similar to the HTML source generated by our traditional ASP sample, but there are several differences:

- An action attribute/value pair was added to our form element.
- A value attribute/value pair was added to each of our option values.
- The following hidden element was added to the form:

```
<input type="hidden" name="__VIEWSTATE"
value="YTB6LTE2NTY1NTY1MF9fX3g=54b44516" />
```

Hmmmm . . . That's weird. Where did all of this extra source code come from, and what function does it perform? Let us explain . . .

How HTML controls work

All of the HTML code that was added came from the ASP.NET engine. Each of these additions are being used by the ASP.NET engine to maintain state across client requests. Absolutely no state is maintained on the server using session variables — definitely a plus for scalability. The hidden __VIEWSTATE field is used to maintain control state and the value is actually a compressed and encrypted value. Typically, you probably won't be able to make much sense of it. But that's OK because ASP.NET handles all of the details for you.

The __VIEWSTATE form field is used to maintain control state, not user state. User state management will be discussed in Session 12, "Maintaining State in ASP.NET."

When an ASP.NET page is requested from the server, several things happen relating to HTML controls. First, the aspx page tries to determine whether the page is a post back. If it is, the __VIEWSTATE property is examined, the posted data is processed, and state is applied to the forms elements. All the __VIEWSTATE field does is contain data about control state when the HTML page is generated.

Put in very simplistic terms, this is what happens. No magic, just some processing that is transparent to the developer.

10 Min.
To Go

Intrinsic HTML controls

As demonstrated in the previous example, the HTML select object can be used as an ASP.NET HTML control. So you may be wondering what other elements can be ASP.NET HTML controls. Each of the following elements can be used as HTML controls:

<form>	<td>
<select>	<th>
<img>	<a>
<textarea>	<button>
<table>	<tr>

<input> (checkbox, image, hidden, file, button, text, submit, radio button)

HTML Control Events

Handling HTML control events is a straightforward process. We can use one of two approaches to handling events:

1. Utilize the ASP.NET Page_Load event.
2. Create custom event handlers.

ASP.NET's Page object provides you with a facility for handling events on the server side using the Page_Load event. Handling events using the Page_Load event requires you to write some code that first checks to see if the request is a post back and then performs the appropriate actions.

The Page_OnLoad event

Listing 8-4 demonstrates how you can handle HTML control events with the Page_OnLoad event.

Listing 8-4 *Using HTML control events with the Page_OnLoad event*

```
<script runat="server" language="VB">
Sub Page_Load(Sender As Object, E As EventArgs)
   If Page.IsPostBack Then
     Select cmbPeople.value
       Case "Bill Gates"
         Response.Redirect("http://www.microsoft.com")
       Case "Larry Ellison"
         Response.Redirect ("http://www.oracle.com")
       Case "Steve Case"
         Response.Redirect ("http://www.aol.com")
       Case Else
     End Select
   End If
End Sub
</script>
<html>
<body>
<form id="frmPeople" method="post" runat="server">
People<br>
<select id="cmbPeople" runat="server">
  <option></option>
  <option>Bill Gates</option>
  <option>Larry Ellison</option>
  <option>Steve Case</option>
</select><br>
<input type="submit" value="Submit">
</form>
</body>
</html>
```

You'll notice at the top of this page a function called Page_Load is invoked. This function is called each time the page is requested by a client. You must check to see whether the page request is a post back (that is, a form has been submitted) by using the Page object's IsPostBack property. If the IsPostBack property returns true, you can check the submitted values — in this case, the value of the cmbPeople select element.

With ASP.NET we can check the value of a form element using its value property. We no longer need to use the Request.Form **syntax.**

The rest of the code is straightforward. Use Visual Basic's Select control structure to redirect the user to a Web site depending on the value selected. Remember that this code is being handled on the server side, so the browser used by the client is inconsequential.

Custom event handlers

In order to create a custom event handler, you need to do two things:

- Create a subroutine that will act as the event handler.
- Wire an HTML control to call the event handler on the server side.

In the following example, we will create a subroutine called Sample_Handler to handle event processing. This subroutine will be called by the Submit button by simply adding the following the runat="server" and onserverclick="Sample_Handler" attribute/value pairs to the control declaration as follows:

```
<input type="submit" value="Submit" id="smbSubmit" runat="server"
onserverclick="Sample_Event">
```

That's all you have to do. Listing 8-5 shows the entire page:

Listing 8-5   *Using a custom event handler*

```
<script runat="server" language="VB">
Sub Sample_Handler(Sender As Object, E As EventArgs)
  Select cmbPeople.value
    Case "Bill Gates"
      Response.Redirect ("http://www.microsoft.com")
    Case "Larry Ellison"
      Response.Redirect ("http://www.oracle.com")
    Case "Steve Case"
      Response.Redirect ("http://www.aol.com")
    Case Else
  End Select
End Sub
</script>
<html>
<body>
<form id="frmPeople" method="post" runat="server">
People<br>
<select id="cmbPeople" runat="server">
  <option></option>
  <option>Bill Gates</option>
  <option>Larry Ellison</option>
  <option>Steve Case</option>
</select><br>
<input type="submit" value="Submit" id="cmbSubmit" runat="server"
onserverclick="Sample_Handler">
</form>
</body>
</html>
```

Done!

REVIEW

HTML controls are server-side ASP.NET controls that render browser-specific HTML. HTML controls reduce the time required to develop HTML that will correctly render on different browsers; and they can be used to maintain state between server requests. HTML controls also allow us, as developers, to capture client-side events and process them on the server.

QUIZ YOURSELF

1. What attribute/value pair must be included in an HTML control declaration? (See "Using HTML controls.")
2. What is the purpose of the hidden VIEWSTATE form field? (See "How HTML controls work.")
3. What is the advantage of using ASP.NET server-side event processing over the more traditional client-side event processing? (See "HTML Control Events.")

Using Web Controls

Session Checklist

✔ Understanding the usefulness of ASP.NET Web controls

✔ Learning how to implement Web controls

**30 Min.
To Go**

I n the previous session, "Using HTML Controls," we discussed how to utilize HTML controls to maintain state between server requests. If you recall, there are two major problems that Web developers commonly face: (1) state maintenance and (2) browser compatibility. HTML controls effectively manage the state maintenance issue, but not the browser compatibility issue. That is where Web controls come in. Web controls are very similar to HTML controls but provide a higher degree of control and programmability.

Web controls do not map one-to-one with HTML controls. Instead, Web controls are abstract controls in which the actual HTML rendered by the control might be quite different from the model that you program against. Web controls include traditional form controls such as buttons and text boxes, as well as complex controls such as tables. They also include controls that provide commonly used functionality, for example displaying data in a grid or choosing dates. Many Web controls can also be bound to a data source such as an ADO.NET DataSet.

Web controls offer all the same advantages as HTML controls plus the following:

- **Type-safe programming capabilities.** Web controls offer a rich programming model that provides type-safe programming capabilities because you, as a developer, can be certain of the type of data a variable contains. Type-safe programming means that a variable is declared as a specific data type (for example integer or string) and can only be assigned values of that type. Type-safe programs are, in most instances, far easier to debug and result in fewer run-time errors.

- **Automatic browser detection.** The controls can detect capabilities and create appropriate output for both basic and rich (HTML 4.0) browsers.

- **Custom templates.** For some Web controls, you can define your own look and feel using templates.

- **More flexible controls.** Some controls offer the ability to specify whether a control's event causes immediate posting to the server or whether it is cached and raised when the form is submitted.
- **Better communication between controls.** This includes the ability to pass events from a nested control (such as a button in a table) to the container control.

At this point, you may be wondering why Microsoft opted to offer both HTML and Web controls. The answer is simple: flexibility. You can use whichever set of controls you feel more comfortable with. HTML controls keep you closer to the content. By contrast, Web controls provide a more consistent programming model, but distance you a little from the actual output.

You use Web controls in the same way that you use HTML controls. The only difference is that they *must* have the runat="server" name/value pair. You don't have to do anything special to access this code library as it's available by default, but you do have to ensure you use the correct tag prefix (or namespace) when using the controls.

In general, Web controls can be grouped into one of four basic categories:

- Intrinsic controls
- List controls
- Rich controls
- Validation controls

Intrinsic Controls

The intrinsic controls are designed to provide replacements for the standard HTML controls. Here is a list of the intrinsic controls:

Button	CheckBox
Hyperlink	Image
Label	LinkButton
Panel	Table
TableCell	TableRow
TextBox	

Using intrinsic controls

We are really fond of Web controls. They are easy to use and immensely programmable. Each control is an object and therefore has its own set of properties, methods, and events. We have found that using Web controls greatly eases the pain of writing repetitive HTML code. You may not feel as closely connected to the HTML when using Web controls, but at least you'll know that your page will render correctly regardless of which browser is used.

Here is a code sample that creates an HTML table using the ASP.NET Table Web control:

```
<html>
<head>
</head>
```

```
<body>
<asp:Table id="tblExample" BorderWidth=1 GridLines="both" runat="server"/>
</body>
</html>
```

When you run the page, you'll notice that nothing is displayed. That's because we haven't added any cells to the data. By examining the HTML output from the page, you should, however, see the HTML table. Here is the HTML generated in IE 5.5:

```
<html>
<head>
</head>
<body>
<table id="tblExample" rules="all" border="1" style="border-width:1px;border-style:solid;">
</table>
</body>
</html>
```

If we further examine the HTML output, we see that there is some HTML that we didn't add. For example, the style and border attributes were created for us by the ASP.NET engine based on the properties we set for the Table Web control (here: BorderWidth and GridLines). This is how browser compatibility is handled. The ASP.NET engine sniffs the browser to determine its capabilities and sends HTML that the browser can handle. This is a simple operation, but it's really a pain if you're forced to do it yourself.

Next, you'll expand on the previous sample page by adding a few rows and columns to the table. There are two ways to accomplish this: you can add TableRow and TableCell Web controls (a) manually or (b) programmatically. Listing 9-1 shows the manual approach.

20 Min. To Go

Listing 9-1 *Using intrinsic controls (manually)*

```
<html>
<head>
</head>
<body>
<asp:Table id="tblExample" BorderWidth=1 GridLines="both" runat="server">
  <asp:TableRow>
    <asp:TableCell>Row 1, Cell 1</asp:TableCell>
    <asp:TableCell>Row 1, Cell 2</asp:TableCell>
    <asp:TableCell>Row 1, Cell 3</asp:TableCell>
    <asp:TableCell>Row 1, Cell 4</asp:TableCell>
    <asp:TableCell>Row 1, Cell 5</asp:TableCell>
  </asp:TableRow>
  <asp:TableRow>
    <asp:TableCell>Row 2, Cell 1</asp:TableCell>
    <asp:TableCell>Row 2, Cell 2</asp:TableCell>
    <asp:TableCell>Row 2, Cell 3</asp:TableCell>
    <asp:TableCell>Row 2, Cell 4</asp:TableCell>
    <asp:TableCell>Row 2, Cell 5</asp:TableCell>
  </asp:TableRow>
</asp:Table>
</body>
</html>
```

You'll notice that all we are doing here is creating rows using the `TableRow` Web control and cells using the `TableCell` Web control. There are two things we would like to mention here. First, the Web controls must be formed correctly, which means that if we open, for example, a `TableCell`, we must close it using the following (XML) syntax:

```
</asp:TableCell>
```

Secondly, it isn't necessary to include the `runat="server"` attribute/value pair when creating the `TableRow` and `TableCell` Web controls in the example because they belong to the Table Web control that did include the `runat="server"` attribute/value pair. As a rule, you should always include it so there's no confusion about what you're doing. (We didn't include the `runat="server"` attribute/value pair for demonstration purposes only.)

Manually adding rows and cells is great if you're using the table for formatting and know exactly how many rows and cells you need. In many cases, however, you don't have this information so it may be better to take the programmatic approach. Listing 9-2 shows the code listing that, when run, creates 10 rows and 50 cells programmatically.

Listing 9-2 *Using intrinsic controls (programmatically)*

```vb
<script language="VB" runat="server">
Sub Page_Load(Sender As Object, E As EventArgs)
    Dim iRowCount As Integer     ' Current row count
    Dim iColumnCount As Integer   ' Total number of columns (columns)

    For iRowCount = 1 To 10
       Dim tRow As New TableRow()
       For iColumnCount = 1 To 5
           Dim tCell As New TableCell()
           tCell.Text = "Row " & iRowCount & ", Cell " & iColumnCount
           tRow.Cells.Add(tCell)   ' Add new TableCell object to row
       Next
       tblExample.Rows.Add(tRow)
    Next

End Sub
</script>
<html>
<head>
</head>
<body>
<asp:Table id="tblExample" BorderWidth=1 GridLines="both" runat="server"/>
</body>
</html>
```

In the body of the HTML, we declare a `Table` Web control. Since we are not initially declaring any `TableRows` or `TableCells`, we end the Table declaration with `/>` rather than `>`. We could have just as easily closed the `Table` Web control using the `</asp:Table>` syntax. Again, a matter of personal preference! At the beginning of the page, we have included a simple script within the Page_Load event that adds rows and cells rows to the table programmatically. Every time the page is called, this script will be executed. Because this is not a book about VB.NET, I won't go into the syntax of the script. The important thing to realize is that by using an object's properties, methods, and events, you can programmatically create other objects at runtime.

Handling intrinsic Web control events

Now may be as good a time as any to talk about handling Web control events. All ASP.NET events are handled on the server rather than the client. This is kind of a new way of thinking for many developers who are used to writing client-side code, but it has the advantage of providing cross-browser compatibility. Each and every Web control has its own set of events. You'll have to refer to your ASP.NET documentation for a complete listing of each control's events. For example, the ASP.NET Button Web control has an OnClick event that is fired when the button is clicked. Listing 9-3 illustrates handling an OnClick event.

Listing 9-3 *Handling OnClick events*

```
<script language="VB" runat="server">
Sub btnTest_Click(Sender As Object, E As EventArgs)
    If tblExample.Rows.Count = 0 Then
        Dim iRowCount As Integer      ' Current row count
        Dim iColumnCount As Integer    ' Total number of cells (columns)

        For iRowCount = 1 To 10
            Dim tRow As New TableRow()
            For iColumnCount = 1 To 5
              Dim tCell As New TableCell()
              tCell.Text = "Row " & iRowCount & ", Cell " & iColumnCount
              tRow.Cells.Add(tCell)    ' Add new TableCell object to row
            Next
            tblExample.Rows.Add(tRow)
        Next
    End If
End Sub
</script>
<html>
<head>
</head>
<body>
<asp:Table id="tblExample" BorderWidth=1 GridLines="both" runat="server"/>
<form runat="server">
<asp:Button id="btnTest" OnClick="btnTest_Click" Text="Insert Rows"
runat="server"/>
</form>
</body>
</html>
```

**10 Min.
To Go**

List Controls

List controls, like intrinsic controls, map closely to HTML elements. The reason they are in their own category is that List controls present the user with a list of options. The general rule here is that there is a parent object that contains multiple child objects. For example a DropDownList control contains one or many List items. The List controls are:

- DataGrid
- DataList
- CheckBoxList
- DropDownList
- ListBox
- RadioButtonList

Since the use of Web controls is uniform regardless of type, I won't go into too much detail here. We recommend that you look at your .NET documentation to get a complete listing of each List control's properties, methods, and events.

The following snippet of code illustrates how to create a DropDownList by manually inserting a List Object:

```
<html>
<head>
</head>
<body>
<form runat="server">
<asp:DropDownList id="cmbPeople" runat="server">
  <asp:ListItem value="0" text=""/>
  <asp:ListItem value="1" text="Bill Gates"/>
  <asp:ListItem value="2" text="Larry Ellison"/>
  <asp:ListItem value="3" text="Steve Case"/>
</asp:DropDownList>
<br/><br/>
<asp:Button id="Button1" Text="Submit" runat="server"/>
</form>
</body>
</html>
```

This is a simple example, but probably requires a little clarification. First, you'll notice that we used the following syntax to declare a ListItem:

```
<asp:ListItem value="1" text="Bill Gates"/>
```

We could have just as easily used:

```
<asp:ListItem value="1">Bill Gates</asp:ListItem>
```

OK, now let's try it programmatically:

```
<script language="vb" runat="server">
Sub Page_Load(Sender As Object, e As EventArgs)
  cmbPeople.Items.Add("")
  cmbPeople.Items.Add("Bill Gates")
  cmbPeople.Items.Add("Larry Ellison")
  cmbPeople.Items.Add("Steve Case")
End Sub
</script>
<html>
<head>
</head>
<body>
<form runat="server">
<asp:DropDownList id="cmbPeople" runat="server"/>
<br/><br/>
<asp:Button id="Button1" Text="Submit" runat="server"/>
</form>
</body>
</html>
```

List controls can be bound to a data source very easily. We'll introduce data binding in Session 22, "Introducing Data Binding."

Cross-Ref

Rich Controls

Rich controls are very different from intrinsic and List Web controls. Intrinsic and List controls can roughly be traced to a single HTML element. Rich controls provide a piece of functionality that requires the use of multiple HTML elements. The ASP.NET rich controls are

- AdRotator
- Calendar

In the "old ASP world," developers would have either (1) written a lot of HTML/ASP code or (2) written an ActiveX control to provide the functionality that is now provided by ASP.NET rich controls. The nice thing is that all state maintenance is managed for us and the user doesn't need to download a component. Very convenient! There should soon be quite an aftermarket for custom rich controls.

Listing 9-4 demonstrates the ease-of-use of the Calendar control.

Listing 9-4   *Using the Calendar control*

```
<html>
<head>
<script language="VB" runat="server">
  Sub Calendar_Change(Source As Object, E As EventArgs)
    If Page.IsPostBack Then

            lblMessage.Text = "You selected " &
ctlCalendar.SelectedDate.ToLongDateString()
    End If
  End Sub
</script>
</head>
<body>
<form id="frmCalendar" runat="server">
<asp:Label id="lblMessage" runat="server" />
<br/><br/>
<asp:Calendar id="ctlCalendar"
  BackColor="white"
    BorderWidth="3"
    BorderStyle="Solid"
    BorderColor="Black"
    CellSpacing="2"
    CellPadding="2"
    ShowGridLines="True"
    TitleStyle-BackColor="white"
    TitleStyle-ForeColor="black"
    DayHeaderStyle-ForeColor="white"
    DayStyle-ForeColor="black"
    SelectedDayStyle-BackColor="red"
    OnSelectionChanged="Calendar_Change"
runat="server" />
</form>
</body>
</html>
```

If you view the source for output, you'll see that Microsoft has really done us a favor by providing rich controls. The great thing about rich controls is that they are infinitely customizable.

The fourth category of HTML controls, Validation controls, deserves a session to itself. So, we'll be discussing those in Session 11, "Validating User Input."

Done!

REVIEW

Web controls are server-side ASP.NET controls that render browser-specific HTML Web controls not only reduce the time required to develop HTML that will correctly render on different browsers, but Web controls can be used to maintain state between server requests. Web controls also allow us, as developers, to capture client-side events and process them on the server.

QUIZ YOURSELF

1. What advantages do Web controls provide over HTML controls? (See session introduction.)
2. What are the four basic categories of Web controls? (See session introduction.)
3. (True/False) Web controls map one-to-one with HTML elements. (See session introduction.)

10

Introducing User Controls

**30 Min.
To Go**

After working through the previous two sessions, you should have a good grasp on the controls, HTML and Web, which are provided with ASP.NET. Although the controls packaged with ASP.NET are very useful, chances are you will run into a situation where creating a custom control might be a good idea. Why? First, the standard ASP.NET controls are developed to meet the most common functional requirements; they were not designed to meet every requirement, or very specific requirements. If an HTML or Web control meets one of your functional requirements but only in a general way, you could end up writing a ton of code in your ASP.NET pages to customize it. Furthermore, if that functionality is required on multiple pages (which from our experience is quite common), maintenance could turn out be a major headache. Second, your pages could require the combination of several ASP.NET controls. Again, if you code this functionality into each ASP.NET page, you're really shooting yourself in the foot. Maintainability! Maintainability! Maintainability!

Both of these common situations can be addressed with the use of User Controls. User Controls provide an easy way to partition and reuse simple, common user interface (UI) functionality across a Web application. Furthermore, User Controls are compiled on demand and cached in server memory so you can gain a bit of a performance boost. User Controls do not need to be authored in the same language as the ASP.NET page in which they are being included. For example, if one developer is creating an ASP.NET using Visual Basic, he or she can include a User Control written in C# or C++. From a business perspective, allowing developers to code in the language with which they're most fluent can drastically improve performance. Plus, your resource pool broadens.

Creating a User Control

Since User Controls will be included in other ASP.NET pages, you should not include <html> and <body> elements around the content. Additionally, User Controls that post events should not contain an HTML Form control. These elements should be placed in the containing page.

Start with a simple example, creating a custom address User Control.

The first thing you need to do is create the UI elements for the control. In your address control you have two textboxes for street address, one textbox for city, a dropdown list for state, and a textbox for Zip Code. Figure 10-1 illustrates what the User Control should look like.

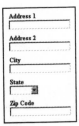

Figure 10-1 *Address User Control UI*

Listing 10-1 shows the HTML that we'll use to construct the address User Control UI.

Listing 10-1 *User Control UI in HTML*

```
<asp:Panel ID="Address" runat="server">
  <asp:Table ID=AddressTable runat="server">
    <asp:TableRow ID=Address1Row runat="server">
      <asp:TableCell ID=Address1Cell runat="server">
        <asp:Label ID=Address1Label text="Address 1" runat="server"
/></BR>
        <asp:Textbox ID=txtAddress1 columns=25 maxlength=50 runat="server"
/>
      </asp:TableCell>
    </asp:TableRow>
    <asp:TableRow ID=Address2Row runat="server">
      <asp:TableCell ID=Address2Cell runat="server">
        <asp:Label ID=Address2Label text="Address 2" runat="server"
/></BR>
        <asp:Textbox ID=txtAddress2 columns=25 maxlength=50 runat="server"
/>
      </asp:TableCell>
    </asp:TableRow>
    <asp:TableRow ID=CityRow runat="server">
      <asp:TableCell ID=CityCell runat="server">
        <asp:Label ID=CityLabel text="City" runat="server" /></BR>
        <asp:Textbox ID=txtCity columns=25 maxlength=50 runat="server" />
```

```
        </asp:TableCell>
      </asp:TableRow>
      <asp:TableRow ID=StateRow runat="server">
        <asp:TableCell ID=StateCell runat="server">
          <asp:Label ID=StateLabel text="State" runat="server" /></BR>
          <asp:DropDownList ID=cmbState runat="server">
            <asp:ListItem selected=true></asp:ListItem>
            <asp:ListItem value=2>California</asp:ListItem>
            <asp:ListItem value=3>Virginia</asp:ListItem>
          </asp:DropDownList>
        </asp:TableCell>
      </asp:TableRow>
      <asp:TableRow ID=ZipCodeRow runat="server">
        <asp:TableCell ID=ZipCodeCell runat="server">
          <asp:Label ID=ZipCodeLabel text="Zip Code" runat="server" /></BR>
          <asp:Textbox ID=txtZipCode columns=10 maxlength=5 runat="server"
/>
        </asp:TableCell>
      </asp:TableRow>
      <asp:TableRow ID=SubmitRow runat="server">
        <asp:TableCell ID=SubmitCell horizontalalign=center runat="server">
          <asp:Button ID=Submit text="Submit" runat="server" />
        </asp:TableCell>
      </asp:TableRow>
    </asp:Table>
  </asp:Panel>
```

If you inspect Listing 10-1 closely, you'll notice that it is simply a collection of ASP.NET Web controls. So, now that we have the UI HTML written, how do we turn it into a simple User Control? Get this . . . instead of giving the file an .aspx extension, simply give an .ascx extension and that's it. You have your first User Control, albeit a very simple one. Go ahead and name your User Control file **address.ascx**.

Now that you have a User Control, you need to include it in an ASP.NET page. In order to do this, you must register the control with the page using the Register directive, which takes the following form:

**20 Min.
To Go**

```
<% @Register TagPrefix="myControl" TagName="Address" src="address.ascx" %>
```

That's pretty self-explanatory with the exception of the TagPrefix and TagName attributes. If you'll recall from Session 9, "Using Web Controls," when adding a Table Web control, for example, to an ASP.NET page, you use the following syntax:

```
<asp:Table . . .runat="server" />
```

You can generalize this declaration using the following syntax:

```
<[TagPrefix]:[TagName] . . .runat="server" />
```

So, when you add your Address control to an ASP.NET page, you would use the following syntax:

```
<myControl:Address . . . runat="server">
```

The following code shows the address.aspx script that will contain the Address User Control:

```
<% @Page Language="VB" %>
<% @Register TagPrefix="myControl" TagName="Address" src="address.ascx" %>
<HTML>
<HEAD>
<TITLE>User Control Example</TITLE>
<STYLE>
      BODY, TABLE, INPUT, SELECT {font-family:trebuchet; font-size:10pt}
</STYLE>
</HEAD>
<BODY>
<FORM ID=frmAddress runat="server">
<myControl:Address ID=AddressControl runat="server" />
</FORM>
</BODY>
</HTML>
```

Adding User Control Properties

One of the things that make Web and HTML controls so useful is that they support properties, methods, and events against which you can program. Guess what? You can customize your User Control by adding your own custom properties, methods, and events to a User Control. Let's start with a few properties.

For this example, you'll be creating your properties using VB. In VB, the syntax for creating a property is

```
[Public|Private] Property [Name] As [Data Type]
    Get
         ' Get Implementation Code
    End Get
    Set
         ' Set Implementation Code
    End Set
End Property
```

Listing 10-2 shows the code for a property for each of our form elements: Address1, Address2, City, StateID, and ZipCode.

Listing 10-2   *Form element properties*

```
<script language="VB" runat="server">
Private m_FontColor As System.Drawing.Color
Private m_Counter As Integer
Public Property Address1 As String
    Get
         Address1 = txtAddress1.text
    End Get
    Set
```

```
        txtAddress1.text = value
    End Set
End Property
Public Property Address2 As String
    Get
        Address2 = txtAddress2.text
    End Get
    Set
        txtAddress2.text = value
    End Set
End Property
Public Property City As String
    Get
        City = txtCity.text
    End Get
    Set
        txtCity.text = value
    End Set
End Property
Public Property StateID As String
    Get
        StateID = cmbState.Items(cmbState.SelectedIndex).Value
    End Get
    Set
        For m_Counter = 0 To (cmbState.Items.Count - 1)
            If cmbState.Items(m_Counter).Value = value Then
                cmbState.SelectedIndex = m_Counter
            End If
        Next
    End Set
End Property
Public Property ZipCode As String
    Get
        ZipCode = txtZipCode.text
    End Get
    Set
        txtZipCode.text = value
    End Set
End Property
Public Property FontColor As System.Drawing.Color
    Get
        FontColor = m_FontColor
    End Get
    Set
        m_FontColor = value
        Address1Label.ForeColor = value
        Address2Label.ForeColor = value
        CityLabel.ForeColor = value
        StateLabel.ForeColor = value
        ZipCodeLabel.ForeColor = value
    End Set
```

Continued

Listing 10-2 *Continued*

```
End Property
Public Property BGColor As System.Drawing.Color
    Get
            BGColor = Address.BackColor
    End Get
    Set
            Address.BackColor = value
    End Set
End Property
</script>
```

Add this code to the top of the Address User Control file. Notice the last two properties listed, FontColor and BGColor. These properties will get and set the font color for all the User Control's labels and the background color of the panel that contains the User Control's controls. Now add the following code to the script block at the top of your ASP.NET page to test your new properties:

```
<script language="VB" runat="server">
Sub Page_Load(Sender As Object, E As EventArgs)
    With AddressControl
            .BGColor = System.Drawing.Color.Blue
            .FontColor = System.Drawing.Color.White
            .Address1 = "100 ASP.NET St."
            .City = "Microsoft"
            .StateID = 3
            .ZipCode = "11111"
    End With
End Sub
</script>
```

Pretty cool, huh? As you can see, the amount of code you'll need to write will be greatly reduced once you create a decent sized library of User Controls. And this is just the beginning; you could expose even more properties to make your controls infinitely customizable.

Writing Custom Control Methods

10 Min. To Go

In addition to creating properties, you can write custom methods for a User Control. Custom methods can be used to populate a list box, validate controls, and so on. The possibilities are endless. In the following example, we will add a method to Address User Control that will validate user input and return a Boolean value (true or false) based on the result of the validation. Include the following code within the `<script>` block in the address.ascx page:

```
Public Function ValidateAddress() As Boolean
    If Trim(txtAddress1.text) = "" Then
         return False
         Exit Function
    End If
    If Trim(txtCity.text) = "" Then
         return False
```

```
        Exit Function
    End If
    If cmbState.SelectedIndex = 0 Then
        return False
        Exit Function
    End If
    If Trim(txtZipCode.text) = "" Then
        return False
        Exit Function
    End If
    return True
End Function
```

As you can see in the `ValidateAddress` method, we do a simple check of a few selected fields and return a Boolean value based on the result. Pretty simple stuff, but it illustrates implementing a User Control method fairly well. To test this method, simply add the following line of code to the ASP.NET page after declaring the server control:

```
<%
Response.Write(AddressControl.ValidateAddress)
%>
```

Implementing User Control Events

User Controls can also respond to events and even respond to ASP.NET events like `Page_OnLoad`.

Try putting the following code in the `<script>` block of address.ascx:

```
Sub Page_Load(Sender As Object, E As EventArgs)
    If Not Page.isPostBack Then
        Dim oItem As New ListItem
        With oItem
            .Value = 10
            .Text = "Georgia"
        End With
        cmbState.Items.Add(oItem)
    End If
End Sub
```

Now try running the ASP.NET page. A `Georgia` item should now appear in the State list box. Imagine writing a little routine in the User Control that could populate controls from a database.

Because User Controls are a collection of ASP.NET controls, you have to use the same methods as with ASP.NET if you want to implement a control event handler. The first thing you want to do is write an event handling method. Add the following method, called `btnSubmit_Click` for example, to the address.ascx file:

```
Private Sub btnSubmit_Click(Sender As Object, E As EventArgs)
    Response.Write("Submit button was clicked!")
End Sub
```

Now in the address.ascx file, change the btnSubmit button control declaration to the following:

```
<asp:Button ID=btnSubmit text="Submit" onClick="btnSubmit_Click"
runat="server" />
```

Try it out now! You see that now, not only is the Web Form submitted, but the btnSubmit_Click event is also processed. It's that simple.

Done!

REVIEW

User Controls are a nice feature of ASP.NET. They essentially enable you to write reusable custom controls based on the standard HTML and Web controls. You can also add custom properties, methods, and events to allow runtime User Control customization and interaction. Using User Controls, you can improve application performance as well as maintainability.

QUIZ YOURSELF

1. What is a User Control? (See session introduction.)
2. What directive can you use in an ASP.NET page to import a User Control? (See "Creating a User Control.")
3. Why shouldn't you include the `<html>`, `<body>`, and `<form>` tags in a User Control? (See "Creating a User Control.")

PART

II

Saturday Morning Part Review

The following set of questions is designed to provide you with feedback on how well you understood the topics covered during this part of the book. Please refer to Appendix A for the answers to each question.

1. SQL is used to create and modify data.

   True/False

2. *Fill in the blanks:* The CRUD activities are _____, _____, _____, and _____.

3. Which of the following SQL statements is used to add data to a table?
   a. CREATE
   b. ADD
   c. INSERT
   d. UPDATE

4. INSERT INTO t_bands (band_title) VALUES (Hootie & The Blowfish) is a valid SQL command. Note: Assume band_title is VARCHAR(100).

   True/False

5. XML is the de facto language for the exchange of data between applications.

   True/False

6. *Fill in the blank:* XML data is stored in a _____ format.

7. XML is compatible with SGML.

   True/False

8. XML was designed to work with only a few applications.

    True/False

9. ASP.NET pages are procedural in nature.

    True/False

10. *Fill in the blank:* When an ASP.NET page is loaded, a structured series of _____ are fired in a set order.

11. *Fill in the blanks:* The first event to be fired when a page is loaded is the _____ event and the last to be fired is the _____ event.

12. Which of the following attributes in the <SCRIPT> element specifies the language used in the code block?

    a. SRC

    b. TEXT

    c. LANGUAGE

    d. LINGO

13. HTML controls maintain their state between client requests.

    True/False

14. HTML controls can be used only when the browser requesting the page is Internet Explorer 4.0 or higher.

    True/False

15. The name of the hidden field to maintain control state between client requests in ASP.NET page is

    a. __VIEWSTATE

    b. __STATEMAINT

    c. __STATE

    d. __VIEW

16. Which of the following is not an intrinsic HTML control?

    a. <form>

    b. <select>

    c. <html>

    d. <table>

17. Web controls map one-to-one with HTML elements.

    True/False

18. Web controls can only be bound to DataSets.

    True/False

19. Web controls must be added to an ASP.NET page at design-time.

    True/False

20. Which of the following is not a List control?

    a. ListBox

    b. DataList

    c. Table

    d. DataGrid

21. ASP.NET User Controls have an .aspx file extension.

    True/False

22. User Controls provide an easy way to partition and reuse simple, common user interface (UI) functionality across a Web application.

    True/False

23. User Controls should include <html>, <body>, and <form> elements.

    True/False

24. Which of the following ASP.NET page directives is used to register a User Control?

    a. Register

    b. Page

    c. Control

    d. Include

PART

III

Saturday
Afternoon

Validating User Input

✔ Understanding the use and implementation of ASP.NET validation controls

✔ Using server- and client-side validation with ASP.NET

✔ Building your own custom validation controls

**30 Min.
To Go**

When developing applications that put a heavy emphasis on end-user data, one of the most tedious and time-consuming activities for a developer is validating user input. Fortunately, ASP.NET provides a series of controls that can perform both client-side and server-side validation. These controls include:

- The RequiredFieldValidator control insures that a user either provides a value for a control or in some way modifies the initial values of a control.

- The CompareValidator control checks to make sure a control contains a specific value or matches the value contained in a second control.

- The RangeValidator control ensures that the user-provided value for a control falls within a specified range, or that the value falls within a range specified by other form controls.

- The RegularExpressionValidator control supports the use of regular expressions to validate control values, providing an extensively flexible technique for validating credit card numbering sequences, e-mail addresses, or any other consistent expressions.

- The CustomValidator control enables the developer to define any server- or client-side function to validate against, therefore covering any remaining validation not provided for in the first four controls.

- The ValidationSummary control allows you to collect all of the validation errors and provide a consolidated listing to the user.

The use of these embedded controls enables you to eliminate hundreds of lines of custom client-side code that you have developed or will develop to perform many of these rudimentary validations. Additionally, you receive the benefit of building upon these basic validation controls to build your own custom validation controls for handling any number of recurring validation tasks.

Common Aspects of Validation Controls

When using the validation controls you should consider several common factors. First, Using validation controls will not normally reduce network traffic. When you use validation controls, validation occurs both at the client as well as at the server. Why? One of the security risks inherent in depending entirely on client-side validation is that malicious users could create their own copy of your page, eliminate the client-side validation, and submit invalid or incorrect values to the business logic of your application. By providing both client- and server-side validation you have the following two advantages:

- Improved performance on most browsers (achieved by not requiring a roundtrip before discovering a blank field or incorrect entry).
- Increased security and confidence that the values submitted to the application logic are within acceptable and, more importantly, expected ranges.

So how do these controls know when to generate client-side code to improve performance or when to eliminate the client-side JavaScript to prevent incompatibility or errors during validation? Natively, these controls automatically detect the user's browser and dynamically deliver JavaScript client-side code where it is appropriate and safe, and enforce server-side validation when the browser may not support client-side validation. However, you can force these controls to always or never use client-side validation with the following page directives:

```
<%@ Page ClientTarget = "DownLevel" %>
```

This will force the validation control to only do validation on the server whereas

```
<%@ Page ClientTarget = "UpLevel" %>
```

forces the controls to do both client-side and server-side validation of all posted values. Be aware that forcing the use of a client-side script with the UpLevel directive will ensure that all browsers, even those that do not support JavaScript, will receive client-side validation. So, be careful in using these directives. Typically, you will be better off letting these controls do the browser sniffing for you.

Display property

When displaying error messages produced during the validation process you will have control over how the message is displayed. Each control has the ability to generate error messages at the point on the page where the validation control is inserted. Additionally, the output can be streamed as HTML or in plain text. This is controlled by the display property of each control. The display property can be set to static, dynamic, or none.

By setting the display property to static, the validation control will allocate an appropriate amount of space on your Web page so that when the error message is displayed, the layout of the page doesn't change.

By setting the display property to dynamic, the validation control will not reserve space on the HTML page for the error message. Therefore, when the error message is displayed, form elements may be moved around to accommodate the error message and thus disrupt the desired look of your form.

By setting the display property to none, no message will be displayed immediately next to the validated control. Why would you ever use this setting? In some situations you may choose to display all validation errors in a consolidated area of the page or in a single message box for the user. In this case you can use the ValidationSummary control to display a summarized list of all error messages rather than displaying them individually next to each control.

Type Property

When comparing values in controls, the values must be of the same type, and you typically will need to explicitly tell the validation control the types being compared. The following type property enumerators are valid: String, Integer, Double, DateTime, and Currency.

Operator Property

When comparing values, the options available for doing the comparison include: Equal, NotEqual, GreaterThan, GreaterThanEqual, LessThan, LessThanEqual, and DataTypeCheck.

These operator properties are relatively intuitive except for DataTypeCheck, which simply evaluates if the values being compared are of the same data type, for instance, that both are strings or integers.

Using Validation Controls

The following examples are all included in the Session 11 folder on the CD. We will look at a single example page for using each of the validation controls.

Let's look at a page that captures basic user information such as the user's name, e-mail address, password, age, and a subscription code that enables the user to subscribe to an online mailing list. Figure 11-1 illustrates the results of using the validation controls to validate required fields, meet regular expression conditions, and to validate field values and types.

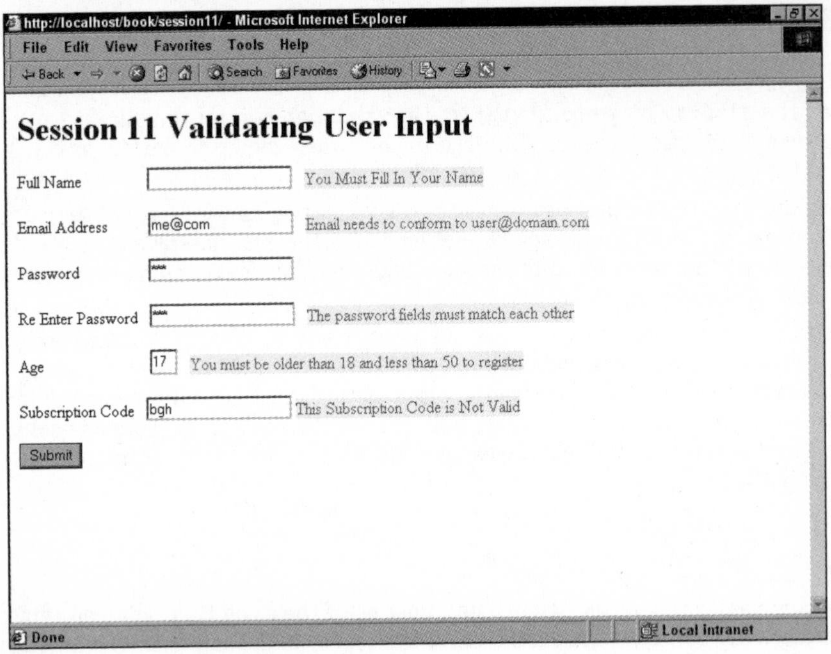

Figure 11-1   Use of validation controls

RequiredFieldValidator

The first thing that you will need to do is insure that the user has at least attempted to complete certain fields. In our example, the only required field is the Full Name field. In order to validate that a user enters information in the Full Name field, you simply insert a RequiredFieldValidator control next to the field you want to validate as shown in Listing 11-1.

Listing 11-1   *Example of Using RequiredFieldValidator Control*

```
<%@ Page Language="vb" %>
<HTML>
    <HEAD>
        <SCRIPT LANGUAGE="VB" RUNAT="server">
        Sub Page_Load(Source As Object, E as EventArgs)
            If Page.IsPostBack Then
                    lblTitle.Text = "Submit was successful"
            Else
                    lblTitle.Text = "Leave the field blank and Submit"
            End If
        End Sub
        </SCRIPT>
    </HEAD>
    <BODY>
        <FORM ID="WebForm1" METHOD="post" RUNAT="server" NAME="WebForm1">
            <P>
```

```
                        <ASP:LABEL ID="lblTitle" RUNAT="SERVER" />
                    </P>
                    <P>
                        Full Name
                        <ASP:TEXTBOX ID="txtName" RUNAT="SERVER"></ASP:TEXTBOX>
                    </P>
                    <P>
                        <ASP:REQUIREDFIELDVALIDATOR
                            ID="valReqName"
                            ERRORMESSAGE="You Must Fill In The <B>Full Name</B> Field"
                            RUNAT="SERVER"
                            CONTROLTOVALIDATE="txtName"
                            BACKCOLOR="#FFFF80"
                            DISPLAY="Static">
                        </ASP:REQUIREDFIELDVALIDATOR>
                    </P>
                    <P>
                        <ASP:BUTTON ID="btnSubmit" RUNAT="SERVER" TEXT="Submit"></ASP:BUTTON>
                    </P>
                </FORM>
            </BODY>
        </HTML>
```

The ControlToValidate property has been set to the id of the control you want to validate, in this case the txtName control. Next, set the ErrorMessage property to a string. In this case, we have added some additional html tags, <B> </B> tags, to provide some bold formatting around the error message. Finally, set the Display property to Static so that the page formatting will remain consistent, regardless if a message is displayed or not.

RegularExpressionValidator

Next, you need to validate the user's e-mail address to make sure that it meets standard Internet e-mail naming conventions. You will do this by utilizing the RegularExpressionValidator control.

A regular expression is a very flexible method of determining if a string value meets certain requirements in terms of its use of upper- or lowercase letters, range of letters, number of characters, use of integers, mix of letters, special characters, or numbers as part of a string.

For example, in the sample registration page, we have created a regular expression to ensure that the user's e-mail conforms to standard e-mail formats. This means that it will contain a series of numbers or letters followed by @ followed by another series of numbers or letters, followed by a period and a final series of numbers or letters.

The expression that tests if the user's input conforms to this standard is set in the property validationexpression as shown in boldface in Listing 11-2.

Listing 11-2   *Implementing RegularExpressionValidator Control*

```
<%@ Page Language="vb" %>
<HTML>
    <HEAD>
        <SCRIPT LANGUAGE="VB" RUNAT="server">
        Sub Page_Load(Source As Object, E as EventArgs)
```

Continued

Listing 11-2   *Continued*

```
            If Page.IsPostBack Then
                    lblTitle.Text = "Submit was successful"
            Else
                    lblTitle.Text = "Enter an invalid email address and Hit the Submit
button"
            End If
        End Sub
      </SCRIPT>
  </HEAD>
  <BODY>
      <FORM ID="WebForm1" METHOD="post" RUNAT="server" NAME="WebForm1">
          <P>
              <ASP:LABEL ID="lblTitle" RUNAT="SERVER" />
          </P>
          <P>
              Email Address
              <ASP:TEXTBOX ID="txtEmail" RUNAT="SERVER"></ASP:TEXTBOX>
              <ASP:REGULAREXPRESSIONVALIDATOR
                  ID="valRegEmail"
                  ERRORMESSAGE="Email needs to conform to <B>user@domain.com</B>"
                  RUNAT="SERVER"
                  CONTROLTOVALIDATE="txtEmail"
                  VALIDATIONEXPRESSION="[\w-]+(\+[\w-]*)?@([\w-]+\.)+[\w-]+"
                  BACKCOLOR="#FFFF80"
                  DISPLAY="Static">
              </ASP:REGULAREXPRESSIONVALIDATOR>
          </P>
          <P>
              <ASP:BUTTON ID="btnSubmit" RUNAT="SERVER" TEXT="Submit"></ASP:BUTTON>
          </P>
      </FORM>
  </BODY>
</HTML>
```

All of the remaining properties are very similar to those used for the `RequiredField Validator` control. The extensive flexibility of the `RegularExpressionValidator` enables you to quickly create custom validators for a wide range of validation routines such as:

- Internet URL = http://([\w-]+\.)+[\w-]+(/[\w- ./?%&=]*)?
- US Phone Number = ((\(\d{3}\) ?)|(\d{3}-))?\d{3}-\d{4}
- US Social Security Number = \d{3}-\d{2}-\d{4}
- US Complex Zip Code = \d{5}(-\d{4})?

20 Min.
To Go

CompareValidator

The `CompareValidator` is self-explanatory. It is used to compare the value of a user control to another user control's value or to a defined value. As illustrated in Listing 11-3, we are using the control to make sure that the second password entered by the user matches the first password entered.

Listing 11-3   *Using the CompareValidator Control*

```
<%@ Page Language="vb" %>
<HTML>
    <HEAD>
        <SCRIPT LANGUAGE="VB" RUNAT="server">
        Sub Page_Load(Source As Object, E as EventArgs)
            If Page.IsPostBack Then
                    lblTitle.Text = "Submit was successful"
            Else
                    lblTitle.Text = "Enter non-identical values and hit the Submit
button"
            End If
        End Sub
        </SCRIPT>
    </HEAD>
    <BODY>
        <FORM ID="WebForm1" METHOD="post" RUNAT="server" NAME="WebForm1">
            <P>
                <ASP:LABEL ID="lblTitle" RUNAT="SERVER" />
            </P>
            <P>
                Password
                <ASP:TEXTBOX ID="txtPassword1" RUNAT="SERVER"
TEXTMODE="Password"></ASP:TEXTBOX>

            </P>
            <P>
                Re Enter Password
                <ASP:TEXTBOX ID="txtPassword2" RUNAT="SERVER"
TEXTMODE="Password"></ASP:TEXTBOX>
                <ASP:COMPAREVALIDATOR
                    ID="valCompPassword"
                    ERRORMESSAGE="The password fields must match each other"
                    RUNAT="SERVER"
                    CONTROLTOVALIDATE="txtPassword2"
                    CONTROLTOCOMPARE="txtPassword1"
                    BACKCOLOR="#FFFF80"
                    DISPLAY="Dynamic">
                </ASP:COMPAREVALIDATOR>
                <ASP:REQUIREDFIELDVALIDATOR
                    ID="valReqName"
                    ERRORMESSAGE="You must complete values in both fields"
                    RUNAT="SERVER"
                    CONTROLTOVALIDATE="txtPassword2"
                    BACKCOLOR="#FFFF80"
                    DISPLAY="Dynamic">
                </ASP:REQUIREDFIELDVALIDATOR>
            </P>
            <P>
                <ASP:BUTTON ID="btnSubmit" RUNAT="SERVER" TEXT="Submit"></ASP:BUTTON>
            </P>
        </FORM>
    </BODY>
</HTML>
```

Note the boldfaced code. We have set the `ControlToValidate` property to the second password field. Once the user has entered the second password, a client-side validation will compare it against the first password field defined by the `ControlToCompare` property.

Additionally, we have set the `Type` property of the comparison to `String` to insure that when the `Operator` property `Equal` is applied that the comparison will work correctly. As already mentioned, you could use any number of operator enumerators to do the comparison as well as any of the property enumerators.

If we wanted to compare a value rather than two controls, you could simply set the `ValueToCompare` property to a specific string rather than use the `ControlToCompare` property.

RangeValidator

This control is useful to compare one control to values of two other controls or to a specific range. In Listing 11-4, we are simply checking to see if the user has entered a valid age range of equal or greater than 18 but less than or equal to 50 years old.

Listing 11-4 *Using a RangeValidator Control*

```
<%@ Page Language="vb" %>
<HTML>
    <HEAD>
        <SCRIPT LANGUAGE="VB" RUNAT="server">
        Sub Page_Load(Source As Object, E as EventArgs)
            If Page.IsPostBack Then
                    lblTitle.Text = "Submit was successful"
            Else
                    lblTitle.Text = "Enter an age <18 or >50 and hit the Submit button"
            End If
        End Sub
        </SCRIPT>
    </HEAD>
    <BODY>
        <FORM ID="WebForm1" METHOD="post" RUNAT="server" NAME="WebForm1">
            <P>
                <ASP:LABEL ID="lblTitle" RUNAT="SERVER" />
            </P>
            <P>
                Age
                <ASP:TEXTBOX ID="txtAge" RUNAT="SERVER" HEIGHT="24"
WIDTH="28"></ASP:TEXTBOX>
                <ASP:RANGEVALIDATOR
                    ID="RangeValidator1"
                    ERRORMESSAGE="You must be older than 18 and less than 50  to
register"
                    RUNAT="SERVER"
                    CONTROLTOVALIDATE="txtAge"
                    BACKCOLOR="#FFFF80"
                    MINIMUMVALUE="18"
                    TYPE="Integer"
                    MAXIMUMVALUE="50">
                </ASP:RANGEVALIDATOR>
```

```
            </P>
            <P>
                <ASP:BUTTON ID="btnSubmit" RUNAT="SERVER" TEXT="Submit"></ASP:BUTTON>
            </P>
        </FORM>
    </BODY>
</HTML>
```

Most of the properties on this control we have used in the previous examples. The new property, in boldface, of MinimumValue establishes the minimum range of the compare. MaximumValue establishes the upper range of the comparison. If you wanted to utilize the values of other controls, you could use the properties MaximumControl and MinimumControl, setting the values equal to the id's of the controls you want to compare against.

Several factors for this control should be noted. If the user leaves a control blank, the control passes the range validation. To force the user to enter a value, add a RequiredField validation control as well. If both MaximumControl and MaximumValue are specified, then the MaximumControl is used. If both MinimumControl and MinimumValue are specified, then MinimumControl will be used to perform the range validation.

**10 Min.
To Go**

CustomValidator

Although the above controls should cover 90 percent of your validation needs, there will be scenarios where you will want to take a value the user enters, apply an algorithm, compare it to a database value, or run it against a Web service to determine if the information is valid. In these cases, you can utilize the CustomValidator control. This control enables you to define both client- and server-side validation routines to compare a control value against. These functions must return Boolean true or false to process the appropriate error message for the control.

For the current example, you are going to compare a subscription code provided by the user against a fixed value. Listing 11-5 illustrates how you can utilize a custom server-side function and a custom client-side function to perform validation.

In Listing 11-5, we have created a server-side function ValidateSubscriptionServer that simply accepts the control value as a string and sets objArgs.IsValid equal to true or false depending upon the result. In this case, you simply check to see if the user control you are validating has a text value equal to abc123. However, you could have also performed a database query or any other type of routine to do the comparison.

Next, we have included a client-side validation routine. The routine is a Javascript 1.0-compliant function called ValidateSubscriptionClient that runs on the client side. Since this function does not have the RunAt = Server attribute, it can have the same name as our server-side function, but will be processed as soon as a user moves their mouse from the Subscription Code field.

Listing 11-5   *Using a CustomValidator Control*

```
<%@   Page Language="vb" %>
<HTML>
    <HEAD>
        <SCRIPT LANGUAGE="VB" RUNAT="server">
```

Continued

Listing 11-5 *Continued*

```
        Sub Page_Load(Source As Object, E as EventArgs)

        End Sub

        Public Sub ValidateSubscriptionServer(objsource As Object, objArgs As
ServerValidateEventArgs)
            If strComp(objArgs.Value, "abc123", CompareMethod.Text) = 0 Then
                objArgs.isValid=True
                lblTitle.Text = "Subscription value accepted  on client and server!"
            Else
                objArgs.isValid =False
                lblTitle.Text = "Subscription value rejected on server!"
            End If
        End Sub
    </SCRIPT>
    <SCRIPT LANGUAGE="javascript">
        function ValidateSubscriptionClient(objSource,objArgs)
            {
            if(objArgs.Value=="abc123")
                {
                objArgs.IsValid= true;
                }
            else
                {
                objArgs.IsValid=false;
                }
             return;
            }
    </SCRIPT>
</HEAD>
<BODY>
    <FORM ID="WebForm1" NAME="WebForm1" METHOD="post" RUNAT="server">
        <P>
            <ASP:LABEL id="lblTitle" RUNAT="SERVER"></ASP:LABEL>
        </P>
        <P>
            Subscription Code
            <ASP:TEXTBOX id="txtSubscription" RUNAT="SERVER"></ASP:TEXTBOX>
            <ASP:CUSTOMVALIDATOR id="CustomValidator1" RUNAT="SERVER"
                ONSERVERVALIDATE="ValidateSubscriptionServer"
                CLIENTVALIDATIONFUNCTION="ValidateSubscriptionClient"
                BACKCOLOR="#FFFF80"
                CONTROLTOVALIDATE="txtSubscription"
                ERRORMESSAGE="This Subscription Code is Not Valid">
            </ASP:CUSTOMVALIDATOR>
        </P>
        <P>
            <ASP:BUTTON id="btnSubmit" RUNAT="SERVER" TEXT="Submit"></ASP:BUTTON>
        </P>
    </FORM>
</BODY>
</HTML>
```

To bind these functions to the Web form, you simply insert a CustomValidator control and set two new properties ClientValidationFunction and OnServerValidate.

In the previous example we have decided to use a server-side function as part of our validation, and set the OnServerValidate property equal to the server-side function ValidateSubscriptionServer. We also have enabled a client-side function, by setting the ClientValidationFunction property equal to the client side function, ValidateSubscriptionClient.

ValidationSummaryx

The last control that is useful for validation is the ValidationSummary control. This control provides you with the option of listing all of the validation errors in a consolidated list for the user, rather than displaying each error message next to the field where the error actually occurred. To use the control, simply plug a ValidationSummary control somewhere on the page your user is likely to reference when reviewing problems with validation:

```
<ASP:VALIDATIONSUMMARY
    ID="valSummary"
    SHOWMESSAGEBOX="False"
    DISPLAYMODE="List"
    HEADERTEXT="Please correct the following errors."
    SHOWSUMMARY="True"
    RUNAT="SERVER">
</ASP:VALIDATIONSUMMARY>
```

The control will automatically display all relevant validation errors in a consolidated area on the page. If you do not want the individual control errors to display, you will need to set each validation control ErrorMessage property to an empty string. Setting the ShowSummary property to False, will prevent the display of each control's error message. Instead, only the content of the HeaderText property will be shown.

In addition, you can choose to display error messages in a pop-up message box by setting the ShowMessageBox property of the ValidationSummary control to True. Be aware that this will only work properly when used in Internet Explorer 4.0 or higher.

The DisplayMode property can be set to List, BulletList, or SingleParagraph to modify the manner in which the list of errors is handled.

Done!

REVIEW

With the use of these controls, you should now be able to eliminate a tremendous amount of client- and server-side validation code previously required when developing ASP pages. Additionally, the ability to construct your own client- and server-side validation controls should provide you with all the flexibility you need to handle 90 percent of your business requirements.

Quiz Yourself

1. When constructing a custom control with custom client-side validation, what client-side language and version should you utilize? (See "Common Aspects of Validation Controls.")

2. What standard ASP.NET validation controls can be combined to perform a value type and value range check on a text field? (See "CompareValidator" and "RangeValidator.")

3. What are the performance impacts of including `<%@ Page ClientTarget = "DownLevel" %>` in pages with validation controls? (See "Common Aspects of Validation Controls.")

Maintaining State in ASP.NET

Session Checklist

✔ Understanding the differences between in-process and out-of-process state maintenance

✔ Implementing ASP State Server or using SQL Server for state maintenance

✔ Using cookies in user state maintenance

**30 Min.
To Go**

I n this session, we will cover the key innovations in state maintenance available in ASP.NET, and demonstrate how these innovations will enable you as a developer to take advantage of the latest in state management to support highly scalable and redundant Web applications.

In ASP.NET, we have optional configuration settings that enable us to select the type of state maintenance we perform, but still allow us to use the familiar methods of state variable access from ASP. In fact, we will not have to change our legacy code to take advantage of the ASP.NET enhancements over ASP with regards to state maintenance. The key differences lie in the way session state management is handled. In ASP, sessions are by default stored in process, which creates significant headaches for developers who develop Web sites that become extremely popular. As the number of users balloon, it becomes apparent that all of those session values used for personalization and customization are killing application performance — and that the possible remedies are limited and costly. In ASP.NET, most if not all of these issues are now very nicely handled using out-of-process state management.

Maintaining State Out of Process for Scalability

In this section, you'll learn how the previously mentioned improvements can be of tremendous help to developers who are implementing applications that require a high degree of scalability.

In ASP, a `Session` object is created and maintained on the Web server from which the page is initiated. In a Web page (for example, somepage.asp) running on server Foo, the embedded ASP code:

```
<% Session("MyFavoriteBeach") = "Trestles" %>
```

will cause the variable `MyFavoriteBeach` to be stored in the memory of server Foo. This variable and all others created during the user session are persisted across multiple Web pages. If you need to retrieve the user's favorite beach, you could simply use the embedded ASP code, for example:

```
<% =Session("MyFavoriteBeach") %>
```

One problem with this approach is that if server Foo crashes or otherwise goes down, all session information is lost, never to be recovered. A second problem with this approach is that it is extremely difficult to share session values with other ASP pages running on other servers. The third problem with the old `Session` object is that it requires the user's browser to support client-side cookies.

 For more information on Windows Load Balancing Services, review Microsoft's WLBS Overview at `http://www.microsoft.com/ntserver/ntserverenterprise/exec/feature/wlbs/default.asp` **or to get information on Network Load Balancing clusters review** `http://www.microsoft.com/windows2000/en/advanced/help/using.htm?id=492.`

All of these factors create massive headaches for ASP developers attempting to build applications that will scale efficiently and support application redundancy, load balancing, and clustering effectively. You are forced to try software solutions such as Windows Load Balancing Services (WLBS), Network Load Balancing clusters or hardware solutions such as Cisco LocalDirector. Unfortunately, these solutions are really designed to handle request-based load balancing where maintaining state on the application server is not a requirement. When you need to use session-based load balancing and store state on the application server, you have to take tremendous performance hits with WLBS by turning on the Affinity option, or if using LocalDirector you have to implement the sticky command which has the same effect — huge performance degradation. In other words, if you modify either LocalDirector or the WLBS to use session-based load balancing, then the benefits of request-based load balancing are eliminated. These options slow the system down by requiring them to maintain a user-to-server mapping and perform a lookup upon each request. It also decreases your ability to provide fault tolerance.

The result of these solutions is like buying a Ferrari and then limiting it to drive around town in stop-and-go traffic at 20 mph, rather than allowing it up on the interstate where it could fly!

The only other way developers can support session maintenance in a Web farm scenario is to do a ton of custom coding, use a back-end database, and then retrieve the session information through the use of cookies; or hidden-form data; or by URL munging the data.

With ASP.NET, Microsoft has gone to great lengths to ease this burden and make our lives as developers much, much simpler! We now have built-in out-of-process and in-process methods to handle state maintenance in ASP.NET, as well as a choice of using client-side cookies or munging the session id.

No More Cookies but Plenty of Milk!

In ASP.NET you can configure your application to store state without the use of cookies, also known as the cookieless method. In this method, ASP.NET simply munges the session id information into the URL of the requested page. This allows you to very easily implement your session information in a standard aspx page on server Foo, pass that information along to a relative path static html page, and then finally pass it back to a third aspx page and maintain state across the session. In order to do this, the session id information is encoded into the URL and thus isn't dependent on the client to store it as a cookie. An example of a munged URL used when the cookieless method is used:

```
http://localhost/session12cookieless/(a5kb53fnuscirn55a4vt1gyt)/Webform2.
aspx
```

The value a5kb53fnuscirn55a4vt1gyt highlighted in bold above is a unique key, which has been "munged" into the URL. This unique key allows the .NET Framework to locate session information specific to the user. In a cookie based implementation a similar value would be stored on the user's hard drive as a cookie.

Advantages

The advantages of this method are:

- Supports state maintenance for all browsers, even those without cookie support.
- Allows you to pass session information between dynamic and static pages.

Disadvantages

The disadvantages of this method include:

- Security risk associated with URL munging the data.
- If implemented in-process, still requires that the user visit the session storing server to retrieve values.

How to make it happen

To implement this method, follow these steps:

1. Open the web.configWeb.config in the virtual directory of your ASP.NET application.
2. Locate the <system.Web> section of the Web.config file, or if none exists, create one.
3. Locate the <sessionstate> element.
4. Set the value of cookieless = true.
5. Save Web.config.

Here is an example of a correctly configured Web.config file enabling cookieless state maintenance:

```
<?xml version="1.0" encoding="utf-8" ?>
<configuration>
   <system.Web>
            <sessionState
            mode="InProc"
            stateConnectionString="tcpip=127.0.0.1:42424"
            sqlConnectionString="data source=127.0.0.1;user id=sa;password="
            cookieless="true"
            timeout="20"
            />
   </system.Web>
</configuration>
```

When modifying the Web.config file be sure to pay particular notice to the capitalization of sections and elements, the file is case sensitive and incorrect capitalization will create errors.

**20 Min.
To Go**

After implementing the method as described above you can now test the use of the cookieless option by turning off cookies in your Web browser, create a virtual directory, add the Web.config file to the virtual directory and create the following three pages illustrated in Listings 12-1, 12-2, and 12-3.

Listing 12-1 *Code for Webform1.aspx*
_____

```
<HTML>
    <HEAD>
        <SCRIPT RUNAT="server" ID="Script1">
        Sub btn1_Click(Sender As Object, E As EventArgs)
            Session("SomeValue") = text1.Value
            span1.InnerHtml = "Session data created/updated! <P>Your session contains:" &
Session("SomeValue") & "</font>"
        End Sub
        </SCRIPT>
    </HEAD>
    <BODY>
        <FORM RUNAT="server" ID="Form1">
            <INPUT ID="text1" TYPE="text" RUNAT="server" NAME="text1"> <INPUT
TYPE="submit" ID="btn1" NAME="btn1" ONSERVERCLICK="Btn1_Click" RUNAT="server"
VALUE="Submit Query">
        </FORM>
        <ASP:HYPERLINK ID="HyperLink1" RUNAT="server" NAVIGATEURL="StaticPage1.htm">Click
here to navigate to a static page.</ASP:HYPERLINK>
        <BR>
        <SPAN ID="span1" NAME="span1" RUNAT="server"></SPAN>
    </BODY>
</HTML>
```

Listing 12-2 *Code for Webform2.aspx*

```
<HTML>
    <HEAD>
        <SCRIPT RUNAT="server" ID="Script1">
        Sub Page_Load()
            span1.InnerHtml = "Session data Recovered! <P>Your session contains: " &
Session("SomeValue") & "</font>"
        End Sub
        </SCRIPT>
    </HEAD>
    <BODY>
        <FONT SIZE="6"><SPAN ID="span1" NAME="span1" RUNAT="server"></FONT>
        <P>
            Click <A HREF="Webform1.aspx">here</A> to modify the session variable
        </P>
        </SPAN>
    </BODY>
</HTML>
```

Listing 12-3 *Code for staticpage1.htm*

```
<HTML>
    <HEAD>
        <TITLE>Static Page</TITLE>
    </HEAD>
    <BODY>
        <P>
            Static HTML Page. Of course there are no values to read, but click
<A HREF="Webform2.aspx">
                here</A> and you will see that session can still be recovered.
        </P>
    </BODY>
</HTML>
```

Open the Webform1.aspx page, and look at the URL in your browser, you should see that upon loading that page ASP.NET has now established a session id embedded in your Web browser. ASP.NET will use this unique key to track all of your session variables. Type in a value that you would like to store, then click the Submit Query button. You will see that the submitted value has been stored. Next, follow the hyperlink to the staticpage1.htm file. Although no session information is available here because it is an .htm file, you will see that the embedded session id remains in your browsers URL. Now follow the hyperlink to the Webform2.aspx page. You will see that the session information has been recovered!

In the previous example, you will notice that we set the mode attribute to InProc. This means that the state will be stored *in process* or in the physical memory of the server it was launched from when the session state was implemented. This means that if the server were to crash, all session information would be lost. This mode is effectively the mode that you operate in under traditional ASP. As we discussed earlier, this provides little in the way of redundancy or failover support needed for highly scalable Web applications.

Out of Process State Management

We will now look at two new methods in ASP.NET that use external state management. This technique stores session values in an external state store instead of the ASP.NET worker process. By storing it out of process, you can make certain that state is stored across worker process restarts (such as when the machine must be restarted) as well as across multiple machines (such as you would commonly face in a Web farm). There are two external state management approaches:

- The first method relies on using SQL Server to store state. This option provides you the most scalability and redundancy but requires you to have SQL Server. There is no Oracle support for this approach as of yet!
- The second method utilizes an "ASP.NET state store." This is a dedicated NT Service that can run on any Windows NT or Windows 2000 server.

Session Management with SQL Server

In this method, ASP.NET will utilize a database called ASPState on a selected SQL Server to store session information. Using this method you can choose to set the property Cookieless to either True or False, at your discretion, since where or how the unique session id is stored has no impact on the method used to store the values associated with the session id. The session id stored in the cookie or alternatively munged in the URL will be the unique key used to query the ASPState database and track session variables.

Advantages

The advantages of this method are:

- Stores session state out of process, allowing you to run your application across multiple servers.
- Supports request-based load balancing.
- Provides extensive redundancy, reliability, and uptime when used in conjunction with clustering and hardware or software load balancing.
- Ability to support periodic "code rot" purges.
- Ability to partition an application across multiple worker processes.
- Ability to partition an application across multiple Web farm machines.

Disadvantages

The disadvantages are:

- Additional network traffic for database queries.
- Maintenance of SQL Server database.

How to make it happen

In order to use the SQL Server session management, you first need to make sure that you have SQL Server installed or available along with the InstallSqlState.sql file that ships with the Premium version of the .NET Framework SDK. You should also have administrative access to SQL Server.

1. You will need to locate the InstallSqlState.sql file that ships with the Premium version of the .NET Framework. This file creates a database for storing state values on a SQL Server Database of your choice. To implement this method, you need to install this script only once on your targeted database. You will need administrative access to SQL Server to execute this script.

2. To run the script, launch a command prompt, Start ⇨ Programs ⇨ Accessories ⇨ Command Prompt.

3. Navigate to the [*Drive*]\WINNT\Microsoft.NET\Framework\[*version*] directory, where [*Drive*] is the installation drive such as C:\ and [*version*] is the version of the .NET Framework installed.

4. Type OSQL –S localhost –U [*Administrator Userid*] –P [*Password*] <InstallSqlState.sql.

5. An illustrative example of a properly formatted command line would be:

   ```
   OSQL -S localhost -U sa -P < InstallSqlState.sql
   ```

6. Press Enter.

To uninstall this database, you can execute the SQL script UninstallSqlState.sql using the same process described in this session.

This will create a database called ASPState on the selected SQL Server instance. We recommend that you restart SQL Server to make sure that the scripts have been applied. Next, we need to update the <system.Web> section of the Web.config file we used earlier in this session.

In order to activate SQL Server State Maintenance set the value of mode="SQLServer". Additionally set the sqlConnectionString="data source=127.0.0.1;user id=sa; password=", where data source is the IP address or name of your SQL Server; user id is an administrative user id, and of course the password for the administrator. Finally save the Web.config file. The following example provides an example of a properly configured Web.config file to support SQL Server State Maintenance:

```
<?xml version="1.0" encoding="utf-8" ?>
<configuration>
   <system.Web>
        <sessionState
             mode="SQLServer"
             sqlConnectionString="data source=127.0.0.1;user id=sa;password="
             stateConnectionString="tcpip=127.0.0.1:42424"
             cookieless="true"
             timeout="20"
        />
   </system.Web>
</configuration>
```

Now you can run the same series of pages that you built earlier in the session, and you should see that they produce exactly the same results. What really should get you excited is to see what happens when you start and stop the SQL Server database when these pages are running to see how the recovery of session information is executed! Now that should make a few Web farm developers real happy!

Session Management with ASP.NET State Server

A second out of process approach to session state management utilizes an NT service and a file-based dictionary rather than a database to store state. This solution is likely to be used by shops that do not utilize SQL Server as their primary database in a Web farm, possibly using Oracle, or for smaller Web farms that do not yet need the scalability of SQL Server.

The ASP.NET State Server runs externally from worker processes in a dedicated .NET State Server process that runs as a Windows NT service. There is no end-user code allowed to run in the same process, thus eliminating the chance of unstable code breaking the service; additionally, no live object references are maintained.

The ASP.NET State Server stores blobs of binary data, either in memory or on disk. The .NET worker processes are then able to take advantage of this simple storage service by saving (using .NET serialization services) all objects contained within a client's Session collection object at the end of each Web request. Whenever the client needs to access the Session collection, the .NET objects will be retrieved as binary streams from the state server by the appropriate worker process. It is then deserialized into a live instance of the object and placed back into a new Session collection object exposed to the request handler. The information stored in the collection is then accessed via the same methods used for in-process and SQL Server approaches described earlier in the session.

Advantages

The advantages of this method are:

- Stores session state out of process, allowing you to run your application across multiple servers.
- Supports request-based load balancing.
- Provides adequate redundancy, reliability, and uptime when used in conjunction with clustering and hardware or software load balancing.
- Ability to support periodic "code rot" purges.
- Ability to partition an application across multiple worker processes.
- Ability to partition an application across multiple Web farm machines.

Disadvantages

The disadvantages are:

- Additional network traffic for data communication.
- Managing a new NT Service.

How to make it happen

To implement this method all you need to do is activate the aspnet state service. To do this, shell out to a command prompt and type, net start aspnet_state. In order to activate ASP State Maintenance, open your Web.config file and modify the <system.Web> section so that the value of mode="StateServer". Additionally set the stateConnectionString= "tcpip=127.0.0.1:42424", where tcpip is the IP address of your SQL Server:Port. Finally save the Web.config file. The following example provides an example of a properly configured Web.config file to support SQL Server State Maintenance.

```
<?xml version="1.0" encoding="utf-8" ?>
<configuration>
   <system.Web>
       <sessionState
             mode="StateServer"
             sqlConnectionString="data source=127.0.0.1;user id=sa;password="
             stateConnectionString="tcpip=127.0.0.1:42424"
             cookieless="true"
             timeout="20"
       />
   </system.Web>
</configuration>
```

Again, you can run the same series of pages that you built earlier in the session and you should see that they produce exactly the same results. And you should get the same results when you simulate a state server system crash by starting and stopping the state server service when these pages are running. As with the SQL Server method, all state is saved and recovered very nicely!

Done!

REVIEW

With the flexibility provided by the ASP.NET framework, you now have multiple options in providing flexible, scalable alternatives to the issue of state maintenance. The new framework enables you to provide a personalized experience to all users of your application, regardless of the various browser implementations that hit your site. And these features are implemented in a manner that allows you to maintain and support your existing personalization engines.

QUIZ YOURSELF

1. How does ASP.NET's state maintenance approach assist customers implementing Web farms? (See "Out of Process State Management.")

2. In what scenarios does it make sense to set cookies to off? (See "No More Cookies but Plenty of Milk!")

3. What are the performance, and reliability differences between using State Server and SQL Server? (See "Out of Process State Management.")

Authentication and Authorization

Session Checklist

✔ Understanding the differences between authentication, authorization, and impersonation

✔ Modifying `Web.config` to support forms and passport based authentication

✔ Using a database to validate a user's credentials

I n this session, we will look at the approaches you can take to handle authentication and authorization in your applications. We will start out by defining the terms authentication and authorization as it relates to ASP.NET. We will also provide an overview on how to implement authentication and authorization within an application's `Web.config` file. Finally we will wrap up with how to use forms based authentication, as well as third party Web service authentication services such as Microsoft Passport.

30 Min. To Go

Introducing the Key Security Mechanisms

It is important in handling security for ASP.NET applications that you understand the three key security mechanisms used to determine how a user gains access to a resource within an ASP.NET application: authentication, authorization, and impersonation.

Authentication is the process of discovering and verifying the identity of a user or service by examining the user's credentials and validating those credentials against some authority such as an LDAP server, a database, an XML file or even a Web service such as Microsoft Passport. Several authentication mechanisms are available for use with the .NET Framework role-based security. ASP.NET natively supports Windows, Cookie, and Passport modes of authentication.

The purpose of *authorization* is to determine whether a user with a specific identity should be provided with a requested type of access to a given resource. This is typically handled by assigning an authenticated user to a predefined role. A role such as end user, super user, power user, administrator or anonymous is defined by the application and given access to execute certain files, run certain functions or add/update/delete certain data.

Impersonation is when an application assumes the user's identity as the request is passed to the application from IIS. Then, access is granted or denied based on the impersonated identity. So, we could establish two accounts in the application called genericUser and superUser, we could then selectively have incoming Web clients run as one of these accounts depending upon the rules established during authorization for each specific user.

Web.config and Security

There are two types of XML configuration files used by ASP.NET, they are called `machine.config` and `Web.config`. The format of these files and elements that they can contain are the same, however the `machine.config` file provides the default configuration for all applications and directories, while the `Web.config` file allows you to modify these defaults for a specific application or virtual directory. The `machine.config` is a located at:

```
[install drive]:\WINNT\Microsoft.NET\Framework\[ASP.NET Version Number]\CONFIG
```

and there is only one copy of this file per Webserver, whereas there may be dozens of `Web.config` files for various applications and subdirectories.

You can establish the conditions for access to a particular directory or application, by modifying the `<system.Web>` section in your application's `Web.config` file. The conditions you set in the `Web.config` file will apply to the directory, which contains it, as well as all of its associated sub directories.

Within the `Web.config` file the `<system.Web>` section establishes the security profile for the application or directories overseen by it. The general syntax for the security section of the `Web.config` file is illustrated in Listing 13-1:

Listing 13-1 *General syntax for the security section of the Web.config file*

```xml
<?xml version="1.0" encoding="utf-8" ?>
    <configuration>
        <location path="[Path of specific file to which system.Web applies]">
          <system.Web>
              <authentication mode="[Windows/Forms/Passport/None]">
                    <forms name="[name]" loginUrl="[url]" protection="[All, None,
Encryption, Validation]" timeout="[time in minutes]" path="[path]" >
                          <credentials passwordFormat="[Clear, SHA1, MD5]">
                              <user name="[UserName]" password="[password]"/>
                          </credentials>
                    </forms>
                    <Passport redirecturl="internal" />
              </authentication>
              <authorization>
                    <allow users="[comma separated list of users]" roles="[comma
separated list of roles]" verb="[GET, POST, HEAD]"/>
                    <deny  users="[comma separated list of users]" roles="[comma
separated list of roles]" verb="[GET, POST, HEAD]"/>
              </authorization>
              <identity impersonate="[true/false]" name="[Domain\Username to operate
under]" password="[password of Domain\UserName]"/>
```

```
            </identity>
          <system.Web>
        </location>
      </configuration>
```

Note the use of camel-casing throughout the Web.config **and** machine. config **file where the first letter of the first word is always lower-case and the first letter of the subsequent word is upper-case, as in "configSections". This is important because the entire file is case sensitive, and errors in case will create application errors.**

The default and optional values for these elements are shown in Table 13-1.

Table 13-1   *Default and Optional Values for Security Section of Web.config*

Element and Default Value	Optional Values	Comment
`<location path="">`	Any string that represents a valid path to a file	If you include a location tag in then the settings contained in the `<system.Web>` section following this tag will only apply to the specific file path named in the path property. This tag is optional and should typically only be used for files not supported by ASP.NET.
`<authentication mode= "Windows">`	Forms, Passport, None	The authentication mode cannot be set at a level below the application root directory.
`<forms name=".ASPXAUTH">`	Any string for storing the cookie	You can use any string you like for the cookie name.
`<forms login Url= "login.aspx">`	Any valid absolute or relative URL	If the mode is set to Forms, and if the request does not have a valid cookie, this is the URL to which the request is directed for a forms-based login.
`<forms protection= "None">`	All, None, Encryption and Validation	The value within the cookie can by encrypted or sent in plain text. For sites that only use forms authentication to identify a user and not for security purposes, then the default None is just fine.

Continued

Table 13-1 *Continued*

Element and Default Value	Optional Values	Comment
`<forms path="/">`	Any valid string	Specifies the path value of the cookie. Cookies are only visible to the path and server that sets the cookie.
`<credentials passwordFormat="sha1">`	Clear, MD5	Tells ASP.NET the password format used to decrypt the password value of the user attribute. Note that just setting this value does not automatically encrypt the password value, instead it is the developers responsibility to add the password value in an encrypted format.
`<Passport redirecturl="internal">`	Any valid URL that provides a login validation	The authentication mode must equal "Passport" for this to apply. When the requested page requires authentication and the user has not signed on with Passport, then the user will be redirected to the supplied "redirecturl".
`<user name="">`	Any valid user name as string	For example use the value "jsmith".
`<user password="">`	Any valid password as string	For example use the value "jsmithspassword".
`<allow users="*">`	Any comma-delimited list of users	By default the special character * indicates that all users are allowed; alternatively, ? indicates that anonymous users are allowed.
`<allow roles= >`	Any comma-delimited list of roles	The special character * indicates that all roles are allowed.
`<deny users="">`	Any comma-delimited list of users	Special characters * for all users and ? for anonymous user can be used.

Element and Default Value	Optional Values	Comment
`<deny roles="">`	Any comma-delimited list of roles	The special character * for all roles can be used.
`<identity impersonate="false">`	True	With impersonation set to "True", the usernames and passwords will be compared against valid NT User Groups to determine access based upon NTFS Access Control Lists.

The ASP.NET Configuration System only applies to ASP.NET Resources, which are those items handled by the xspisapi.dll. By default items not handled by this DLL, such as TXT, HTML, GIF, JPEG, and ASP files, are not secured by the `Web.config`. To secure these items use the IIS admin tool to register these files, or use the `<location>` tag to specify a specific file or directory.

The following example grants access to Tony, while denying it to Jason and anonymous users:

```
<?xml version="1.0" encoding="utf-8" ?>
<configuration>
   <system.Web>
     <authorization>
         <allow users="Tony" />
         <deny users="Jason" />
         <deny users="?" />
     </authorization>
   <system.Web>
</configuration>
```

Next we'll look at how users and roles may refer to multiple entities using a comma-separated list:

```
<allow users="Tony, Jason, DomainName\tcaudill" />
```

As you can see, the domain account (`DomainName\tcaudill`) must include both the domain and user name combination.

Special identities

In addition to identity names, there are two special identities: *, which refers to all identities, and ?, which refers to the anonymous identity. So, to allow Jason and deny all other users you could set the configuration section as shown in the following code sample:

```
<?xml version="1.0" encoding="utf-8" ?>
<configuration>
    <system.Web>
        <authorization>
            <allow users="Jason" />
```

```
            <deny users="*" />
        </authorization>
    <system.Web>
</configuration>
```

Using request types to limit access

You can also limit access to resources based upon the request type, GET, POST, and HEAD. The following example lets everyone do a POST, but only Jason can perform a GET request:

```
<?xml version="1.0" encoding="utf-8" ?>
<configuration>
    <system.Web>
        <authorization>
            <allow verb="GET" users="Jason" />
            <allow verb="POST" users="*" />
            <deny verb="GET" users="*"/>
        </authorization>
    <system.Web>
</configuration>
```

When it is determined that a user should be denied, then the default 401 code is displayed.

**20 Min.
To Go**

New Tricks for Forms-based Authentication

The most common type of authentication that you will want to implement with ASP.NET is forms-based cookie authentication. In this approach, we use a simple Web form combined with a modification to the Web.config file to provide user authentication.

Let's look at an example of using forms-based authentication to validate users against a database.

The first step is to create the Web.config file as shown in the following example:

```
<?xml version="1.0" encoding="utf-8" ?>
<configuration>
    <system.Web>
        <authentication mode="Forms">
            <forms name="CookieFormApplication" loginUrl="login.aspx" />
        </authentication>
        <authorization>
            <deny users="?" />
        </authorization>
        <sessionState mode="InProc" cookieless="false" timeout="20"/>
    </system.Web>
</configuration>
```

In this example we are setting the authentication mode to use forms based authentication, establishing that all non-authenticated users should be denied access and that users will be redirected to the login.aspx to obtain authentication.

We will use an xml file, users.xml, to validate the users during the login session. The following example shows the format of the xml file used to validate the users credentials.

```
<Users>
  <User>
    <UserEmail>joe@smith.com</UserEmail>
    <UserPassword>jsmith</UserPassword>
  </User>
  <User>
    <UserEmail>bill@johnson.com</UserEmail>
    <UserPassword>bjohnson</UserPassword>
  </User>
</Users>
```

Once you have created the `users.xml` file, populate it with some sample user name/password pairs for testing. Next, you can create the `login.aspx` form. The `login.aspx` form will collect the user name and password of the user and then compare these values against the xml file. If they match, an authentication cookie will be sent to the user. Should the username not be found in the XML file then the user is redirected to another page that allows them to add a new username/password to the xml file. Listing 13-2 provides a sample of the `login.aspx` form.

Listing 13-2 *Example of login.aspx using forms-based authentication*

```
<%@ Import Namespace="System.XML" %>
<%@ Import Namespace="System.IO" %>
<%@ Import Namespace="System.Web.Security " %>
<%@ Import Namespace="System.Data.SqlClient" %>
<%@ Import Namespace="System.Data.OleDB" %>
<%@ Import Namespace="System.Data" %>
<%@ Page Language="vb" debug="True"%>
<HTML>
    <HEAD>
        <TITLE>Session 13 Cookie Authentication </TITLE>
        <SCRIPT LANGUAGE="VB" RUNAT="Server">

    Sub btnLogin_Click(ByVal Sender As Object, ByVal E As EventArgs)


        Select Case ValidateUserXML(txtusername.text,txtpassword.text)
            Case "Success"
                FormsAuthentication.RedirectFromLoginPage (txtusername.text,
chkPersistForms.Checked)
            Case "PasswordFailed"
                lblMessage.Text = "Sorry your password verification for the user " &
txtusername.text &" failed."
            Case "NoSuchUser"
                    Response.Redirect("adduser/adduser.aspx?username=" & txtusername.text)
        End Select

    End Sub
    Sub btnAddNewUser_Click(ByVal Sender As Object, ByVal E As EventArgs)
                Response.Redirect("adduser/adduser.aspx?username=Enter User Name")
    End Sub
    Function ValidateUserXML(ByVal username as String, ByVal password as String) as String

        Dim cmd as String
```

Continued

Listing 13-2 *Continued*

```
        cmd = "UserEmail='" & username & "'"
        Dim ds as New DataSet
        Dim fs as new
FileStream(Server.MapPath("users.xml"),FileMode.Open,FileAccess.Read)
        Dim reader as new StreamReader(fs)
        Dim pass as string
        Dim user as string
        ds.ReadXml(reader)
        fs.Close()
        Dim users as DataTable
        Users = ds.tables(0)
        Dim Matches() as DataRow
        Matches = Users.Select(cmd)
        If Matches.length >0 Then
                Dim row as DataRow
                row = matches(0)
                pass = row.item("UserPassword")
                user = row.item("userEmail")
                if pass = password then
                        Return "Success"
                else
                        Return "PasswordFailed"
                end if
        Else
                Return "NoSuchUser"
        End If
    End Function

        </SCRIPT>
    </HEAD>
    <BODY>
        <FORM ID="WebForm1" METHOD="postPOST" RUNAT="server">
            <P>
                <STRONG>Session 13 Forms Authentication</STRONG>
            </P>
            <P>
                Please enter your username and password information below and then select
the Login Button.
            </P>
            <P>
                <ASP:LABEL ID="lblMessage" RUNAT="SERVER"></ASP:LABEL>
            </P>
            <P>
                Email
                <ASP:TEXTBOX ID="txtUserName" RUNAT="SERVER" TOOLTIP="Please enter your
Username here"></ASP:TEXTBOX>
            </P>
            <P>
                Password
                <ASP:TEXTBOX ID="txtPassword" RUNAT="SERVER" TEXTMODE="Password"
TOOLTIP="Please enter your password here."></ASP:TEXTBOX>
            </P>
```

```
            <P>

                <ASP:CHECKBOX ID="chkPersistForms" RUNAT="SERVER" TEXT="Select to Persist
Cookies"></ASP:CHECKBOX>
            </P>
            <P>
                <ASP:BUTTON ID="btnLogin" RUNAT="SERVER" TEXT="Login"
ONCLICK="btnLogin_Click"></ASP:BUTTON>
                <ASP:BUTTON ID="btnAddUser" RUNAT="SERVER" TEXT="Add New User"
ONCLICK="btnAddNewUser_Click"></ASP:BUTTON>
            </P>
        </FORM>
    </BODY>
</HTML>
```

The login form displays a login page to the user. When the user selects the Login button, the btnLogin_Click() method is called. btnLogin_Click() calls a function that compares the e-mail address entered to the e-mail field to the users.xml file. If a valid e-mail is found, then the password of the user is tested. Once a match is discovered, then the FormsAuthentication.RedirectFromLoginPage () method is called to redirect the user back to the originally requested page or resource while also writing the authentication cookie to the browser.

To test this functionality out, create another file called default.aspx as shown below, establish a virtual directory for all of the above described files (default.aspx, login.aspx, users.xml, Web.config) and browse to the default.aspx page:

```
<%@ Page Language="vb"%>
<HEAD>
<SCRIPT Language = "VB" Runat="Server">

    Sub btnLogout_Click(ByVal Sender As Object, ByVal E As EventArgs)
        FormsAuthentication.Signout
      Response.Redirect("default.aspx")
    End Sub
</SCRIPT>
<HTML>
<BODY>
<H1> You successfully logged in and gained access</H1>


    <FORM Runat="Server">
          <asp:Button id=btnLogout runat="SERVER" Text="LogOut"
OnClick="btnLogout_Click">
          </asp:Button>
        </P>
    </FORM>
</BODY>
</HTML>
```

And that does it — you have tested the user name and password against an xml file, authenticated the user, and forwarded the user to the appropriate resource. When you compare this approach against a similar scenario in ASP 3.0, it is clear that ASP.NET is streamlining these basic functions for the developer.

**10 Min.
To Go**

Using the Passport Authentication Provider

Passport authentication is a service supported by Microsoft that provides a centralized authentication service for single sign-on and core profile services. Using Passport authentication is not mandatory, but the benefits of using such a service are apparent when you look at the number of Internet users handled by the Microsoft HotMail or MSN Service. These users already have profiles established as part of these services; and you can use this data for your own public Web sites. Additionally it simplifies users' experience with your site, in that they do not need to go through a second registration process, but instead use an existing profile. Should a new visitor not have a Passport profile, the service provides methods to register the user for a new Passport userid.

The `PassportAuthenticationModule` provider supplies a wrapper around the Passport Software Development Kit (SDK) for ASP.NET applications. It requires installation of the Passport SDK and provides Passport authentication services and profile information from an `IIdentity`-derived class called `PassportIdentity`. This provides an interface to the Passport profile information as well as methods to encrypt and decrypt Passport authentication tickets.

The general process for implementing Passport authentication in an ASP.NET application is as follows:

1. Establish a PREP Passport Account. In order to test the SDK you will need to create a PREP Passport Account that effectively creates a testing account for development purposes. This can be done at `https://current-register.passporttest.com/`

2. Download, install, and configure the Passport SDK. It can be found at `http://www.passport.com/devinfo/Start_Goals.asp`. When installing, be sure to select the installation options for Development/Testing unless you are planning on implementing a production environment. This option will install a sample application of AdventureWorks that utilizes the Passport Authentication Scheme. However this version utilizes standard ASP rather than the ASP.NET Passport approach.

3. Create a new PREP Site ID by following the instructions at `http://siteservices.passport.com/`

4. Create a virtual directory on your default Web site to store the `Web.config` and `login.aspx` files discussed below.

5. Make sure that your site has access to the Internet. The passport service operates by using the public site http://current-login.passporttest.com.

6. Create a `Web.config` file and set up Passport as the authentication as shown in the following example.

```
<?xml version="1.0" encoding="utf-8" ?>
<configuration>
   <system.Web>
      <authentication mode="Passport">
         <passport redirectUrl="login.aspx">
         </passport>
      </authentication>
      <authorization>
         <deny users="*">
```

```
            </deny>
        </authorization>
        <sessionState mode="InProc" cookieless="false" timeout="20"/>
    </system.Web>
</configuration>
```

1. @NL:Next you will need to create a basic ~~login.aspx~~ file which the user will be sent to by default when they first request a file from your site, as shown in the following example:

```
<%@ Page Language="vb" %>
<%@ Import Namespace="System.Web"%>
<%@ Import Namespace="System.Web.SessionState"%>
<%@ Import Namespace="System.Web.Security"%>
<%@ Import Namespace="System.Web.HttpUtility"%>
<SCRIPT LANGUAGE="VB" RUNAT="SERVER">
Sub Page_Load(ByVal Sender As System.Object, ByVal e As System.EventArgs)

    Dim oPassport As Web.Security.PassportIdentity
    Dim sReturnURL As String
    Dim sLogoURL As String
    Dim sAuthURL As String

    'Create a new PassportIdentity object
    oPassport = New Web.Security.passportidentity

    'Dynamically generate the ReturnURL as this page
    sReturnURL = Server.URLEncode("http://" & Request.ServerVariables("SERVER_NAME") &
Request.ServerVariables("SCRIPT_NAME"))

    'Establish the PassportIdentity.LogoURL
    slogourl = opassport.LogoTag2(sReturnURL, 3600, True, Nothing, 1033, True, Nothing,
Nothing, True)

    'Determine the users Authenticated Status
    If oPassport.IsAuthenticated() Then
        Response.Write("<H3>You are Authenticated, Click Below To SignOut. Note that unless
you have a valid Passport Contract with Microsoft, SignOut functionality may not work
properly.</H3>")
    Else
        Response.Write("<H3>You are Not Authenticated, Click Below To Login.</H3>")
    End If

    'Dynamically display the appropriate Passport Login or Logout Logo
    Response.Write(sLogoURL)
END SUB
</SCRIPT>
<HTML>
    <BODY>
    </BODY>
</HTML>
```

In this example, we are using PassportIdentity to do all of the authentication labor. First we create a variable sReturnURL, which describes what URL that Passport should redirect the user to after a successful login or logout. We then use the sReturnURL to create the string variable slogourl using the PassportIdentity.LogoTag2() method, which will dynamically display a login or logout graphic depending on the status of the user's session.

To determine if a user is in fact already authenticated we use the `PassportIdentity`. `IsAuthenticated` property, which returns `True` if a user is authenticated or `False` otherwise. Depending upon the user's state, we display a message indicating if they are logged on or not. If they are logged in, then the passport service will automatically create the Passport sign-out hyperlink, otherwise we insert the string of html stored in the `slogourl` value, creating a dynamic hyperlink to the Passport sign-in page.

Done!

REVIEW

In this session, we reviewed how to handle simple forms-based authentication, as well as how to implement basic Passport authentication. The forms-based examples show how to use a database to look up a user's credentials. The passport example shows how to use a Web service to validate authentication. You should continue exploring authorization and impersonation to add further granular security capabilities to your end solution.

QUIZ YOURSELF

1. What security and privacy issues are associated with using Passport authentication? (See "Introducing the Key Security Mechanisms.")

2. Provide an example `Web.config` file that only allows POST requests from the user John in domain corporate. (See "Web.config and Security.")

3. What alternatives are there to using a database to look up user credentials? (See "New Tricks for Forms-based Authentication.")

ASP.NET Caching

Session Checklist

✔ Implementing Page Output Caching

✔ Using Fragment Caching

✔ Caching Data Objects

**30 Min.
To Go**

I n ASP.NET there have been tremendous improvements in providing a framework that scales much better than previous versions of ASP. *Caching* is another area where Microsoft has gone to great lengths to provide ASP.NET developers control over their application performance and scalability.

What is caching? Caching improves overall system performance by storing frequently accessed or computationally expensive data in memory. Once a page or piece of data has been compiled and delivered, it is stored in memory. Subsequent requests access the cache rather than reinitiating the process that originally created it.

Caching is one of three state management approaches you can use in ASP.NET.

- Session state is used to store data, such as personalization data, that you want available to the user each time a page is accessed. You need to be efficient about using this approach, however, as the session information isn't shared across users.

- Application state is used to store data that needs to be available to the entire application. The approach and methods for application state are the same as for session state, however the visibility of data is global across all application users.

- In caching, we are able to make any object or piece of data globally available to all users and have robust methods for optimizing how long this data is stored and what dependencies affect the optimal delivery of the data.

In this session, we will first cover how you can implement caching using the same Response object properties and methods that were available in ASP. Then, we will cover how ASP.NET implements page and data output caching to improve the scalability and responsiveness of your applications.

ASP.NET Updates to the ASP Response Model

In previous versions of ASP, the Response object used the Expires, ExpiresAbsolute, and CacheControl properties to support caching. While these methods and properties can still be used and implemented in the same way, you need to understand how to update the syntax of your ASP pages to reflect the new ASP.NET framework.

In ASP, using the Response.Expires property will insert an HTTP Header that tells the client browser to request another copy of the page only if it has been a specified number of minutes since the last request. So, by inserting the following code in your page:

```
<%Response.Expires = 10%>
```

You will ensure that after the first request, the browser will only request the page from the server if it hasn't been requested in the last ten minutes. In ASP.NET this can be handled in the following manner:

```
<%Response.Cache.SetExpires(DateTime.Now.AddSeconds(600))%>
```

This method will set the cache to expire in 600 seconds or 10 minutes from the point that the first request for the page from any client was initiated. This method gives you very fine control over the expiration of the page as it takes full advantage of the new DateTime object, which provides a tremendous amount of flexibility in the calculation and formatting of date and time values.

Additionally you could set this same expiration rule using the OutPutCache page directive as follows:

```
<%@ OutputCache Duration="600"%>
```

Caching with ASP.NET

ASP.NET supports three types of caching:

- **Page output caching**, which involves storing the dynamic response generated by a request in memory.
- **Fragment caching**, which involves storing a portion of a page in a non-user-specific key to improve access to this content as part of other dynamic or static pages.
- **Page data caching**, which involves the storing of arbitrary objects across multiple requests.

Page Output Caching

Page output caching is typically utilized when you want to store the entire output of a dynamically created or static page in the cache of the server, the client, or a proxy server for rapid access across multiple requests. When the page is cached in the output cache, all subsequent requests for that page are served up from the output cache without activating the page that originally instantiated it.

So, if you had a page default.aspx and had set the page to cache the response for a fixed period of 30 seconds from the last request, and you wanted that cached output to be stored on any cache-enabled device in the request stream such as the Web server or proxy-servers, you could set the OutputCache page directive as follows:

```
<%@ OutputCache Duration="30" Location="Any" VaryByParam="None">
```

Or I could use the following code that just replicates the above page directive,

```
<%
Response.Cache.SetExpires(DateTime.Now.AddSeconds(30))
Response.Cache.SetCacheability(HttpCacheability.Public)
%>
```

In the next section we will address two approaches for implementing the expiration/validation policy: absolute cache expiration and sliding cache expiration.

Absolute cache expiration

When using the OutputCache page directive, you can specify that the content is expired a specified number of seconds after it was first requested. All further requests after the initial request will simply receive the content stored in the output cache; and the page will not be processed until the time frame specified has expired. Lets look at the following example contained on CD in the Session14 folder under the file named "AbsoluteCache.aspx." In this example we illustrate a programmatic method for handling absolute cache expiration, rather than using the OutputCache page directive discussed earlier. By using this programmatic approach, we can establish a final date for a page to expire rather than simply a span of time from when it was first initiated. In this example we are expiring the page on a specific date of December 31, 2009.

Sliding cache expiration

The Cache object can utilize a Boolean property called SetSlidingExpiration. When this property is set to True, every time a *new* request is received for the page — for instance when a new user visits the page or when an existing page visitor selects the refresh button in his or her browser — then the page is initiated and the output cache expiration is reset based upon the code, as shown in Figure 14-1.

 See the example SlidingCache.aspx on the CD in the Session 14 folder.

When the user selects the Click Here To Refresh hyperlink, the output page is retrieved from the output cache and redisplayed, thus no values on the page change. However, if the user selects the Refresh button from the toolbar, simulating a NEW request, then the page skips retrieving the page out of cache, and instead recompiles the page and resets the expiration on the output cache, even though the expiration time has not been reached! In other words, it slides the expiration.

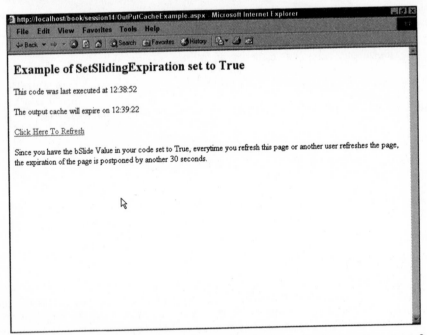

Figure 14-1 *An example of sliding expiration when a user requests a page from the output cache*

The code in Listing 14-1 shows the source of the SlidingCache.aspx page shown in Figure 14-1.

Listing 14-1 *Source of the SlidingCache.aspx file*

```
<%@ Page Language="VB" Debug="False" Trace="False" %>
<HTML>
    <HEAD>
        <SCRIPT LANGUAGE="VB" RUNAT="server">
        Sub Page_Load(ByVal Sender As System.Object, ByVal e As System.EventArgs)
            SetOutPutCache()
        End Sub
        Sub SetOutPutCache
            Dim dt As Date ' Creates a new DateTime Object
            Dim bSlide as Boolean ' creates a Boolean Variable to Hold the Sliding
Expiration State
            Dim dSec as Double
            dSec = 30 'Set the expiration delay in Seconds
            dt=datetime.now.addseconds(dSec) ' This calculates the time 20 seconds from
the time the Page is compiled

            bSlide = True

            Response.Cache.SetExpires(dt) 'Sets the cache to expire in 20 seconds
```

```
                Response.Cache.SetCacheability(HTTPCacheability.Public)
                Response.Cache.SetSlidingExpiration(bSlide) 'Sets the state of Sliding
        Expiration
                lblSlide.Text = bSlide
                lbldt.Text=datetime.Now.ToLongTimeString
                lblExpire.Text =dt.ToLongTimeString
                Select Case bSlide
                Case True
                    dInfo.InnerHTML = "<p>Since you have the bSlide Value in your code set to
        True, everytime you refresh this page or another user refreshes the page, the expiration
        of the page is postponed by another " & dSec & " seconds."
                Case False
                    dInfo.InnerHTML = "<p>Since you have the bSlide Value in your code set to
        False, no matter how you refresh this page or how another user refreshes the page, the
        page will expire at " & dt.ToLongTimeString & "."
                End Select
              End Sub
        </SCRIPT>
        </HEAD>
        <BODY>
            <H2>
                Example of SetSlidingExpiration set to
                <ASP:LABEL ID="lblSlide" RUNAT="SERVER"></ASP:LABEL>
            </H2>
            <P>
                This code was last executed at
                <ASP:LABEL ID="lbldt" RUNAT="SERVER"></ASP:LABEL>
            <P>
                The output cache will expire on
                <ASP:LABEL ID="lblExpire" RUNAT="SERVER"></ASP:LABEL>
            <P>
                <A HREF="SlidingCache.aspx">Click Here To Refresh </A>
                <DIV ID="dInfo" RUNAT="server">
                </DIV>
            <P>
            </P>
        </BODY>
    </HTML>
```

When `Cache.SetSlidingExpiration` is set to `False`, the page is always retrieved from the output cache for all existing users as well as for new requests.

To test this try changing

```
bslide=True
```

to

```
bslide=False
```

in Listing 14-1. This turns off the sliding expiration functionality. Therefore, all requests for the page, new or existing will be served from the output cache until you get past the expiration time of 30 seconds; the next request after this expiration time produces a reset of the expiration value. You can test this by looking at the code generation time stamp on the output page.

Fragment Caching

Fragment caching is an approach that caches a portion of a page in memory rather than the entire page as is done when using page output caching. Suppose you have a heavily accessed evaluation or survey form, whose content is static for each user, but whose answers you would like to track based upon a unique userid or value stored or passed in the URL. Using page output caching is not going to provide you much benefit, because it depends upon a unique URL string for caching the output. In our scenario, *every* request for the page content will generate a unique URL.

Please refer to the FragmentOutputExample.aspx page in the Session 14 folder on the accompanying CD. This example illustrates storing the static survey form in a file called SurveyForm.htm. The first time the page is loaded, SurveyForm.htm is opened and its text is inserted into a cache variable sMyForm. An absolute expiration of 10 seconds is applied to the cached variable, so that all requests occurring 10 seconds after the initial request will load this fragment of the page from cache, rather than loading it from disk.

When you look at the content of the SurveyForm.htm page, you can see that it is a simple survey form that does not change from user to user. Instead, its results need to be uniquely stored based upon the userid information passed in the URL. You can handle this scenario nicely in ASP.NET by caching the fragment of static information in a data cache and retrieving the static data during the generation of the dynamic page (see Listing 14-2).

Listing 14-2 *Using fragment caching*

```vb
<%@ Import Namespace="System.IO.StringWriter"%>
<%@ Import Namespace="System.IO.File"%>
<%@ Import Namespace="System.IO"%>
<%@ Import Namespace="System"%>
<%@ Page Language="vb" %>
<HTML>
    <HEAD>
        <META HTTP-EQUIV="Content-Type" CONTENT="text/html; charset=windows-1252">
        <SCRIPT LANGUAGE="VB" RUNAT="server">
            Sub Page_Load(ByVal Sender As System.Object, ByVal e As System.EventArgs)
                ' Checks to see if the Form is in Memory
                Dim bCheckCache as Boolean
                bCheckCache =CheckCache("sMyForm")
                Select Case bCheckCache
                    Case True ' Set the lblCached to True
                        lblCached.Text = "True"
                    Case False 'Set the lblCached to False
                        lblCached.Text ="False"
                End Select
            End Sub
            Function CheckCache(sItem as String)
                'Checks for the existince of a Cached Item
                Dim bCached as Boolean
                If Cache.Get(sItem) = Nothing Then
                    bCached = False
                Else
                    bCached = True
```

```
                    End If
                    Return bCached
                End Function
                Function GetCachedForm(sFileName as String, sCacheItem as String)
                    'Dim String for Cached HTML Form
                    Dim sMyForm as String
                    'Dim StreamReader to Read HTML From File
                    Dim sr As StreamReader
                    'See if Cache Exists
                    If CheckCache(sCacheItem) Then
                        sMyForm = Cache.Get(sCacheItem)
                    'Otherwise if it doesn't read in survey to cache
                    Else
                        sr = File.OpenText(server.MapPath(sFileName)) 'Open File
                        While sr.peek <> -1 'Loop Through File
                            sMyForm = sMyForm & sr.ReadLine() 'Load Line of Text from File
                        End While
                        sr.close() ' Close FileStream
                        sr = Nothing 'Optional Destroy Object
                        Cache.Insert(sCacheItem,sMyForm,Nothing, datetime.Now.AddSeconds(10),
timespan.zero) 'Insert the HTML Form
                    End If
                    Return sMyForm
                End Function
                Sub btnSubmit_Click(sender As Object , e As
System.Web.UI.WebControls.CommandEventArgs)
                    'Insert Code to Write Survey Information to Log File or Database
                End Sub
                </SCRIPT>
    </HEAD>
    <BODY>
        <FORM ID="FragmentOutputExample" METHOD="get"
ACTION="FragmentOutputExample.aspx">
            <H2>
                Example of Fragment Caching a Form
            </H2>
            <BR>

            <%Response.write(GetCachedForm("SurveyForm.htm", "sMyForm"))%>

            <ASP:BUTTON ID="btnSubmit" RUNAT="SERVER" TEXT="Button"
ONCOMMAND="btnSubmit_Click"></ASP:BUTTON>
            <BR>
            <P>
            </P>
            <HR SIZE="1">
            <P>
                Was the above form in Cache?  
                <ASP:LABEL ID="lblCached" RUNAT="SERVER"></ASP:LABEL>
            </P>
            <P>
                Page Compiled at:<%=datetime.now.tolongtimestring()%>
            </P>
        </FORM>
    </BODY>
</HTML>
```

As can be seen in Listing 14-2, we first test to see if the static form text is in cache. If it is not stored in memory, we proceed to open the static html file, load the text into a string, and then store that string in cache, setting an absolute expiration of 10 seconds. All subsequent requests for this page for the next 10 seconds will achieve a higher performance because the static page fragment will be pulled from memory. However, the developer can still leverage the dynamic components of the container page to combine userid's or other user-specific data with the form's response so that the resulting data can be uniquely identified.

Page Data Caching

ASP.NET additionally exposes the `Cache` object in the `System.Web.Caching` namespace, which provides direct access to the ASP.NET cache engine. The `Cache` object provides a collection that allows you to access all information stored in the cache. We can utilize this capability to support the storage and retrieval of arbitrary objects across HTTP requests.

Because the ASP.NET cache is private to each ASP.NET application, when the application is restarted all cache information is lost. However, all active data in the cache is stored in memory, so we can pass data between pages within the same application. The cache is thread-safe, which means that it implements automatic locking so that concurrent access isn't typically an issue. However, because all pages can access the cache, you can have scenarios in which user B will view from cache an item that was modified by user A on the same or a different page. Thus, page data caching works closer to the way variables established in the `Application_OnStart` event work, rather than session variables that are unique to a user session.

You can thus use this feature to store data such as database queries or custom objects; and you can share these across users of your application. The ASP.NET cache provides methods for expiring this content based upon the following factors:

- **Expiration:** You can expire cached data items just as you can expire pages as shown in the page output caching examples earlier. You can expire a data item at a specific time such as noon on December 31, 2002. You can also expire an item 60 seconds after its initial request, or relative to the last time it was requested, a sliding cache.

- **File and Key Dependency:** You an also expire a cached data item based upon the status or state of an external file, or another cached data item. As soon as the dependency rule you set up is violated, the cached item is invalidated and removed. Another process will then be required to reestablish the cached data.

- **Scavenging:** This refers to the process whereby the ASP.NET cache engine attempts to remove infrequently referenced cache data when memory constraints come into play. When using scavenging you can set up rules that the cache engine should follow to determine the relative cost of creating the item and how frequently it should be accessed to remain useful.

Each of these approaches can be used alone or in combination to provide robust handling of cached data.

Expiration

10 Min. To Go

When you are using the data cache, the rules for expiration, dependency, and scavenging are established when you first insert an object into the cache. If you wanted to add your name to the cache, with no expiration, scavenging, or dependency rules, you would simply use something like this:

```
<% Cache.Insert("sMyName", "Tony Caudill") %>
```

To retrieve this value from the cache, you would use:

```
<%
Dim sMyName as String
sMyName = Cache.Get("sMyName")
%>
```

If you attempted to write the value of the cached item to your output page prior to using the Cache.Insert method, you would receive an error message, Attempted to dereference a null object reference. So, you need a way to check if the cached item is in fact cached prior to referencing that item. You can do this by seeing if the cached item is equal to Nothing, as illustrated in the following code:

```
<% @ Page Language ="VB" Runat="Server"%>
<%
   Dim sMyName as String ' Creates a new String Object
   If Cache.Get("sMyName") = Nothing Then
     Cache.Insert("sMyName","Tony Caudill") ' Insert the value
   End If
     sMyName = Cache.Get("sMyName") ' Get the value

%>
```

Displaying all items currently in the data cache

As you use the data cache more frequently, you will find that it is helpful to obtain a listing of all items that it contains. Because these items are stored in a collection, it is easy to obtain. Open up the example in your Session 14 folder named datacacheexample.aspx. Figure 14-2 shows the output.

In this example, we have included a report at the bottom of the page that lists all the key/value pairs inserted into the cache. This is fairly easily done using the ShowCache() subroutine in the DataCacheExample.aspx page as illustrated in Listing 14-3.

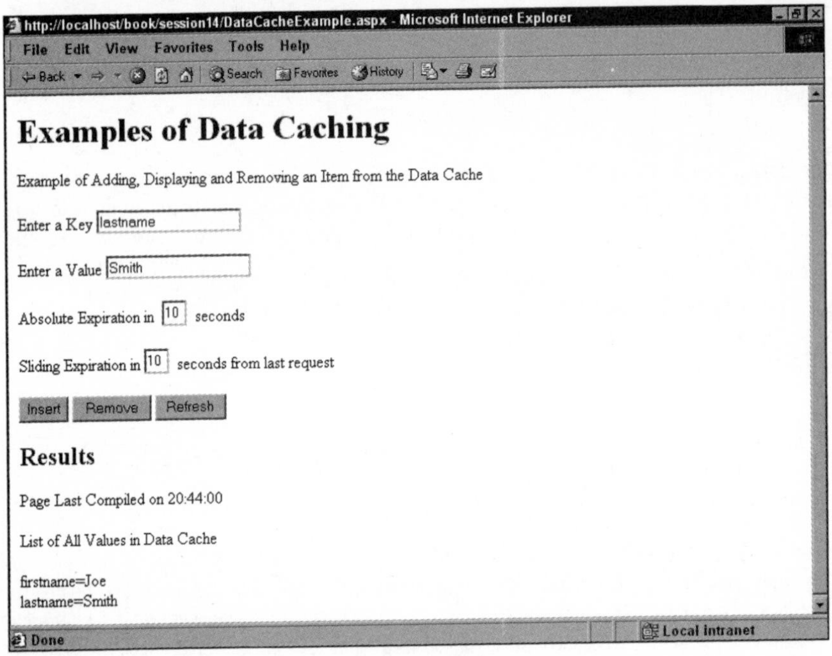

Figure 14-2   Output from DataCacheExample.aspx

Listing 14-3   *Segment of code from DataCacheExample.aspx for retrieving key/value pairs stored in Cache*

```
Public Sub ShowCache()
    Dim oItem As Object
    Dim sText As String
    For Each oItem In Cache
        If Left(oItem.key, 7) <> "System." Then
            sText = sText & oItem.Key & "=" & Cache(oItem.Key) & "<br>"
        End If
    Next
        divDisplay.InnerHTML =sText
    lblcompile.Text = datetime.Now.ToLongTimeString
End Sub
```

You simply loop through all of the items stored in the cache collection and filter out all items that start with the text System. You then attach the resulting key/value pairs into a string and display them after the <DIV> tag at the bottom of the page.

Explicitly removing an item from the data cache

You may have occasion to remove an item from cache. In the DataCacheExample.aspx file, we've included a subroutine that will remove a key/value pair based upon what key the user has entered in the form:

```
Public Sub BtnRemoveClick(ByVal sender As Object, ByVal e As
System.EventArgs)
    Cache.Remove(txtKey.Text.ToString)
    showcache()
End Sub
```

Once the subroutine has removed the selected key/value pair, it then calls the `show-cache()` method which regenerates the full listing of all key/value pairs that we discussed above.

To expire data from the cache automatically we can use the `absoluteExpiration` and the `slidingExpiration` parameters of the `Cache.Insert` method. These options are addressed below.

Using the absoluteExpiration parameter

To expire a piece of data at an absolute time or a specified number of seconds after it was inserted, use the following syntax, highlighted in bold in Listing 14-4, when you insert the data for the first time:

Listing 14-4 *Example of using absolute expiration*

```
<%@ Page Language="vb" %>
<HTML>
    <HEAD>
        <SCRIPT LANGUAGE="VB" RUNAT="server">
        Sub Page_Load(ByVal Sender As System.Object, ByVal e As System.EventArgs)
            Dim sMyName as String ' Creates a new String Object
            Dim dt as DateTime
            dt.Now.AddSeconds(30)'Set DateTime you need data to expire
            If Cache.Get("sMyName") =  Nothing Then
                Cache.Insert("sMyName", "Tony Caudill",Nothing,dt,TimeSpan.Zero)
            End If
            sMyName = Cache.Get("sMyName")
            Response.Write(sMyName)
        End Sub
        </SCRIPT>
    </HEAD>
<HTML>
    <BODY>
    </BODY>
</HTML>
```

By setting the value of the dt variable to be equal to the current system time plus 30 seconds (`dt.Now.AddSeconds(30)`)and by setting the `TimeSpan` variable equal to zero (`TimeSpan.Zero`), we have provided an absolute expiration of the data cache variable MyName to occur exactly 30 seconds from the time the data is inserted into the cache. No matter how many times it is read during the 30 seconds, it will cease to exist when the time has elapsed. In order to reestablish it in the cache, you would need to perform another `Cache.Insert` statement.

Using the slidingExpiration parameter

To expire the data from the last time it was accessed, you can use the `slidingExpiration` parameter as in Listing 14-5:

Listing 14-5   *Example of using sliding expiration*

```
<%@ Page Language="vb" %>
<HTML>
    <HEAD>
        <SCRIPT LANGUAGE="VB" RUNAT="server">
        Sub Page_Load(ByVal Sender As System.Object, ByVal e As System.EventArgs)
            Dim sMyName as String ' Creates a new String Object
            Dim dt as DateTime
            Dim ts as TimeSpan
            ts.FromSeconds(30)
            If Cache.Get("sMyName") =  Nothing Then
                Cache.Insert("sMyName", "Tony Caudill",Nothing,dt.MaxValue,ts)
            End If
            sMyName = Cache.Get("sMyName")
            Response.Write(sMyName)
        End Sub
        </SCRIPT>
    </HEAD>
<HTML>
    <BODY>
    </BODY>
</HTML>
```

In the code above, we used `dt.MaxValue` to indicate that there was no absolute expiration, and `ts.FromSeconds(30)` to indicate that the item should expire on a sliding basis, 30 seconds from the time it was last accessed. This will ensure that the data remains cached once every 30 seconds as long as the page is accessed.

File and Key Dependency and Scavenging

File and Key Dependency-based caching are most likely to be used when you are storing global configuration information in an XML or other physical file that is read from very frequently but changes infrequently. You can create a file dependency that initiates a cache update whenever the date/time stamp on the file is updated.

When inserting an object into cache you can use the optional methods `CacheItemPriority`, `CacheItemPriorityDecay`, and `CacheItemRemovedCallback` to build rules for scavenging the expiration of cached items. By setting the `CacheItemPriority`, you are setting the relative cost of the object, as expressed by the `CacheItemPriority` enumerator. This value is used by the cache when it evicts objects. All things being equal, objects with a lower cost are removed from the cache before objects with a higher cost, in order to save memory or other application resources. By setting a cached items `CacheItemPriority` value to a selection such as `AboveNormal`, the cache will remove these items only after lower priority items have been removed. This provides you very granular, rule-based control in sophisticated caching scenarios. An example of using these optional methods are illustrated below which shows storing a DataSet object for absolute expiration in 2 minutes, and giving it a high priority and slow decay so that it will have priority over other cached items should resources become constrained:

```
Cache.Insert("DataSet", oDA, Nothing, DateTime.Now.AddMinutes(2), TimeSpan.Zero,
CacheItemPriority.High, CacheItemPriorityDecay.Slow, onRemove)
```

Done!

REVIEW

ASP.NET provides a much more robust caching model, than was previously available in ASP. This should allow you tremendous flexibility in designing and optimizing your application to the needs of your end users. The ability to store just about anything in cache including XML, files, and even objects as part of the data cache opens up nearly unlimited possibilities for you as a developer.

Remember that when you are storing items in cache, you are increasing the demands on available memory, so be sure to monitor your application servers for memory utilization as you expand the use of these features in your application framework.

QUIZ YOURSELF

1. When would you want to set SlidingCache to True in an application? (See "Sliding cache expiration.")
2. Describe the differences between page output caching and data caching? (See "Page Output Caching" and "Page Data Caching.")
3. Under what scenarios would data caching be useful? (See "Page Data Caching.")

Introducing ADO.NET

Session Checklist

✔ Understanding the core differences between ADO and ADO.NET

✔ Knowing when to use ADO.NET

✔ Understanding the benefits of ADO.NET for n-tier application development

**30 Min.
To Go**

I n this session, we cover the major factors that are key to understanding ADO.NET and its usefulness for n-tier platform development. We take a brief tour of the history of ADO and then expand into why the move to n-tier application development has required the delivery of an enhanced data access layer that more appropriately supports disconnected datasets and cross-platform sharing of data and schemas.

A Brief History of Microsoft Data Access

The days of homogenous operating environments are numbered. Most of today's Internet applications are deployed in heterogeneous environments that consist of loosely coupled platforms. These new environments pose new challenges for sharing common services and system scalability. To address the requirements of these heterogeneous environments, Microsoft has developed ADO.NET.

There are three key requirements related to data access that have evolved in the expanded use of distributed computing:

- Robust data exchange among heterogeneous computing environments.
- Native support for the transmission of data sets across firewalls using HTTP.
- Requirement to rapidly scale while supporting a centralized data store.

ADO.NET is an evolution of the ADO model for data access. ADO was an extremely effective, easy-to-use model that provided the ability to interact with multiple types of structured data. However, the core element of the ADO model, the RecordSet object, was becoming extremely fat. Originally operating as a simple way to interact with a SQL result set, the `RecordSet` object had grown to support disconnected sets of data, data shaping of multiple datasources, and a complex SQL generation layer that could support optimistic locking. In short, the `RecordSet` object was the universal data access object for COM-oriented environments.

As Internet applications evolved, it became clear that their true strength would be their ability to operate as loosely coupled systems. These systems can easily communicate and exchange data across a heterogeneous environment and through an infrastructure whose primary common transmission protocol was HTTP. ADO depends heavily on COM and specifically on Advanced Data Table Gram (ADTG) as the native transmission format, which requires conversion of this binary format to derivative forms such as XML in order to support robust transmission across HTTP. ADO.NET provides the needed evolution by natively supporting XML, a text-based format, as the transmission format. This evolution provides the ability to access middle-tier business logic on any platform or standard — CORBA, COM, and so on — supporting XML, and have the services of these middle-tier applications made available to one another through the serialization and deserialization of XML for data interchange. When the transmission occurs through an XML-based standard there is a significant reduction in the amount of effort and data conversion required to access data in a heterogeneous environment.

Today's Internet application systems need to be highly scalable and redundant. As systems scale, one of the primary limitations becomes the ability of the relational database management system (RDBMS) to maintain and support open connections to the middle-tier business objects. Typically there is a fixed limit to the number of open connections that can be supported by the RDBMS. In a distributed environment, it is likely that you will have a higher number of middle-tier components desiring simultaneous connections to the data store. To the extent that these components require an open connection for sorting, filtering, and manipulating the data, scalability is tremendously limited. ADO.NET natively supports a disconnected approach that involves pulling down the core set of data and then performing all filters, sorts, and manipulations on the middle tier. Because of its XML-based nature, it can also transmit the manipulated data set to another component for further processing before finally submitting it back to the original data store for update. In the ADO model, the extent of the disconnected manipulation was limited and thus impacted scalability — you had to programmatically handle connection opens and closes. In ADO.NET these happen automatically.

Differences between ADO and ADO.NET

**20 Min.
To Go**

The previous section discussed at a high level some of the fundamental changes in the ADO.NET framework that are driven by a move to highly distributed, loosely coupled, and thinly connected applications. This section provides a more detailed look at the differences between ADO and ADO.NET.

Transmission formats

ADO utilized a very efficient and compact binary format, the Advanced Data Table Gram (ADTG) format, to provide transmission of data between applications. This limited the direct transmission of a set of data to applications that could support this format, in this case COM applications. The transmission of data was further limited in the world of the Internet as there was not an easy method for sending this binary format efficiently across firewalls that often only supported HTTP. These factors effectively limit the full functional use of ADO to COM environments.

ADO.NET, by contrast, natively supports the text-based XML format for transmission of data. As a text-based, open, and widely accepted standard, XML can and is supported in COM, CORBA, and numerous other computing environments. As a text-based format, it can be readily communicated across HTTP, providing a simple method to transmit structured data across corporate firewalls.

Connected versus disconnected datasets

ADO (ActiveX Data Objects) is an application programming interface (API) for accessing data primarily in a connected (cursor-based) scenario. ADO provides the capability of using a connection-oriented approach to creating, updating, and deleting data through pessimistic locking. This is a preferred approach in a two- and three-tier environment. ADO optionally enables you to operate with a client-side cursor providing a disconnected method as well, and thus provides a solution for n-tier development.

ADO.NET is an API to access data and information in a disconnected manner. It is thus not very useful in a client/server environment, and in fact is optimized for use in a n-tier environment in which maintaining open connections to the datasource are typically ineffi- cient and ineffective.

COM marshaling versus text-based data transmission

When operating in a purely COM environment it is clear that the ADO model provides a very rich and attractive programming interface. Its ability to use multiple cursor types and con- nections, and to easily shape, sort, filter, and modify data on multiple-relational and non- relational sources is apparent. However, the ADO model is only an advantage if all systems that are interacting with each other are COM based. These very same benefits are a liability in a distributed and heterogeneous environment where mainframe, UNIX, and numerous other non-windows-based platforms are involved. In the ADO world, the transmission of a disconnected recordset from one component to another involves COM marshaling and forces the receiving component to support COM to accept the transmission. Therefore only COM objects can use ADO recordsets. And while ADO did provide the capability to save content to XML and rebuild from an external XML file, the default XML schema employed was optimized for use in an ADO environment (as opposed to transmission to non-COM based systems). With ADO.NET, the native support of XML overcomes these issues and provides an approach for transmission of almost any data type between almost any type of platform. This allows mainframe systems to communicate with COM-based middleware and then have the result modified by a CORBA-based Java Servlet while having the data roundtrip back and updating a centralized relational or nonrelational datasource.

Variant versus strongly typed data

ADO by default will utilize variant data types to comply with script-based environments. This means that the data types will not be evaluated until runtime, and that they must be evaluated prior to committing them back to the originating datasource in most cases.

ADO.NET utilizes a strongly typed data, which ensures that conversion of data from one type to another is accurate and complete, and that methods for calculations based upon ADO.NET provide a more accurate and less error-prone scenario.

Data schema

ADO can represent data relationships and constraints that may exist in the original relational data store by expressing them through an XML schema. However, this ability is limited because the schema was optimized to support interaction in a COM-only environment. ADO.NET natively supports full transformation of a data schema into a disconnected datasource. This provides for a more universal and leaner data set because it doesn't carry the datasource-specific data previously carried by the ADO XML approach.

**10 Min.
To Go**

ADO.NET Managed Provider Versus SQL Managed Provider

The ADO.NET Managed Provider is used to connect to OLEDB Providers and ODBC drivers, and thus tends to have more overhead and lower performance than the SQL Managed Provider, which has been optimized to work with SQL Server. The SQL Managed Provider in fact doesn't use ODBC and instead talks directly with SQL Server without assistance from OLEDB. Microsoft has provided this capability for one reason — performance. Microsoft claims that the speed of moving data between SQL Server and an ASP.NET application can increase by as much as 300 percent using the SQL Managed Provider because of the optimized direct communication provided.

Why ADO.NET?

ADO.NET should be your strategic choice for n-tier application development in a COM environment. While it is fairly easy for you to run your ADO code in an *.aspx page as .NET provides backward compatibility, you will not be able to take advantage of some key benefits of the .NET framework such as databinding. ADO uses RecordSet objects that follow guidelines that are no longer suitable in .NET. Therefore, you cannot use a RecordSet object to populate an ASP.NET or Windows Forms datagrid by attaching it as a datasource. Instead, you will be required to iteratively loop through the RecordSet object and populate these databound controls manually.

Additionally, by using the ADO.NET framework, you are inherently preparing your application for much more robust activity. Even if you are not using XML extensively within your application today, by using the ADO.NET framework you have set yourself up for success in the future.

ADO.NET clearly provides some key advantages in applications that require a readily transportable disconnected data store or need to support a highly scalable middle tier. However, there is one core feature that ADO.NET doesn't support, the use of server-side cursors. A server-side cursor requires that an open connection be maintained between the application and the database. In client/server applications, this was a fairly common approach and there are a number of applications and situations where you still should use server-side cursors. However, most Web-based systems just don't need to maintain an open connection to the database. So, what do you do if your current application code uses server-side cursors? You should first examine why you need this type of connection, and then balance this against the loss of scalability and flexibility that results. You should consider the option of dropping dynamic, server-side cursors in favor of static, client-side cursors, which are the preferred cursors within the ADO.NET framework. If you can't change your code to employ client-side cursors, then you may be stuck with ADO.

Done!

REVIEW

We have covered at a high level how the shift to a distributed computing environment has created a need for a leaner, more robust data access solution, ADO.NET. You should now understand some of the key differences between ADO and ADO.NET and be able to better determine how your own applications may be impacted by ADO.NET.

QUIZ YOURSELF

1. In what scenario is ADO.NET not a suitable approach? (See "Why ADO.NET?")
2. What is the native transport format for ADO.NET? (See "A Brief History of Microsoft Data Access.")
3. How is ADO.NET an advantage when dealing with transporting data across corporate firewalls? (See "Transmission formats.")

Navigating the ADO.NET Object Model

Session Checklist

✔ Understanding the relationship between an object and an object model

✔ Learning to navigate an object model

✔ Understanding the relationship between objects in the ADO.NET object model

30 Min. To Go

Y ou have probably heard the term *object-oriented programming* (OOP). It is and has been *the* buzzword for several years; and although it is a frequently (over?) used phase, almost everyone you ask will describe the concept of OOP differently.

OOP is effectively a method of developing application code based on objects in order to promote code reusability, maintainability, and extensibility. An *object* is defined by a class and is actually an instance of a class. Multiple objects can be created based on the same class. A class is a structure that contains both *properties*, what the class is, and *methods*, what the class does. Most people will tell you that the classes you create for an application should be abstract representations of real-world entities. For example, you might have a class called "Band" that represents a musical group. OK, so how do you take a class and create an object? Well, that's usually handled by the programming language for which you are creating the object. The facility for creating an object from a class is generally referred to as a factory and is basically a means of manufacturing an object based on a class definition.

Don't concern yourself with the details of how a factory works, just be aware that object creation is not magic, there is code somewhere that handles it for you. In Visual Basic .NET, you can create an object using the New keyword as follows:

```
Dim oConn As New ADOConnection
```

In this case, a new object called oConn will be created that is an instance of the ADOConnection class.

So now that you know what an object is, let's talk about object models. An *object model* gives structure to a hierarchical grouping of functionally related objects. For example all of the objects under the ADO.NET object model umbrella in some way provide data access functionality. An object model typically expresses the fact that some objects are "bigger" or more important that others — these objects can be thought of as containing other objects, or being made up of other objects.

Suppose you want to build an application that will store information about music groups. In order to facilitate the development of this application, you want to develop a group of classes, in the form of an object model, that other developers can use to write application code. In your object model, you might want to create a Band class that can contain other classes like Album, Member, and RecordCompany classes. Figure 16-1 shows the object model for this situation.

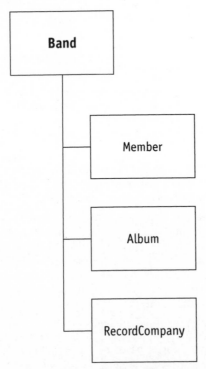

Figure 16-1 *An object model for an application that stores information about music groups*

As you can see in Figure 16-1, the Band class can contain a Member, an Album, and a RecordCompany object. Let's say that the Band class has the following properties and methods:

Properties	Methods
Name	Add
Member	Update
Album	Delete
RecordCompany	Dispose

In the previous scenario, the Member, Album, and RecordCompany properties are actually classes. Classes can be properties of other classes. So in the previous example, a Band object can contain a Member class, an Album class, and a RecordCompany class. To make things easy, say that the Member, Album, and RecordCompany classes all implement just one property: Name. (Don't worry about the methods right now.) So, now that you know how the classes are related and what properties and methods they contain, you can write the following code (in Visual Basic) to create your objects and navigate the object model:

```
Dim oBand As New Band
oBand.Name = "Hootie & The Blowfish"
oBand.Member.Name = "Darius Rucker"
oBand.Album.Name = "Cracked Rear View"
oBand.RecordCompany.Name = "Atlantic"
oBand.Add
oBand.Album.Name = "Fairweather Johnson"
oBand.Update
oBand.Dispose
oBand = Nothing
```

You'll notice that, as a developer, when you work with an object model (well actually objects in general) you don't need to concern yourself with implementation details. For example, we know that when we call the Band class's Add method, a record is added to a table in our data store for the band, but we have no idea how. We don't need to know how. That's the beauty of objects.

**20 Min.
To Go**

OK, going back to your example. It's neat, but not too realistic. Frequently an object of one type, in this example the oBand object, can contain many objects of another type, such as Member and Album. This situation can be handled in one of two ways. You can either implement the Member and Album properties as collection objects or you can create two more classes, Members and Albums, that sit between the Band class and the Member and Album classes. The more OOP-like approach would be the latter in order to increase reusability and maintainability. Figure 16-2 shows the new object model.

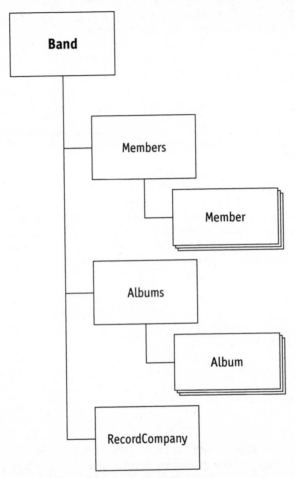

Figure 16-2 *Object model with collection classes*

The Band class should now implement the following properties and methods:

Properties	Methods
Name	Add
Members	Update
Albums	Delete
RecordCompany	Dispose

Notice that the Band class's Member and Album properties have now become Members and Albums respectively. You can infer here that these properties are collection properties. A collection property represents a collection class, which is effectively a container for or group of another type of class. In your example, the Band class's Members property is actually a link to your Members collection class, which can contain several Member objects. The same holds true for the Albums property and class.

Assume the Members and Albums classes implement the same properties and methods:

Properties	**Methods**
Item	Add
Count	Remove
	Dispose

So, now that you know how the classes are related (by examining the object model) and what properties and methods each class implements, you can navigate your object model with the code shown in Listing 16-1.

Listing 16-1 *Navigating the Band object model*

```
Dim oBand As New Band
Dim oMember As New Member
Dim oAlbum As New Album
Dim x As Integer

oBand.Name = "Hootie & The Blowfish"
oMember.Name = "Darius Rucker"
oBand.Members.Add(oMember)

oMember = New Member
oMember.Name = "Mark Bryan"
oBand.Members.Add(oMember)

oAlbum.Name = "Cracked Rear View"
oBand.Albums.Add(oAlbum)

oAlbum = New Album
oAlbum.Name = "Fairweather Johnson"
oBand.Albums.Add(oAlbum)

For x = 0 To (oBand.Members.Count - 1)
    Response.Write(oBand.Members.Item(x).Name)
Next

For x = 0 To (oBand.Albums.Count - 1)
    Response.Write(oBand.Albums.Item(x).Name)
Next

oBand.Add

oAlbum.Dispose
oAlbum = Nothing
oMember.Dispose
oMember = Nothing
oBand.Dispose
oBand = Nothing
```

As you can see, navigating an object model is straightforward. You create your objects, set their properties, and call their methods. In Listing 16-1, all you are doing is creating a few objects, specifically Member and Album objects, and adding them to their parent object's collection properties, specifically Members and Albums.

So you may be asking yourself, "What in the world does all this have to do with ADO.NET?" Well, ADO.NET provides an object model that you can program against in order to access your data store. The ADO.NET object model is a little larger and a lot more functionally robust than your example, but they work the same way. ADO.NET is simply a collection of objects that offer properties and methods used to access data. Figure 16-3 shows the ADO.NET object model.

10 Min. To Go

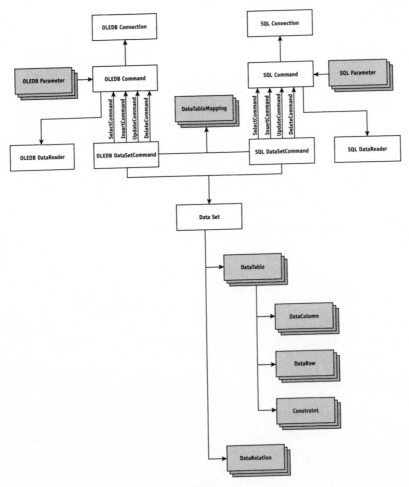

Figure 16-3 The ADO.NET object model

At first glance, the task of navigating the ADO.NET object may seem a little daunting. Rest assured that if you apply the lessons you learned earlier in this session you will have no problem at all.

To make this discussion a little more manageable, break the ADO.NET object model into smaller pieces. Figure 16-4 shows a diagram that represents one fragment of the ADO.NET object model, the DataSet. The DataSet is a new ADO object that is a memory-resident database that you can use to access, update, delete, and add data to your data store.

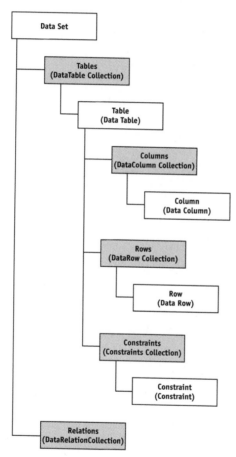

Figure 16-4   *The DataSet object*

As you can see, the DataSet object model consists of numerous objects and collections (in gray). Without going into too much detail about the Dataset object's properties and methods (and the properties and methods of the many objects that comprise the Dataset object), here's how you can leverage your knowledge of object models to fully exploit the power of the DataSet object.

The first thing you need to do is create a `dataset` object. There are many ways to do this, explicitly or by using a `DataSetCommand` object's methods. You can use Visual Basic's New keyword as follows:

```
Dim oDS As New DataSet
```

Now that you have a `dataset` object, `oDS`, you can gain access to its constituent objects. The `Tables` collection has the `Count` property, which returns an integer value representing the number of tables in your dataset object. Try it out:

```
Dim x As Integer
x = oDS.Tables.Count
```

As you can see, you use the `DataSet` object to access your `Tables` collection through the `Tables` property. Unfortunately, because your dataset is empty, you can't go much further than the `Tables` collection. Instead, you can build a `Table`, a `DataTable`, object using the `DataRow` and `DataColumn` objects.

First you'll declare the object as follows:

```
Dim oDataSet As DataSet
Dim oTable As DataTable
Dim oRow As DataRow
Dim oColumn As DataColumn
```

Then create a table object and add it to your dataset object, `oDataSet`:

```
oDataSet = New DataSet("Music")
oTable = New DataTable("t_bands")
oDataSet.Tables.Add(oTable)
```

These three lines of code have done a great deal. In the first line, you created a `DataSet` object and named it `Music`. How does that work? Well, objects have something called a constructor to which you can pass parameters to initialize the object's properties. Often, an object has several constructors that all accept different parameters. As you can see, when constructing your `DataSet`, `oDataSet`, `DataTable`, and `oTable` objects, you are passing strings that represent the object's name. After initializing the `DataSet` and `DataTable` objects, you added `oTable` to `oDataSet`'s `TableCollection` object through the `Tables` property.

OK, now that you have a dataset and a datatable, you can create a column (or two) and add it to `oTable`'s `ColumnCollection` through the `Columns` property:

```
oColumn = New DataColumn
With oColumn
    .ColumnName = "band_id"
    .DataType = System.Type.GetType("System.Int32")
    .AllowDBNull = False
    .Unique = True
    .AutoIncrement = True
    .AutoIncrementSeed = 1
```

```
      .AutoIncrementStep = 1
   End With
   oTable.Columns.Add(oColumn)
```

All you've done in the previous code snippet is (1) create a new `DataColumn` object named `oColumn`, (2) set several of the column's properties, and (3) added `oColumn` to `oTable` through its `Columns` property by calling its `Add` method. Notice that when you created `oColumn`, you didn't pass any parameters to its constructor. That's OK. You can always set the properties explicitly, which you did with, for example, the `ColumnName` property. Don't concern yourself right now with all the properties and methods described in these examples. Try to focus more on how all of these objects are related. Add another column to `oTable`:

```
   oColumn = New DataColumn
   With oColumn
      .ColumnName = "band_title"
      .DataType = System.Type.GetType("System.String")
      .AllowDBNull = False
      .Unique = True
   End With
   oTable.Columns.Add(oColumn)
```

So at this point, you have a dataset, `oDataSet`, which contains one `DataTable` object, `oTable`, which in turn contains two `DataColumn` objects. Actually that's not exactly true. To be more exact, you have a `DataSet` that contains a `TableCollection` object that contains one `DataTable` object that contains a `ColumnsCollection` object that contains two `DataColumn` objects. To illustrate this point, set the primary key on `oTable`:

```
   oDataSet.Tables("t_bands").PrimaryKey = New DataColumn()
   {oTable.Columns("band_id")}
```

Don't worry about the syntax to the right of the equals sign, you get to that in Session 21, "Introducing DataSets, Part II." If you look at the syntax on the left of the equals sign, you can see that you are navigating through the hierarchy of `DataSet` objects to get to the `PrimaryKey` property on the `DataTable` named t_bands.

Now that you have successfully created the structure of `oTable`, let's add some data. To add data to a `DataTable` object, you need to use the `DataRow` class.

```
   oRow = oTable.NewRow
   oRow("band_title") = "Hootie & The Blowfish"
   oTable.Rows.Add(oRow)
```

In the previous code you (1) created a new `DataRow` object, `oRow`, based on `oTable`'s structure using its `NewRow` method, (2) added data to the `band_title` column, and (3) added `oRow` to `oTable` through the `RowsCollection`'s `Add` method.

So that is how you can navigate the `DataSet` object model. The rest of the ADO.NET object model is essentially the same. The objects may have different properties and methods, but, at the end of the day, they're all related in a very elegant hierarchical manner.

Note

We should mention one more thing about the ADO.NET objects. As you can see in Figure 16-3, several classes are offered in two flavors, OLEDB and SQLClient. Two examples of this are the OLEDBConnection and SQLConnection classes. Each of these "flavors" is referred to as a Managed Provider. What does this mean? Well, if you are using SQL Server 7.0 or higher, use the SQLClient classes (that is, SQLConnection, SQLCommand, and so on), otherwise use the OLEDB classes (i.e., OLEDBConnection, OLEDBCommand). You can certainly use the OLEDB classes to access a SQL Server database, but you loose a little performance because the SQL Managed Providers communicate directly with the SQL Server internal API, skipping the intermediate level represented by OLEDB.

Done!

REVIEW

In this session, you learned about classes, objects, collections, and object models. An object is an instance of a class. An object model is a hierarchical grouping of objects that are functionally related. The ADO.NET object model provides us, as developers, with an easy-to-use programming model to access practically any type of data store. Many of the objects that make up ADO.NET come in two flavors, ADO and SQL, which are referred to as Managed Providers. With respect to ADO.NET, a Managed Provider is effectively a class that is optimized to work with a particular type of data store.

QUIZ YOURSELF

1. What is an object model? (See session introduction.)
2. How are objects and classes related? (See session introduction.)
3. What is a Managed Provider? (See session introduction.)

PART

III

Saturday Afternoon
Part Review

The following set of questions is designed to provide you with feedback on how well you understood the topics covered during this part of the book. Please refer to Appendix A for the answers to each question.

1. The required field validator can be used with a label control.
   True/False

2. What is a regular expression that can be used to validate an e-mail address?

3. More than one validation control can be used together to validate a single user input field.
   True/False

4. What version of JavaScript should be used for client-side validation?
   - a. 1.0
   - b. 1.1
   - c. 2.0
   - d. 2000

5. If browsers do not support client-side cookies, what state maintenance approach can be used?
   - a. Cookieless
   - b. Client-side
   - c. Server-side
   - d. None of the above

6. *Fill in the blank:* Use of SQL Server for state maintance uses _____ state maintenance.

7. List two advantages of using .NET State Server.

   _____

   _____

8. List two advantages of using SQL Server for state maintenance.

   _____

   _____

9. *Fill in the blank:* _____ is the process of discovering and verifying the identity of a user or service by examining the user's credentials and validating those credentials against some authority.

10. *Fill in the blank:* _____ is when an application assumes the user's identity when the request is passed to the application from IIS.

11. What section of the config.Web file is used for storing a list of authorized users?

    a. <authorization>

    b. <personal>

    c. <credentials>

    d. None of the above

12. *Fill in the blank:* To deny all users access to your ASP.NET application, add a <deny users="*"/> declarations to the _____ section of your config.Web file.

13. Which of the following forms of caching involves storing the dynamic response generated by a request in memory?

    a. Page output caching

    b. Fragment caching

    c. Page data caching

    d. None of the above

14. Which of the following forms of caching involves the storing of arbitrary objects across multiple requests?

    a. Page output caching

    b. Fragment caching

    c. Page data caching

    d. None of the above

15. How do you set the `TimeSpan` variable equal to zero?

16. When are the rules for expiration, dependency, and scavenging established?

17. The RecordSet is a supported object type in .NET.
    True/False

18. Server-side cursors are supported in .NET.
    True/False

19. .NET can support multiple tables and their relationships in a single object.
    True/False

20. Server-side cursors negatively impact the scalability of an application, in terms of concurrent users.
    True/False

21. A class is an instance of an object.
    True/False

22. *Fill in the blank:* _____ is effectively a method of developing application code based on objects in order to promote code reusability, maintainability and extensibility.

23. An object model is a hierarchical grouping of objects that provides related functionality.
    True/False

24. *Fill in the blank:* With VB .NET the _____ keyword is used to instantiate a new object.

PART

IV

Saturday Evening

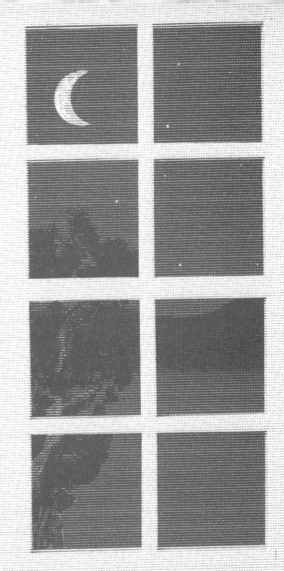

Opening a Connection

Session Checklist

✔ Connecting with ADO.NET

✔ Opening a connection

✔ Understanding transaction management with ADO.NET

**30 Min.
To Go**

Before you can access any part of a database, you need to establish a connection to it. You can use either the OleDbConnection or SqlConnection object to represent that connection. Throughout our discussion of ADO.NET, we are going to use a simple analogy to try and relate ADO.NET objects to something most people use everyday — a telephone. This will help you visualize what is actually happening when you use the ADO.NET objects. In the telephone analogy, a connection is analogous to picking up your telephone, dialing the number, and waiting for someone on the other end to answer.

Note

> **For the remainder of this session, we will focus on the OLEDB Managed Provider Connection object,** OleDbConnection. **The** OleDbConnection **and** SqlConnection **objects map one to one. So, if you are using a SQL Server database and would like a moderate performance boost, you can use the** SqlConnection **object.**

By creating an instance of an OleDbConnection object, and specifying data source-specific information in its properties, you can build a predefined link between the data consumer (your ASP.NET application) and the data provider (your database). Then, once you have established the connection to the data source, you can use the connection, in concert with other ADO.NET objects, to execute commands directly against the data source, to execute stored procedures, and to retrieve and manipulate data.

The OleDbConnection object also offers you the benefit of connection pooling — a mechanism that keeps connections pooled after you have explicitly closed them. Repeatedly opening and closing connections may consume Web server resources and can be a time-consuming process. Connection pooling is effectively a method of improving performance when a Web server is regularly accessed.

Creating a Connection

With ADO, ADO.NET's predecessor, you, as the developer, could create Connection objects explicitly or through another object such as a Command object. That is no longer the case. With ADO.NET you must explicitly open your connections using one of its constructors. Some developers might be taken aback by this feature, however, we recommend that developers create their connection objects explicitly for two reasons: (1) the code is easier to maintain and (2) connection pooling can be utilized.

In order to use the OLEDB Managed Provider objects, such as OleDbConnection, OleDbCommand, and so on, you need to include the OleDb namespace in your ASP.NET page. To do this, you use the Import construct at the top of your ASP.NET page:

```
<%@ Import Namespace="System.Data.OleDb" %>
```

For all you Visual Basic programmers out there, using a namespace is like adding a Reference to your project.

Table 17-1 lists the various namespaces you are likely to use in order to access the ADO.NET objects.

Table 17-1 *Namespaces Used to Access ADO.NET Objects*

Namespace	Contains
System.Data	ADO.NET base objects
System.Data.OleDb	Managed OLDDB data store objects
System.Data.SqlClient	SQL Server-specific implementation of the ADO.NET objects
System.Data.SqlTypes	SQL Server data types

Now you're ready to create your connection object. In the following code, we've used VB to create a connection object called oConn:

```
<%@ Import Namespace="System.Data.OleDb" %>
<script language="VB" runat="server">
  Dim oConn As New OleDbConnection
</script>
```

The ADO.NET Connection objects, OleDb and Sql, have several constructors. A constructor is essentially the syntax you use to instantiate an object. Any given object can have several constructors, like the Connection objects, or no constructors, like the DataReader objects, which need to be instantiated or created by another object. In the previous code snippet, we demonstrated the use of the OleDbConnection's default constructor that does not accept any parameters. The Connection objects have another constructor that accepts a connection string as its only parameter.

If you think back to your telephone analogy, what we have done thus far is pick up the telephone. Now that you have picked up the phone, it's time to make a call or open a connection.

Opening a Connection

20 Min. To Go

In order to open a connection to a data source, you need to know a little about the database. Kind of like making a phone call, you need to have a phone number. When opening a connection, you need to supply several pieces of information depending on the Relational Database Management System (RDBMS) you are using. Some of these pieces of information could be server name or IP address, database name, user name, and password. With this crucial information, you will construct a connection string that is effectively a collection of name/value pairs, separated by semicolons, which tell the Connection object how to connect to your database. The information that you use to construct your connection string will vary depending on the type of database to which you are trying to connect. Table 17-2 lists some of the most common parameters you will use to build a connection string.

Table 17-2 *Parameters Used to Construct a Connection String*

Parameter	Description
Provider	The OLEDB provider used to access the database.
Data Source	The IP address or name of the server on which the database resides.
Database	The name of the database to be used once the connection is open.
User ID	The user ID for the account used to access the database.
Password	The password for the account used to access the database.

All of the parameters listed in Table 17-2 are optional with the exception of the Provider parameter.

Here is a snippet of code that opens, using the OleDbConnection object's Open method, a connection to a SQL Server database named "Music" that is located on my local machine:

```
<%@ Page LANGUAGE="VB"%>
<%@ Import Namespace="System.Data" %>
<%@ Import Namespace="System.Data.OleDB" %>
<SCRIPT LANGUAGE="VB" RUNAT="server">
Sub Page_Load(Sender As Object, E As EventArgs)
    Dim oConn As OleDBConnection
    Dim sConnString As String
    sConnString = "Provider=SQLOLEDB;Data Source=(local);Initial
Catalog=Music;User ID=music;Password=music"
```

```
   oConn = New OleDBConnection(sConnString)
   oConn.Open()
   oConn.Close()
End Sub
</SCRIPT>
<HTML>
<BODY>
Opening a Connection!
</BODY>
</HTML>
```

In the previous code listing, the connection string, sConnString, contains a user ID/password combination. You may need to alter the user ID/password combination to get the code to run successfully on your computer.

We constructed a string, sConnString, that we passed to the connection's Open() method. The Open() method in turn parses this string and attempts to open a connection to the database. The Open() method is equivalent to an operator in our telephone analogy. The operator takes the phone number you dial and attempts to place the call. The connection string contains several very important pieces of information including Provider, Data Source, Initial Catalog, User ID, and Password. The Provider specifies which method you are using to connect to the database, the Data Source indicates on which server your database resides, the Initial Catalog represents the name of the database you are attempting to access, and the User ID and Password are the credentials you need to pass to the RDBMS in order to gain access. The OleDbConnection object actually has a read-only property for each of these pieces of information. So, you can easily gather a connection's settings using these properties as shown in Listing 17-1.

Listing 17-1   *Inspecting a Connection's Properties*

```
<%@ Page Language="VB" debug="true" %>
<%@ Import Namespace="System.Data" %>
<%@ Import Namespace="System.Data.OleDb" %>
<SCRIPT LANGUAGE="VB" RUNAT="server">
Sub Page_Load(Sender As Object, E As EventArgs)
  Dim oConn As New OleDbConnection
  Dim sConnString As String

  sConnString = "Provider=SQLOLEDB;Data Source=(local);Initial
Catalog=Music;User ID=music;Password=music"
  With oConn
    .ConnectionString = sConnString
    .Open()
    Response.Write(.Provider & "<BR>")
    Response.Write(.DataSource & "<BR>")
    .Close()
  End With
End Sub
```

```
</SCRIPT>
<HTML>
<BODY>
Opening a Connection!
</BODY>
</HTML>
```

Let's talk about the `Provider` property for a second. There are actually several ways to connect to a database in the Microsoft world. You can use OLEDB or you can use ODBC. What's the difference? The major difference, from a developer's viewpoint, is performance. OLEDB communicates directly with the data source whereas ODBC, in most instances, must go through the OLEDB provider for ODBC in order to access the data source. So, OLEDB provides a little better performance.

In the previous examples, we used OLEDB. When accessing a database via OLEDB, a data source-specific provider needs to be specified via the `Provider` property. Because, in our examples, we were accessing a SQL Server database, we used the SQLOLEDB provider. To obtain a provider for the data source you need to access, try contacting the product's vendor or Microsoft. The most common providers, for example Oracle, SQL Server, and Microsoft Access, are readily available.

Connecting to a database via ODBC and ADO is very simple. You simply create a *data source name* (DSN) on the server from which you are accessing the data source and then add a "DSN=*value*" name/value pair to your connection string.

Creating a DSN is fairly straightforward and well documented. For details see www.15seconds.com **or** www.4guysfromrolla.com.

However, it's not quite as simple with ADO.NET. You cannot connect to a database via ODBC directly with the `OleDbConnection` or `SqlConnection` objects. As a matter of fact, you can't use the `SqlConnection` to a database via ODBC at all. The .NET SQL Server data provider uses its own protocol to communicate with SQL Server therefore it does not support the use of an ODBC DSN because it does not add an ODBC layer. You can use the .NET OleDb data provider in conjunction with a Universal DataLink (UDL) file to connect to a database via ODBC; however, this is not the approach we recommend. To this point, we have neglected to mention a third .NET data provider, ODBC. To access the ODBC data provider, use the following namespace:

```
System.Data.ODBC
```

You may need to download the .NET update that includes the ODBC data provider from www.microsoft.com.

Suppose you've created a DSN to a Music database, named "Bands." To access the database via ODBC, you would use the following code:

```
<%@ Page LANGUAGE="VB"%>
<%@ Import Namespace="System.Data" %>
<%@ Import Namespace="System.Data.ODBC" %>
<SCRIPT LANGUAGE="VB" RUNAT="server">
Sub Page_Load(Sender As Object, E As EventArgs)
    Dim oConn As OdbcConnection
    Dim sConnString As String
    sConnString = "DSN=Bands"
    oConn = New OdbcConnection(sConnString)
    oConn.Open()
    oConn.Close()
End Sub
</SCRIPT>
<HTML>
<BODY>
Opening a Connection with ODBC!
</BODY>
</HTML>
```

You'll notice that the code is very similar to the previous OLEDB examples. Actually, the only difference is how you construct the connection string. Instead of providing all of the database information, such as location, Data Source, and name, Database, you simply supply a DSN name/value pair. You've also already provided the User ID or Password when you created the DSN.

You'll notice in all of the examples, we call a Close method. This method closes the connection that we have opened. *Always close connections!!!!!* We can't emphasize this enough. When you close the connection, it is returned to the connection pool and can be used by another request.

Now that the connection is open, what can we do with it? Well, to be quite honest not too terribly much. With the ADO.NET connection objects you can't directly execute SQL commands against a data source like you could with ADO. In order to create, update, delete, or retrieve data from our data source, you must utilize other ADO.NET objects such as the DataReader and DataAdapter objects, both of which we'll discuss in Sessions 19 and 20, respectively. The connection does, however, provide several properties and methods to manage transactions.

**10 Min.
To Go**

Using Transactions

By definition, a *transaction* is an atomic unit of work that either fails or succeeds. There is no such thing as a partially completed transaction. Since a transaction is composed of many steps, each step in the transaction must succeed for the transaction to be successful. If any one part of transaction fails, the entire transaction fails. When the transaction fails, the system needs to return, or roll back, to its original state.

To demonstrate why you may want to use transactions, we will present a sample scenario. Imagine that you own your own bank. A customer wants to transfer $5,000 from checking to savings. So you get on your computer and begin the transaction. Behind the scenes, the following "units" of work need to be completed:

1. Subtract $5,000 from customer's checking account.
2. Add $5,000 to customer's saving's account.

This is a very simple scenario, but we think it illustrates the need for transactions. If either of these steps fails, but the other succeeds, we have a major problem. If step 1 succeeds, but step 2 is not successful, you will have a very upset customer on your hands. If step 1 fails, but step 2 succeeds, you will have a very satisfied customer, but some upset shareholders. Either way, bad news! So you need to ensure that either both steps are successful or that the system returns to its state prior to beginning the transaction.

This is how ADO.NET supports transactions. The ADO.NET connection objects provide the BeginTransaction method, which, when called, returns a transaction object (either SQLTransaction or OLEDBTransaction).

The BeginTransation method begins a transaction. When called, the BeginTransaction method returns a Transaction object (either an OleDbTransaction or SQLTransaction). It is through the Transaction objects that you can manage your transactions. The Transaction objects support numerous properties and methods (like any object). We will only discuss a few of them in this book. If you need more information, we suggest taking a quick glance at your .NET Framework documentation. The Transaction object's Commit method commits the transaction, which means that all the steps in the transaction have completed successfully and the new state should be persisted. The transaction object's RollBack method returns your data store to its pre-transaction state if one or more of the steps in the transaction fail.

So, the basic framework for a transactional ASP.NET page may look like this:

```
Dim oConn As OleDBConnection
Dim oTransaction As OleDbTransaction
Dim sConnString As String
sConnString = "DSN=Bands"
oConn = New OLEDBConnection(sConnString)
oConn.Open()

oTransaction = oConn.BeginTransaction()

Try
    [Transaction Steps]
    oTransaction.Commit()
        Exit Try

Catch
    oTransaction.RollBack()
End Try
```

We begin the transaction with the BeginTransaction method and then attempt to complete each of the steps of the transaction. Because the steps are within a try . . . catch structure, if a step fails, the transaction will be rolled back using the RollbackTransaction method. If all the steps are completed successfully, the transaction is committed with the CommitTransaction method. The try . . . catch structure is new to VB.NET and, as you can see, is very useful.

Transactions should only be used when writing to your data store. You could retrieve data from your data store using transactions, but this would really serve no purpose since you are not attempting to preserve the integrity of your data. Transactions do incur a bit of a performance penalty, so use them only when necessary.

Done!

REVIEW

With the ADO.NET connection objects, SQLConnection and OleDbConnection, you, as a developer, can easily connect to relational and non-relational data sources. The ADO connection objects were designed to be very lightweight — and thereby quickly created and destroyed. The connection objects also provide transaction management facilities through the transaction objects, which are vital for enterprise application development.

QUIZ YOURSELF

1. What is the main function of the connection objects? (See session introduction.)
2. What is the major difference between ODBC and OLEDB? (See "Opening a Connection.")
3. What is a transaction and why are they important for enterprise application development? (See "Using Transactions.")

Executing Commands

Session Checklist

✔ Understanding the function of the Command objects in ADO.NET

✔ Executing SQL commands against a data store

✔ Appending parameters to a Command object

✔ Filling a DataReader using the Command object's Execute method

**30 Min.
To Go**

I n Session 17, "Opening a Connection," we introduced the ADO.NET Connection objects. In this session, we build upon our previous discussion of connections and introduce the OledbCommand objects. ADO.NET offers two flavors of command objects: OledbCommand and SqlCommand. Just like the connection object, you can use either object to access a SQL Server database, but need to use the OleDbCommand object to access any other data source. However, using the SqlCommand object with SQL Server does provide some performance gain.

So, what is a command? A *command* is an instruction — in this case to create, retrieve, update, or delete data in your data store. Most importantly, the Command objects enable you to fill the DataReader objects with data.

In the telephone analogy we used earlier, you are the Command object. When the person on the other end answers the phone, you might say, "May I please speak with Tony?" You have issued a command or request. Or you might say, "Can I have directions to your restaurant?" in which case you are asking for information to be returned to you.

For the remainder of this session, we will focus on the OleDb Managed Provider Command object, OleDbCommand. For the most part, the OleDbCommand and SqlCommand objects map one-to-one. So if you are using a SQL Server database and would like to improve performance, you can use the SqlCommand object. To utilize the SqlCommand object, you will need to import the System.Data.SqlClient namespace.

Building a Command

There are many ways of building, or constructing, a command object with ADO.NET. You can explicitly set the command object's properties, pass parameters into the command object's constructor, or a combination of the two. Following are several examples of how to initialize (or construct) an OleDbCommand object:

```
oCmd = New OleDbCommand()
oCmd = New OledbCommand(sSQL)
oCmd = New OledbCommand(sSQL, oConn)
```

In the previous listing, oConn is an OleDbConnection object and sSQL is a query command string.

Listing 18-1 shows an example of how you might build a command that returns all of the rows in the t_bands table in the Music database:

Listing 18-1   *Building a Command*

```
<%@ Page Language="VB" %>
<%@ Import Namespace="System.Data" %>
<%@ Import Namespace="System.Data.OleDb" %>
<SCRIPT LANGUAGE="VB" RUNAT="server">
Sub Page_Load(Sender As Object, E As EventArgs)
  Dim oConn As OledbConnection
  Dim oCmd As OledbCommand
  Dim sSQL As String

  sSQL = "SELECT * FROM t_bands"

  oConn = New OledbConnection
  oConn.ConnectionString = "Provider=SQLOLEDB;Data Source=(local);Initial
Catalog=Music;User ID=music;Password=music"
  oConn.Open()

  oCmd = New OledbCommand(sSQL, oConn)

  oConn.Close
  oConn = Nothing
End Sub
</SCRIPT>
<HTML>
<BODY>
Building a Command with ADO.NET!
</BODY>
</HTML>
```

You'll notice in the previous sample that we build the OleDbCommand by passing two parameters to its constructor. The first parameter is a string representing the SQL command we want to execute. The second parameter is an OleDbConnection object.

The OleDbCommand object has several properties that you can explicitly set. Some of these properties are Connection, CommandText, CommandType, and CommandTimeout.

Connection property

**20 Min.
To Go**

The Connection property is used to set or get the connection against which to execute the command. You must pass a valid OleDbConnection object to the Connection property or you will receive an error.

Listing 18-2 shows an example of how you might explicitly set the Connection property by passing it a valid OleDbConnection object.

Listing 18-2   *Explicitly setting a Command object's Connection properties*

```
<%@ Page Language="VB"%>
<%@ Import Namespace="System.Data" %>
<%@ Import Namespace="System.Data.OleDb" %>
<SCRIPT LANGUAGE="VB" RUNAT="server">
Sub Page_Load(Sender As Object, E As EventArgs)
  Dim oConn As OleDbConnection
  Dim oCmd As OleDbCommand
  Dim sSQL As String
  Dim sConnString As String

  sSQL = "SELECT * FROM t_bands"
  sConnString = "Provider=SQLOLEDB;Data Source=(local);Initial
Catalog=Music;User ID=music;Password=music"

  oConn = New OleDbConnection
  With oConn
      .ConnectionString = sConnString
      .Open()
  End With

  oCmd = New OledbCommand(sSQL)
  With oCmd
      .Connection = oConn
  End With

  oConn.Close()
End Sub
</SCRIPT>
<HTML>
<BODY>
Building a Command with ADO.NET!
</BODY>
</HTML>
```

CommandText property

The CommandText property gives you a means of holding your command (as a string) for later execution. It can contain a SQL statement, a stored procedure name, or a table name. For example, you can assign a simple SQL statement to the CommandText property as follows:

```
oCmd.CommandText = "SELECT band_id, band_title, music_type_id, record_company_id FROM t_bands"
```

Alternatively, you could assign a stored procedure name to the CommandText property and tell the Command object you are using a stored procedure by setting the CommandType property accordingly:

```
oCmd.CommandText = "prGetBands"
oCmd.CommandType = CommandType.StoredProcedure
```

CommandType property

The CommandType property gets the CommandText or sets how it is interpreted. The possible values, or enumerations, of the CommandType property are

- StoredProcedure
- TableDirect
- Text

When the CommandType property is set to StoredProcedure, the CommandText property is interpreted as a stored procedure. Go figure! If the CommandType is set to TableDirect and the CommandText property is set to a valid table name, then all the rows and columns for the specified table are returned. This is generally not a good idea, for performance reasons, when executing the command against a large database. Finally, if the CommandType property is set to Text, then the CommandText is executed as a SQL text command.

Listing 18-3 presents an example of how to execute a stored procedure called prCountBands.

Listing 18-3 *Executing a stored procedure*

```
<%@ Page Language="VB" debug="true" %>
<%@ Import Namespace="System.Data" %>
<%@ Import Namespace="System.Data.OleDb" %>
<SCRIPT LANGUAGE="VB" RUNAT="server">
Sub Page_Load(Sender As Object, E As EventArgs)
  Dim oConn As OledbConnection
  Dim oCmd As OledbCommand
  Dim sSQL As String
  Dim iBandCount As Integer

  oConn = New OledbCOnnection("Provider=SQLOLEDB;Data
Source=(local);Initial Catalog=Music;User ID=music;Password=music")
  oConn.Open()
```

```
   oCmd = New OleDbCommand(sSQL, oConn)
   oCmd.CommandType = CommandType.StoredProcedure
   oCmd.CommandText = "prCountBands"
   iBandCount = oCmd.ExecuteScalar()

   oConn.Close()

   lblBandCount.Text = iBandCount
End Sub
</SCRIPT>
<HTML>
<BODY>
There are <asp:Label ID="lblBandCount" Text="" Runat="server" /> bands in
the database.
</BODY>
</HTML>
```

CommandTimeout property

The CommandTimeout property gets or sets the time, in seconds, to wait while executing the command before terminating the attempt and generating an error. The syntax for setting the CommandTimeout property follows:

```
oCmd.CommandTimeout = 60
```

The default value for the CommandTimeout property is 30 seconds. The CommandTimeout property is not inherited from the command's Connection. The command object's CommandTimeout property and the connection object's CommandTimeout property are completely disparate properties. The Command object's CommandTimeout property sets the maximum amount of time, in seconds, for a command to attempt to execute before returning an error. The Connection object's ConnectionTimeout works the same way. The connection object attempts to open the connection for a designed amount of time before returning an error.

 Setting the CommandTimeout **property's value to 0 indicates that the command will attempt to execute indefinitely. We do not recommend this!**

Appending parameters

The OleDbCommand object supports a *collection* property named Parameters. The Parameters property is actually a OleDbParameterCollection object that can contain more than one OleDbParameter object. The Parameters property enables you to append parameters to the Command object. Parameters are generally attached to commands that are executing stored procedure that require input parameters. For example, you could write the following stored procedure to return a band's title based on its band_id:

```
CREATE PROCEDURE prGetBandTitle
  @iID AS INT = 0
AS
  SELECT band_title from t_bands WHERE band_id = @iID
  RETURN
```

So how do you append parameters? First you create an `OleDbParameter` object. An `OledbParameter` object can be constructed in several ways. For now, we'll focus on constructing the `OleDbParameter` object by setting its properties explicitly rather than passing them into the `OleDbParameter` object constructor. The properties we'll set are `ParameterName`, `DBType`, and `Value` as follows:

```
oParam = New OleDbParameter()
oParam.ParameterName = "@iID"
oParam.DBType = OleDbType.Integer
oParam.Value = 1
```

The `OledbParameter` object supports an `Add()` method that you can call to append the `OLEDBParameter` to your `OLEDBCommand` as shown in Listing 18-4.

Listing 18-4 *Appending a parameter to a command*

```
<%@ Page Language="VB" %>
<%@ Import Namespace="System.Data" %>
<%@ Import Namespace="System.Data.OleDb" %>
<SCRIPT LANGUAGE="VB" RUNAT="server">
Sub Page_Load(Sender As Object, E As EventArgs)
  Dim oConn As OleDbConnection
  Dim oCmd As OleDbCommand
  Dim oParam As OleDbParameter
  Dim sSQL As String

  oConn = New OleDbConnection("Provider=SQLOLEDB;Data
Source=(local);Initial Catalog=Music;User ID=music;Password=music")
  oConn.Open()

  oCmd = New OleDbCommand(sSQL, oConn)
  oCmd.CommandType = CommandType.StoredProcedure
  oCmd.CommandText = "prGetBandTitle"

  oParam = New OleDbParameter()
  oParam.ParameterName = "@iID"
  oParam.DBType = OleDbType.Integer
  oParam.Value = 1

  oCmd.Parameters.Add(oParam)
End Sub
</SCRIPT>
<HTML>
<BODY>
Appending a Parameter to a Command with ADO.NET!
</BODY>
</HTML>
```

You'll notice in Listing 18-5 that we first created the OleDbCommand, oCmd, object. Next, we constructed the OleDbParameter, oParam, object, and set its properties. Finally, we attached the OledbParameter to the OleDbCommand object using the Parameters collection's Add () method with the following line of code:

```
oCmd.Parameters.Add(oParam)
```

The Parameter object supports many properties and methods and can become very complex. You should check your .NET documentation for a more detailed look at the OleDbParameter and SqlParameter objects.

Executing a Command

**10 Min.
To Go**

Now that you know how to construct an OLEDBCommand object, it is time that you ask it do something. The OLEDBCommand object has many useful methods, including the ExecuteReader(), ExecuteNonQuery(), and Prepare() methods.

ExecuteNonQuery method

The ExecuteReader() and ExecuteNonQuery() methods are similar in that they both execute commands against a data source. The main difference is the number of rows returned when the command is executed. As indicated by its name, the ExecuteNonQuery() method does not return any rows from the datasource; you probably won't use this command when executing a SQL SELECT command. It could, however, be useful when executing INSERT, UPDATE or DELETE commands depending on your requirements. The ExecuteNonQuery() method does not require, or for that matter accept any parameters in its constructor. Here is a sample of calling the ExecuteNonQuery method:

```
oCmd = New OleDbCommand()
oCmd.Connection = oConn
oCmd.CommandType = CommandType.Text
oCmd.CommandText = "UPDATE t_bands SET band_title = 'Hootie and The
Blowfish' WHERE band_title = 'Hootie & The Blowfish'"
oCmd.ExecuteNonQuery()
```

You'll notice that we are executing a SQL UPDATE command so we probably don't want any records returned. The ExecuteNonQuery() method does return the number of rows, as an integer, that were affected by the executed command. So if you wanted to determine how many records were affected by a command, you could use the following code:

```
Dim iAffected As Integer
iAffected = oCmd.ExecuteNonQuery()
```

Prepare method

The Prepare() method is used to create a prepared, or compiled, version of the command on the datasource. This method is generally used only when the CommandType property is set to Text; but it does improve performance when executing large SQL commands or dynamically generated SQL commands that contain parameters. The syntax for preparing a command is

```
oCmd.Prepare()
```

ExecuteReader method

The ExecuteReader() method executes the CommandText against the command's Connection and builds an object capable of forward-only data reads. This object is an OleDbDataReader. The syntax is

```
oDR = oCmd.ExecuteReader()
```

where oDR is an OleDbDataReader object. Simple! Once you have populated the OleDbDataReader object by calling the OleDbCommand's ExecuteReader() method, you have access to the data. We cover DataReader objects in detail in Session 19, "Using DataReaders." Listing 18-5 demonstrates how to populate a datareader via the command object's Execute method.

Listing 18-5   *Populating a DataReader with a command*

```
<%@ Page Language="VB" %>
<%@ Import Namespace="System.Data" %>
<%@ Import Namespace="System.Data.OleDb" %>
<SCRIPT LANGUAGE="VB" RUNAT="server">
Sub Page_Load(Sender As Object, E As EventArgs)
  Dim oConn As OleDbConnection
  Dim oCmd As OleDbCommand
  Dim oDR As OleDbDataReader

  oConn = New OleDbConnection("Provider=SQLOLEDB;Data
Source=(local);Initial Catalog=Music;User ID=music;Password=music")
  oConn.Open()

  oCmd = New OleDbCommand()
  With oCmd
      .Connection = oConn
      .CommandType = CommandType.StoredProcedure
      .CommandText = "prGetBands"
      oDR = oCmd.ExecuteReader()
  End With

  While oDR.Read()
      lstBands.Items.Add(New
ListItem(oDR.Item("band_title"),oDR.Item("band_id")))
  End While

  oDR.Close()
  oConn.Close()
End Sub
```

```
</SCRIPT>
<HTML>
<BODY>
<asp:ListBox ID="lstBands" Size="1" Runat="server" />
</BODY>
</HTML>
```

In Listing 18-6, we use the following line of code to populate the DataReader object with the results of the query:

```
oDR = oCmd.ExecureReader()
```

Once the DataReader is populated, we iterate through the DataReader and add an Item to the ListBox server control, lstBands, for each record using the following statement:

```
lstBands.Items.Add(New
ListItem(oDR.Item("band_title"),oDR.Item("band_id")))
```

This method of populating controls with data is very fast, but not very flexible as the DataReader objects provide for forward-only navigation.

Done!

REVIEW

The ADO.NET Command objects, OleDbCommand and SqlCommand, are used to execute commands against a data source. With the Command objects you can execute SQL statements to insert, update, delete, or select data as well as create database objects such as stored procedures, tables, or triggers. Additionally, using the command object's ExecuteReader() method, we can fill a DataReader object for forward-only navigation.

QUIZ YOURSELF

1. What is the main function of a Command object? (See session introduction.)
2. What Command property do you use to add parameters to a Command object? (See "Appending parameters.")
3. What are the differences between the ExecuteReader () and ExecuteNonQuery () methods? (See "ExecuteNonQuery method.")

Using DataReaders

Session Checklist

✔ Understanding the function of the DataReader objects in ADO.NET

✔ Filling a DataReader using the Command object's Execute method

✔ Moving through a DataReader

**30 Min.
To Go**

In the previous session, we introduced the ADO.NET Command objects. In this session, we build upon the previous discussion of Command objects and further discuss the ADO.NET DataReader objects. As usual, ADO.NET offers two flavors of DataReader objects: OleDbDataReader and SqlDataReader. Just like the Connection and Command objects, you can use either to access a SQL Server database, but need to use the OleDbDataReader object to access any other data source.

Introducing DataReaders

So, what is a DataReader? A DataReader object is effectively a forward-only collection of records from your data source. The interesting thing about DataReaders is that they do not have a public constructor per se. The DataReader is created via a Command object's ExecuteReader method. Another interesting thing to note about DataReader objects is that, unlike many other ADO.NET objects, they can't be disconnected — that is, they always need an active connection. Thus, you can't, for example, pass them between business objects. The purpose of the DataReader is to provide data for display, that's it. The DataReader objects are lightweight and very fast so they are ideal for this purpose.

Looked at in terms of our telephone analogy, the DataReader is analogous to a recording you might get when say calling a restaurant and requesting directions. When you're listening to the directions and feverishly trying to write everything down you might often miss something. The problem is, you can't go back because the recording is forward-only. I guess you could call back! Same with a DataReader. It's forward only!

When creating a DataReader, start by declaring a variable as follows:

```
Dim oDR As OleDbDataReader
```

The next thing you need to do is construct your Connection and Command objects.

For more details on constructing Connection and Command objects, refer to Sessions 17 and 18.

Next, initialize the DataReader object by calling the Command object's ExecuteReader method as follows:

```
oDR = oCmd.Execute()
```

Now that is easy! Let's bring it all together . . . The following example illustrates how to (1) construct and open a Connection, (2) construct a Command, and (3) call the Command's ExecuteReader method and pass the result to a DataReader, as shown in Listing 19-1.

Listing 19-1 *Constructing a DataReader*

```
<%@ Page Language="VB" %>
<%@ Import Namespace="System.Data" %>
<%@ Import Namespace="System.Data.OleDb" %>
<SCRIPT LANGUAGE="VB" RUNAT="server">
Sub Page_Load(Sender As Object, E As EventArgs)
   Dim oConn As OleDbConnection
   Dim oCmd As OleDbCommand
   Dim oDR As OleDbDataReader

   oConn = New OleDbConnection("Provider=SQLOLEDB;Data
Source=(local);Initial Catalog=Music;User ID=music;Password=music")
   oConn.Open()

   oCmd = New OleDbCommand()
   With oCmd
        .Connection = oConn
        .CommandType = CommandType.Text
        .CommandText = "SELECT * FROM t_bands"
        oDR = .ExecuteReader()
   End With
End Sub
</SCRIPT>
<HTML>
<BODY>
Creating a DataReader with ADO.NET
</BODY>
</HTML>
```

Using DataReader Properties

OK, so now that you have your DataReader object, what can you do with it? Well, just like all other objects, the DataReader object has numerous properties and methods. We'll start with the properties:

20 Min.
To Go

Item property

The Item property returns the value for a given column in its native format. In order to reference the value of a column, you need to pass a string representing the column name or an integer representing the column's index. Take for example the following table called t_bands:

band_id	band_title	music_type_id	record_company_id
1	Hootie & The Blowfish	1	1
2	Toad the Wet Sprocket	1	1

You could reference the band_title field in either of the following ways:

```
oDR.Items("band_title")
oDR.Items(1)
```

You'll notice that we passed a one (1) to the DataReader object's Items property. To clarify, the 1 is the column index or location of the column in the row from which we want to retrieve the data. We used 1 as the index, because the numbering of column indexes begins with 0.

FieldCount property

The FieldCount property, which is obviously read-only, returns the number fields, as an integer, in the current record. Here is some sample syntax for getting the FieldCount:

```
Dim iFCount As Integer
iFCount = oDR.FieldCount
```

One possible application of the FieldCount property is to iterate through the columns in a DataReader and write out the column's value as shown in Listing 19-2.

Listing 19-2 *FieldCount property application*

```
<%@ Page Language="VB" %>
<%@ Import Namespace="System.Data" %>
<%@ Import Namespace="System.Data.OleDb" %>
<SCRIPT LANGUAGE="VB" RUNAT="server">
Sub Page_Load(Sender As Object, E As EventArgs)
  Dim oConn As OleDbConnection
```

Continued

Listing 19-2

Continued

```
    Dim oCmd As OleDbCommand
    Dim oDR As OleDbDataReader
    Dim iFieldCount As Integer
    Dim x As Integer

    oConn = New OleDbConnection("Provider=SQLOLEDB;Data
Source=(local);Initial Catalog=Music;User ID=music;Password=music")
    oConn.Open()

    oCmd = New OleDbCommand()
    oCmd.Connection = oConn
    oCmd.CommandType = CommandType.Text
    oCmd.CommandText = "SELECT * FROM t_bands"
    oDR = oCmd.ExecuteReader()

    iFieldCount = oDR.FieldCount

    While oDR.Read()
        Dim oRow As New TableRow()
        For x = 0 To (iFieldCount - 1)
            Dim oCell As New TableCell()
            oCell.Text = oDR.Item(x)
            oRow.Cells.Add(oCell)
        Next
        tblExample.Rows.Add(oRow)
    End While

    oDR.Close
    oConn.Close
End Sub
</SCRIPT>
<HTML>
<BODY>
<asp:Table ID="tblExample" BorderWidth=1 GridLines="both" Runat="server"/>
</BODY>
</HTML>
```

In Listing 19-2, all we've done is open our OleDbDataReader object, obtain the number of fields in the DataReader using the FieldCount property, and iterate through the rows of the DataReader using the Read method. (We discuss the Read method later in this session.) For each row, we loop through the fields and create a table cell containing the columns' value. Simple!

IsClosed property

The IsClosed method returns a Boolean value indicating whether the DataReader is closed. A value of true means that the DataReader is closed.

RecordsAffected property

The RecordsAffected property returns the number of rows that are changed, inserted, or deleted by the Command object that opens the DataReader. 0 is returned from the RecordsAffected property if no records were affected by the command object, and –1 is returned for SELECT commands. The RecordsAffected property is not set until the DataReader object is closed. The isClosed and RecordsAffected are the only DataReader properties that can be accessed after the DataReader has been closed.

Listing 19-3 illustrates how you can use the isClosed and RecordsAffected properties to display information about the Command that was executed to create a DataReader object.

Listing 19-3 *Displaying command information*

```
<%@ Page Language="VB" %>
<%@ Import Namespace="System.Data" %>
<%@ Import Namespace="System.Data.OleDb" %>
<SCRIPT LANGUAGE="VB" RUNAT="server">
Sub Page_Load(Sender As Object, E As EventArgs)
  Dim oConn As OleDbConnection
  Dim oCmd As OleDbCommand
  Dim oDR As OleDbDataReader
  Dim oParam As OleDbParameter
  Dim iBandID As Integer = 0

  If Page.IsPostBack Then iBandID = lstBands.SelectedItem.Value

  oConn = New OleDbConnection("Provider=SQLOLEDB;Data
Source=(local);Initial Catalog=Music;User ID=music;Password=music")
  oConn.Open()

  oCmd = New OleDbCommand()
  With oCmd
      .Connection = oConn
      .CommandType = CommandType.StoredProcedure
      .CommandText = "prBandDelete"
      oParam = New OleDbParameter
      With oParam
          .ParameterName = "BandID"
          .OleDbType = OleDbType.Integer
          .Value = iBandID
      End With
      .Parameters.Add(oParam)
      Try
          oDR = .ExecuteReader()
          lstBands.Items.Clear
          lstBands.Items.Add(New ListItem("",0))

          While oDR.Read()
```

Continued

Listing 19-3

```
                    lstBands.Items.Add(New
ListItem(oDR.Item("band_title"),oDR.Item("band_id")))
            End While
        Catch err As Exception
            Response.Write("The following error occurred:<BR>" &
err.Message & "<BR>")
        End Try
    End With

    oDR.Close
    oConn.Close

    If oDR.isClosed Then
        If oDR.RecordsAffected > 0 Then lblDeleted.Text = "You deleted " &
oDR.RecordsAffected & " bands from the database."
    End If
End Sub
</SCRIPT>
<HTML>
<BODY>
<FORM ID="frmBandDelete" Runat="server">
<asp:ListBox ID="lstBands" Size="1" AutoPostBack="true" Runat="server"/>
<BR/><BR/>
<asp:Label ID="lblDeleted" Text="" ForeColor="Red" Runat="server"/>
</FORM>
</BODY>
</HTML>
```

You'll notice that Listing 19-3 uses a ListBox Web Control, lstBands, to allow a user to select a band that he or she would like to delete from the t_bands table. When the Web Form containing lstBands is submitted, the id of the band is gathered and passed to OleDbCommand, oCmd, as an OleDbParameter, oParam. The prBandDelete stored procedure, which deletes the selected band and returns a recordset containing the remaining bands, is then executed by calling the Command object's ExecuteReader method. Following is the code for the prBandDelete stored procedure.

```
CREATE PROCEDURE prBandDelete
    @BandID INT = 0
AS
    IF @iBandID > 0
        BEGIN
            DELETE FROM t_songs WHERE album_id IN (SELECT
album_id FROM t_albums WHERE band_id = @iBandID)
            DELETE FROM t_albums WHERE band_id = @iBandID
            DELETE FROM t_band_members WHERE band_id = @iBandID
            DELETE FROM t_bands WHERE band_id = @iBandID
        END

    SELECT
        band_id, band_title
```

```
OM
      t_bands
DER BY
      band_title
```

You will need to create the `prBandDelete` **stored procedure in the Music database in order to get this example to work correctly.**

When the `ExecuteReader` method is called, an `OleDbDataReader`, oDR, is constructed and then iterated through the data to repopulate the `lstBands` ListBox. After repopulating `lstBands`, we inspect to see that the DataReader has been closed, using the `isClosed` property. We then use the `RecordsAffected` property to display the number of records that were deleted from t_bands table.

Using DataReader Methods

**10 Min.
To Go**

Now that you know the properties you are likely to use most often, let's move onto the DataReader's methods. The `DataReader` objects provide a plethora of methods.

Read method

We've touched on the Read method in an earlier example (Listing 19-2). The Read method advances the `DataReader` object to the next record each time it is called. In the "Old World" of ADO you would have had to use a combination of several properties and methods, including `EOF` and `MoveNext`, to perform the same function as the DataReader's Read method. Since the DataReader provides for forward-only navigation, the Read method really minimizes the amount of code you need to write to get to your data. We do not provide a Read method example here as you can refer to several of the previous examples to see it in action.

GetValue method

The `GetValue` method returns the value of a specified field in its native format. You can effectively use the `GetValue` method in place of the `Item` property. The `GetValue` method accepts either an integer representing a column index or a string representing a column name. For example, if the first column (index of 0) of our table is called band_id, we can use the following statement to get its value:

```
iID = oDR.GetValue(0)
```

Or, we can use the following:

```
iID = oDR.GetValue("band_id")
```

Since band_id is set as an integer in our table, the value returned from the `GetValue` method will return an integer, its native format.

Get[Data Type] methods

The DataReader object provides a multitude of what we call the Get[Data Type] methods, including the GetString, GetInt32, and GetBoolean methods. The Get[Data Type] methods return the data in a column as the specified data type. For example, the GetString method will return the data in a column in the form of a string. However, no data type conversion is performed, so the data type of the column must be of the data type specified. Unlike the GetValue method, the Get[Data Type] methods only accept a column index, also called an ordinal reference, as a parameter. The following statements demonstrate the GetString method:

```
Dim sBandName As String
sBandName = oDR.GetString(0)
```

GetOrdinal method

The GetOrdinal method returns a column's ordinal reference value, or index, as an integer when passed a column name. For example, the following code returns 0 because band_id is the first column in the t_bands table:

```
Dim iOrdinal As Integer
iOrdinal = oDR.GetOrdinal("band_id")
```

GetName method

The GetName method is the exact opposite of the GetOrdinal method. It returns a column's name as a string when passed its index. For example, the following code snippet will return band_id:

```
Dim sName As String
sName = oDR.GetName(0)
```

Close method

As the name implies, the Close method closes a DataReader object. Unlike other objects, closing the DataReader object is mandatory when you're done using it. You will get an error if you don't close your DataReader and then attempt to alter your Connection object. Closing a DataReader's Connection object immediately closes the DataReader. The syntax is very simple:

```
oDR.Close()
```

That covers the DataReader's major properties and methods.

There are other DataReader **methods and properties. However, chances are you may never use them. For a complete listing, refer to the .NET documentation.**

Done!

REVIEW

The ADO.NET DataReader objects, OleDbDataReader and SqlDataReader, are a collection of rows retrieved from a data source. The DataReader object provides forward-only navigation and must always be connection to your data source via a Connection object. While a DataReader object is in use, no other operations can be performed on its associated Connection object. To create a DataReader object, you must call the ExecuteReader method of the OleDbCommand or SqlCommand object rather than directly using a constructor.

QUIZ YOURSELF

1. What is the main function of a DataReader object? (See "Introducing DataReaders.")

2. How is a DataReader object constructed? (See "Introducing DataReaders.")

3. Can a DataReader object be disconnected from its Connection object? (See "Introducing DataReaders.")

SESSION

20

Introducing DataSets, Part I

**30 Min.
To Go**

Thus far in our discussion of ADO.NET, we have covered the Connection, Command, and DataReader objects. In this session, we will cover the DataSet object, probably the most innovative and exciting of the ADO.NET objects. The DataSet object, much like a DataReader, is designed to handle the actual data from a database. The DataSet also provides access to multiple tables, rows, and columns. Figure 20-1 illustrates the hierarchy of DataSet objects.

Each DataSet object can contain multiple tables, DataTable objects, as well as the relationships, DataRelation objects, between these tables. A DataSet object is effectively an off-line copy of your data store. The major advantage of the dataset is that because it's designed for disconnected data, you can pass multiple tables, along with their relationships, around the tiers of your Web application. Not only can you pass DataSet objects around your Web application, you can also pass them to other systems for processing in the form of XML, and then retrieve and update your data store with the updated DataSet. The DataSet object makes the promise of disconnected data a reality.

In our discussion of DataSet objects, we will introduce several other objects that are very closely related to the dataset, including the DataAdapter, DataTableMapping, DataView, DataRelation, and DataTable objects.

In the past, data processing has been primarily connection-based. Now, in an effort to make multi-tier applications more efficient, data processing in general and particularly ASP.NET data processing is turning to a message-based approach that revolves around chunks of data in the form of datasets. At the center of this approach is the DataAdapter object, which provides a bridge to retrieve and update data between a DataSet and a data store. The DataAdapter object provides this bridge via the Fill method to load data from a data source into the DataSet and uses the Update method to send changes made in the DataSet to the data source.

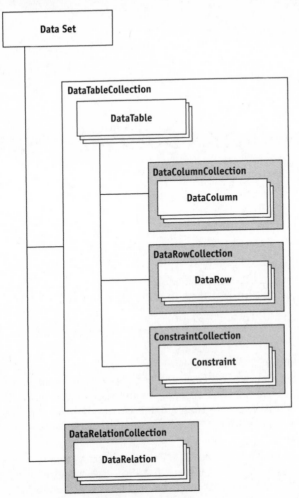

Figure 20-1 *Dataset object model*

Again Microsoft has provided two flavors of the DataAdapter, SqlDataAdapter and OleDbDataAdapter. If you are connecting to a SQL Server database, you can use the SqlDataAdapter object in conjunction with the SqlConection and SqlCommand objects to increase overall performance. Throughout this session, however, we will use the OleDbDataAdapter object in the examples.

Constructing a DataAdapter Object

As with many ADO.NET objects, there are several ways to construct a DataAdapter object. The default constructor is as follows:

```
oDA = New OleDbDataAdapter()
```

You'll notice that no parameters are passed using the default method. The DataAdapter's properties need to be set explicitly after construction. With the second method, we construct a DataAdapter with a specified select OleDbCommand object as follows:

```
oDA = New OleDbDataAdpater(oCmd)
```

The third method initializes a new instance of a DataAdapter with a select command string (for example a SQL statement) and a valid OleDbConnection object as follows:

```
oDA = New OleDbDataAdapter(sSQL, oConn)
```

Finally, we can initialize an OleDbDataAdapter with a select command string and a connection string as follows:

```
oDSComd = New OLEDBDataAdapter(sSQL, sConnString)
```

This method of constructing a DataAdapter object differs from the previous because a connection to the database specified in the connection string is created when the DataAdapter is executed.

In the following snippet of code, we demonstrate initializing a DataAdapter object by passing a command string and an OleDbConnection object:

```
<%@ Page Language="VB" %>
<%@ Import Namespace="System.Data" %>
<%@ Import Namespace="System.Data.OleDb" %>
<SCRIPT LANGUAGE="VB" RUNAT="server">
Sub Page_Load(Sender As Object, E As EventArgs)
  Dim oConn As OleDbConnection
  Dim oDA As OleDbDataAdapter

  oConn = New OleDbConnection("Provider=SQLOLEDB;Data
Source=(local);Initial Catalog=Music;User ID=music;Password=music")
  oConn.Open

  oDA = New OleDbDataAdapter("SELECT * FROM t_bands", oConn)
  oDA = Nothing
  oConn.Close()
  oConn = Nothing
End Sub
</SCRIPT>
```

The DataSet object provides several very useful properties, most of which revolve around manipulating DataSet content.

SelectCommand property

The SelectCommand property gets or sets a Command object used to select records in a DataSet. In following code snippet, we will create an OleDbDataAdapter object and set the SelectCommand:

```vb
<%@ Page Language="VB" %>
<%@ Import Namespace="System.Data" %>
<%@ Import Namespace="System.Data.OleDb" %>
<SCRIPT LANGUAGE="VB" RUNAT="server">
Sub Page_Load(Sender As Object, E As EventArgs)
    Dim oConn As OleDbConnection
    Dim oCmd As OleDbCommand
    Dim oDA As OleDbDataAdapter

    oConn = New OleDbConnection("Provider=SQLOLEDB;Data
Source=(local);Initial Catalog=Music;User ID=music;Password=music")
    oConn.Open()

    oCmd = New OleDbCommand("SELECT * FROM t_bands", oConn)

    oDA = New OleDbDataAdapter()
    oDA.SelectCommand = oCmd
End Sub
</SCRIPT>
```

You notice in the previous example that we (1) create an OleDbConnection object, (2) create an OleDbCommand object, (3) construct an OleDbDataAdapter object, and (4) set the OleDbDataAdapter object's SelectCommand equal to the previously created OleDbCommand object.

When the SelectCommand property is set to a previously created Command object, as in the previous example, the Command object is not cloned. The SelectCommand merely maintains a reference to the Command object — as shown in the following example. We set the SelectCommand property without explicitly creating a Command object:

```vb
<%@ Page Language="VB" %>
<%@ Import Namespace="System.Data" %>
<%@ Import Namespace="System.Data.OleDb" %>
<SCRIPT LANGUAGE="VB" RUNAT="server">
Sub Page_Load(Sender As Object, E As EventArgs)
    Dim oConn As New OleDbConnection
    Dim oDA As New OleDbDataAdapter

    With oConn
        .ConnectionString = "Provider=SQLOLEDB;Data Source=(local);Initial
Catalog=Music;User ID=music;Password=music"
        .Open
    End With
```

```
oDA.SelectCommand = New OleDbCommand
With oDA.SelectCommand
.CommandType = CommandType.Text
    .CommandText = "SELECT * FROM t_bands"
.Connection = oConn
End With

oDA = Nothing
oConn.Close
oConn = Nothing
End Sub
</SCRIPT>
```

Make sense? In effect, we're creating the SelectCommand explicitly.

UpdateCommand, DeleteCommand, and InsertCommand properties

The UpdateCommand property is used to get or set the command used to update records in the data source. The UpdateCommand is effectively the Command object used to update records in the data source for modified rows in the DataSet. When a DataAdapter object's Update method is called and (1) the UpdateCommand property is not set and (2) primary key information is present in the DataSet, the UpdateCommand will be generated automatically.

To keep things brief here, just say that the DeleteCommand and InsertCommand properties are used to get or set the command used to delete or insert, respectively, records in the data source when the Update method is called.

We'll return to the DataAdapter properties later. But first, take a look at the methods you can use to create DataSet objects.

Fill method

The Fill method is probably the DataAdapter method you will use most frequently. Simply stated, the Fill method adds data from your data source to a dataset. The Fill method accepts a variety of parameters including the DataSet object to fill, a string representing the alias for the newly created DataSet object, an integer representing the lower bound of records to retrieve, and an integer representing the upper bound of records to retrieve from our data source. Here are some examples:

- oDSCmd.Fill(oDS)
- oDSCmd.Fill(oDS, "Band Information")

In the previous sample, the only parameter that is required is the DataSet. Listing 20-1 details how to create a DataSet called "Band Information" and bind it to a DataGrid, dgBands, control.

Listing 20-1 *Creating a DataSet and binding it to a DataGrid control*

```
<%@ Page Language="VB" %>
<%@ Import Namespace="System.Data" %>
<%@ Import Namespace="System.Data.OleDb" %>
<SCRIPT LANGUAGE="VB" RUNAT="server">
Sub Page_Load(Sender As Object, E As EventArgs)
  Dim oConn As OleDbConnection
  Dim oDA As OleDbDataAdapter
  Dim oDS As New DataSet

  oConn = New OleDbConnection("Provider=SQLOLEDB;Data
Source=(local);Initial Catalog=Music;User ID=music;Password=music")
  oConn.Open

  oDA = New OleDbDataAdapter("SELECT * FROM t_bands", oConn)
  oDA.Fill(oDS, "Band Information")

  dgBands.DataSource = oDS
  dgBands.DataBind()

  oDS.Dispose()
  oDS = Nothing
  oDA.Dispose()
  oDA = Nothing
  oConn.Close()
  oConn = Nothing
End Sub
</SCRIPT>
<HTML>
<BODY>
<asp:DataGrid id="dgBands" runat="server"
        BorderColor="#000000"
        BorderWidth="2"
        GridLines="Both"
        CellPadding="5"
        CellSpacing="0"
        Font-Name="Arial"
        HeaderStyle-BackColor="#C0C0C0"
/>
</BODY>
</HTML>
```

As you can see, we simply create and open a connection to the Music database, create a DataAdapter object, and fill the DataSet by calling the Fill method. If you run this example, you may be a little surprised by the output. Instead of a list of bands from the t_bands table, you actually get a list of the tables in the DataSet. That is because in the process of binding the DataSet, oDS, to the DataGrid control, dgBands, we set the DataGrids DataSource property as follows:

```
dgBands.DataSource = oDS
```

The DataSet's `Tables` property, in this case, returns a collection of `OleDbDataTable` objects in the DataSet object. More on that in the next Session, "Introducing DataSets, Part II," but in the meantime, if you want a list of the bands in the t_bands table, simply set the dgBands object's DataMember property as follows:

```
dgBands.DataSource = oDA.dgBands.DataMember("Band Information")
```

**10 Min.
To Go**

Update method

The Update method calls the respective insert, update, or delete command for each inserted, updated, or deleted row in the DataSet. There are three different ways to call the Update method — you can pass:

- An array of `DataRow` objects
- A DataSet object
- A DataSet object and a string representing a table name

If you make changes to any of the tables in your DataSet, you could use the following syntax to send the changes to the `Music` database:

```
oDA.Update(oDS, "t_bands")
```

Dispose method

The `Dispose` method, when called, disposes of the `DataAdapter` object.

That's about all we'll cover for the `DataAdapter` object.

The `DataAdapter` **object has many more properties and methods that we didn't cover in this discussion. For more details, refer to the .NET documentation.**

Using DataSet Objects

As we mentioned before, a `DataSet` object is a memory-resident database that provides a consistent programming model regardless of the data source. A `DataSet` object represents a complete set of data including related tables, constraints, and relationships among the tables. The `DataSet` object is a very complex object and has numerous properties, methods, and collections. We'll start our discussion of datasets with the properties.

DataSetName property

The `DataSetName` property is used to get or set the name of the `DataSet` object. This is fairly straightforward, as shown in the following example:

```
oDS.DataSetName = "MyDataSet"
```

Suppose that oDS is a DataSet object. In order to retrieve the name of a DataSet, you may use:

```
Dim sName As String
sName = oDS.DataSetName
```

CaseSensitive property

The CaseSensitive property gets or sets a value (as a Boolean) indicating whether string comparisons within DataTable objects are case sensitive. The CaseSenstive property affects operations such as sorting, filtering, and searching a DataTable. The default value for this property is False. If you want to set the property to True, use the following syntax:

```
oDS.CaseSensitive = True
```

By default, setting the CaseSensitive property for a DataSet also sets each of its DataTable object's CaseSensitive property to the same value. However, the DataSet's CaseSensitive property can be overridden by a DataTable's CaseSenstive property. In order to retrieve the CaseSensitive property you may use the following code:

```
Dim bCase As Boolean
bCase = oDS.CaseSensitive
```

Done!

REVIEW

The ADO.NET DataSet object, is a very complex, yet exciting object. The DataSet is a memory-resident database that provides a consistent programming model regardless of its data source. The DataSet is designed to work in a disconnected environment, so passing a DataSet from one system to another is expected. In order to create a DataSet, you can use a DataAdapter, OleDbDataAdapter, or SqlDataAdapter object.

QUIZ YOURSELF

1. What are some of the differences between the Command and DataAdapter objects? (See session introduction.)
2. What is a DataSet and how does it differ from a DataReader? (See session introduction.)
3. How is the DataAdapter method used to populate a DataSet? (See "Fill method.")

PART

IV

Saturday Evening
Part Review

The following set of questions is designed to provide you with feedback on how well you understood the topics covered during this part of the book. Please refer to Appendix A for the answers to each question.

1. Which namespace can be used to access the OleDbConnection objects?
   a. System.Web
   b. System.Data.Connections
   c. System.Data.ADO
   d. System.Data.OleDb

2. Which namespace can be use to manipulate XML data?
   a. System.XML
   b. System.Data.Connections
   c. System.Data.ADO
   d. System.Data.OleDb

3. OleDbConnection and SqlConnection objects must be created explicitly.
   True/False

4. Which of the following `OleDbConnection` properties is used to obtain the database to which an `OleDbConnection` object is connected?

   a. `Provider`

   b. `DataSource`

   c. `Database`

   d. `UserID`

5. A `Command` object is basically a facility for executing commands against a datasource.

   True/False

6. In order to create an `OleDbCommand` object, an `OleDbConnection` object must be specified in its constructor.

   True/False

7. Which `OleDbCommand` class property is used to specify the SQL command or stored procedure to execute?

   a. `ActiveConnection`

   b. `Command`

   c. `CommandText`

   d. `ExecuteString`

8. *Fill in the blank:* The `SqlCommand` class's _____ property gets or sets how the `CommandText` is interpreted

9. A `DataReader` object is a forward-only collection of records from a data source.

   True/False

10. *Fill in the blank:* The `OleDbDataReader` object is created via the _____ object's `Execute` method.

11. A `SqlDataReader` object has a constructor.

    True/False

12. The `OleDbDataReader` allows forward and backward row navigation.

    True/False

13. A `DataSet` can contain multiple tables, but not the relationships between the tables.

    True/False

14. The DataAdapter objects provide a bridge to retrieve and update data between a DataSet and a data store.

    True/False

15. *Fill in the blank:* The OleDbDataAdapter's _____ property gets or sets a Command object used to select records in a DataSet.

16. *Fill in the blank:* The SqlDataAdapter's _____ method adds data from a datasource to a DataSet.

☑ Friday

☑ Saturday

☑ **Sunday**

PART

V

Sunday Morning

Introducing DataSets, Part II

Session Checklist

✔ Learning to construct a DataSet without a DataAdapter object

✔ Learning to navigate the DataSet's object model

✔ Understanding the relationship between DataSet, DataTable, DataRow, and DataColumn objects

**30 Min.
To Go**

I n the previous session, we began our discussion of DataSet objects, the cornerstone of ADO.NET. You learned that a dataset is effectively a disconnected copy of a database and that you can populate a DataSet using a DataAdapter object. In this session, you're going to attack some of the DataSet object's constituent, or child, objects, including the DataTable, DataColumn, and DataRow objects.

Constructing a DataSet

Before we get started with its constituent objects, lets step back for a moment and discuss how to construct a DataSet object. In Session 20, "Introducing DataSets, Part I," you learned how to construct a DataSet with a DataAdapter object. Oddly enough, you don't actually need a DataAdapter object to create a DataSet object. Creating a DataSet object is fairly straightforward as shown in the following example:

```
Dim oDS As DataSet
oDS = New DataSet()
```

There's another way to explicitly create a DataSet and that is by passing a name for the DataSet into the constructor as follows:

```
Dim oDS As DataSet
oDS = New DataSet("MyDataSet")
```

In Session 20, you learned to set the DataSet's name using the `DataSetName` property. The following example does the same thing as passing the name of the DataSet into the constructor:

```
Dim oDS As DataSet
oDS = New DataSet()
oDS.DataSetName = "MyDataSet"
```

Tables property

As you might suspect, the `DataSet` object is actually a container class. So what does a DataSet contain? Well, many things, but most importantly a collection of `DataTable` objects in the form of a `DataTableCollection` object. In order to access a DataSet's `DataTable` objects, we need to go through the DataSet's `Tables` property. Make sense? Figure 21-1 helps you visualize the relationships among all the objects.

As you can see in Figure 21-1, the DataSet is a hierarchy of containers, collections, and objects.

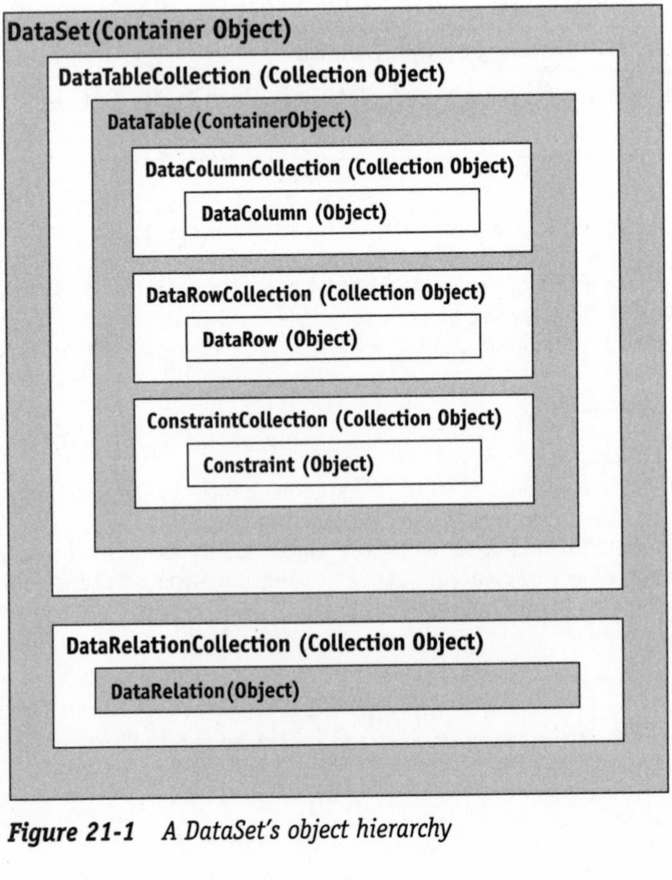

Figure 21-1   *A DataSet's object hierarchy*

A DataSet can contain one or more `DataTable` objects (among other things) in the form of a `DataTableCollection` object and, in turn, a `DataTable` object can contain one or more `DataColumn` and `DataRow` objects. So, when you access a DataSet's `Tables` property, you are actually accessing a `DataTableCollection` object. Try this out:

```
<%@ Page Language="VB" %>
<%@ Import Namespace="System.Data" %>
<%@ Import Namespace="System.Data.OleDb" %>
<SCRIPT LANGUAGE="VB" RUNAT="server">
Sub Page_Load(Sender As Object, E As EventArgs)
    Dim oDS As DataSet
    Dim oDTC As DataTableCollection
    oDS = New DataSet("MyDataSet")
    oDTC = oDS.Tables

    lblTableCount.Text = oDTC.Count
End Sub
</SCRIPT>
<HTML>
<BODY>
MyDataSet contains <asp:Label Id="lblTableCount" Text="" Runat="server" />
tables.
</BODY>
</HTML>
```

This example illustrates our "Hierarchy Theory." As you can see, you created a DataSet and called it "MyDataSet" with the following line:

```
oDS = New DataSet("MyDataSet")
```

You also created a `DataTableCollection` object and initialized it with the DataSet's `Tables` property as follows:

```
oTS = oDS.Tables
```

Now that you have a reference to the DataSet's `DataTablesCollection` object, you can access its properties and methods. In this example, you simply write out the number of tables in the `DataTableCollection` object using its `Count` property as follows:

```
lblTableCount.Text = oDTC.Count
```

You actually could have accomplished this using the few lines of code that follow:

```
Dim oDS As DataSet
oDS = New DataSet("MyDataSet")
lblTableCount.Text = oDs.Tables.Count
```

As you can see, even though you are using a `DataTableCollection` object's properties and methods, you don't necessarily need to explicitly create a `DataTableCollection` object. You can just go though the `DataSet` object.

By the way, when you run the previous two examples, the Count property should return a value of zero because you haven't actually added any DataTable objects to the DataTableCollection object.

TablesCollection Object

Now that you know what the DataTableCollection object is and how to access it explicitly and via the DataSet object, let's take a look at its properties and methods.

Count property

Because we have already used the Count property in a previous example, we'll keep this explanation short and sweet. The Count property, which is read-only, returns the number of DataTable objects in the DataTableCollection object.

20 Min. To Go

Item property

Item is probably the DataTableCollection property you will use most frequently. The Item property gets a specified DataTable from the DataTableCollection. In order to get the desired table you either pass an integer representing the table's index or a string representing the table's name to the Item property. Listing 21-1 illustrates how you might use the Item property:

Listing 21-1 *Using the Item property*

```
<%@ Page Language="VB" %>
<%@ Import Namespace="System.Data" %>
<%@ Import Namespace="System.Data.OleDb" %>
<SCRIPT LANGUAGE="VB" RUNAT="server">
Sub Page_Load(Sender As Object, E As EventArgs)
   Dim oConn As New OleDbConnection
   Dim oCmd As New OleDbCommand
   Dim oDA As New OleDbDataAdapter
   Dim oDS As DataSet
   Dim i As Integer
   Dim x As Integer

   With oConn
        .ConnectionString = "Provider=SQLOLEDB; Data Source=(local);
Initial Catalog=Music; User ID=music; Password=music"
        .Open
   End With

   With oCmd
        .Connection = oConn
        .CommandType = CommandType.Text
        .CommandText = "SELECT * FROM t_bands"
   End With
```

```
oDS = New DataSet("Music")

oDA.SelectCommand = oCmd
oDA.Fill(oDS, "t_bands")

oDA.SelectCommand.CommandText = "SELECT * FROM t_music_types"
oDA.Fill(oDS, "t_music_types")

oDA.SelectCommand.CommandText = "SELECT * FROM t_record_companies"
oDA.Fill(oDS, "t_record_companies")

For i = 0 To oDS.Tables.Count - 1
        Response.Write(oDS.Tables.Item(i).TableName & "<BR>" & chr(13))
        For x = 0 To oDS.Tables.Item(i).Columns.Count - 1
                Response.Write("    " &
oDS.Tables.Item(i).Columns.Item(x).ColumnName & "<BR>" & chr(13))
        Next
Next

oDS.Dispose()
oDS = Nothing
oDA.Dispose()
oDA = Nothing
oCmd.Dispose()
oCmd = Nothing
oConn.Close()
oConn = Nothing
End Sub
</SCRIPT>
<HTML>
<BODY>
</BODY>
</HTML>
```

For a complete listing of the `DataTableCollection`'s **properties, please
refer to the .NET documentation.**

Contains method

The `Contains` method returns a Boolean value indicating whether the DataTableCollection
and thereby the DataSet contain a specified table. The `Contains` method accepts, as input,
a string representing the table's name. Here's a quick example:

```
Dim bValid As Boolean
bValid = oDS.Tables.Contains("t_bands")
```

Based on previous DataTableCollection examples, `bValid` should be true.

The `IndexOf` method returns the index of the specified table. The method accepts either a string representing a DataTable's name or a `DataTable` object as input parameters, as shown in the following example:

```
Dim iIndex As Integer
iIndex = oDS.Tables.IndexOf("t_bands")
```

The `Clear` method, as the name implies, removes all tables from the `DataTableCollection` object.

CanRemove method

The `CanRemove` method returns a Boolean value indicating whether a specified table can be removed from the `DataTableCollection` object. The `CanRemove` method accepts a `DataTable` object as its input parameter.

Remove method

The `Remove` method removes the specified table from the `DataTableCollection` object. The `Remove` method can accept either a table's name or a `DataTable` object as its input parameter. Here's an example:

```
oDS.Tables.Remove("t_bands")
```

Add method

The `Add` method adds a table to the DataTableCollection. The `Add` method can be used in one of three ways. You can call the `Add` method and not pass it any input parameters. In this case a DataTable is added to DataTableCollection and assigned a default name. You can also pass only a string representing the table's name. In this case, a DataTable is added to the DataTableCollection and assigned the specified name. Or you can call the `Add` method and pass it a `DataTable` object. In this case, the specified DataTable is added to the DataTableCollection. Here's a quick example:

```
oDS.Tables.Add("Bands")
```

That's it for the `DataTableCollection` object. Basically the DataTableCollection provides access to the `DataTable` object's in a DataSet.

Now that you know how to get to your tables, let's see what you can do with them.

DataTable Objects

The DataTable object is a central object in the ADO.NET library and effectively represents a data source's data. You can manually fabricate a DataTable using its properties and methods, or you can have it automatically filled using DataSet commands.

In order to manually construct a DataTable we can use the following code:

```
Dim oDT As DataTable
oDT = New DataTable()
```

You can also pass a string representing the DataTable's name to the constructor as follows:

```
oDT = New DataTable("MyTable")
```

As will all ADO.NET objects, the DataTable object has a variety of properties and methods. I'll start with the properties.

CaseSensitive property

The CaseSensitive property is a Boolean value that indicates whether string comparison within a table is case sensitive. The property's default value is set to the parent DataSet object's CaseSensitive property. The CaseSensitive property affects string comparisons in sorting, searching, and filtering. Here's an example:

```
oDS.Tables.Item(0).CaseSensitive = False
```

In this statement you are going through a DataSet object's Tables property to access a DataTableCollection object. You will then use the DataTableCollection's Item property to access the DataTable in the collection with an index of zero. Once you have drilled down to the DataTable, you can access its properties, in this case the CaseSensitive property.

ChildRelations property

If you have more than one table in your DataSet, chances are that you'll want to relate them in some way. The ChildRelations property gets a collection of child relations for a DataTable in the form of a DataRelationCollection object. This is a little complicated and we can't go into it too much in this session. Data relationships are further discussed in Session 25, "Data Shaping with ADO.NET."

Columns property

The Columns property gets the collection of columns that belong to a DataTable in the form of a DataColumnCollection object. The relationship between the Columns property and a DataTable is very similar to the relationship between the Tables property and a DataSet. The Columns property exposes a DataColumnCollection through which you can access a DataTable's columns. Here's sample syntax demonstrating how you can access a DataTable's columns using the Columns property:

```
Dim oDCC As DataColumnCollection
oDCC = oDS.Tables(0).Columns
```

Constraints property

The Constraints property gets the collection of constraints maintained by a DataTable object in the form of a ConstraintCollection object. If you'll recall from our discussion on database design in Session 3, "Designing A Database," a table can have zero, one, or multiple constraints. Some typical constraints you'll find on a given table are foreign key and unique constraints. We'll return to the Constraints property in Session 25, "Data Shaping with ADO.NET."

DataSet property

If a DataTable belongs to a DataSet, the DataSet property returns a reference to the parent DataSet. You might find this property useful when processing a form. In the following code snippet, assume that you have submitted an HTML form that contains a DataGrid control, dgExample, which is bound to a DataTable. Here's the syntax:

```
Dim oDS As DataSet
Dim oDT As DataTable
oDT = cType(dgExample.DataSource, DataTable)
oDS = oDT.DataSet
```

DefaultView property

The DefaultView property gets a customized view of the DataTable in the form of a DataView object. A DataView object is a databindable, customized view of a DataTable used for sorting, filtering, searching, editing, and navigating a DataTable. We'll talk more about this in Session 22, "Introducing Data Binding."

ParentRelations property

The ParentRelations property is very similar to the ChildRelations property except that it gets the parent relationships rather than the child relationships. (We guess that kind of makes sense.) The ParentRelations property gets a collection of parent relations for a DataTable in the form of a DataRelationCollection object. More in Session 25, "Data Shaping with ADO.NET."

PrimaryKey property

The PrimaryKey property gets or sets an array of columns that function as primary keys for a DataTable. In most cases you'll be getting the primary key columns rather than setting them. In cases where you need to manually create a custom DataTable object, you'll set the PrimaryKey property. The PrimaryKey property returns an array of DataColumn objects. Likewise, when you are setting the PrimaryKey property, you need to pass it an array of DataColumn objects. Here's an example of getting the primary key columns on a DataTable:

```
Dim aPK() As DataColumn
   Dim x As Integer

   oDT = oDS.Tables("t_bands")
aPK = oDT.PrimaryKey

For x = LBound(aPK) to UBound(aPK)
   Response.Write("PRIMARY KEY " & x & ": " & aPK(x).ColumnName & "<BR/>"
& chr(13))
Next
```

In this example, you gain access to the Tables collection via the DataSet and then initialize an array, aPK, using the DataTable object's PrimaryKey property. We then use a For loop to iterate through the array.

Rows property

The Rows property provides access to the collection of rows that belong to the table. This property is similar to the Columns property, but instead of returning a collection of DataColumn objects, it returns a collection of DataRow objects. It is through the Rows property that you can gain access to a DataTable's constituent DataRow objects' properties and methods. A DataTable's DataColumn objects represent the DataTable's structure whereas the DataRow objects represent the DataTable's data.

Additionally, it is through the DataRow object that you can gain access to the data in your DataTable objects. Listing 21-2 demonstrates iterating through the DataRowCollection (returned by the Rows property) in a DataTable and writing its contents to a .NET Table control.

**10 Min.
To Go**

Listing 21-2 *Iterating through a table's rows*

```
<%@ Page Language="VB" %>
<%@ Import Namespace="System.Data" %>
<%@ Import Namespace="System.Data.OleDb" %>
<SCRIPT LANGUAGE="VB" RUNAT="server">
Sub Page_Load(Sender As Object, E As EventArgs)
  Dim oConn As OleDbConnection
  Dim oDA As OleDbDataAdapter
  Dim oDS As DataSet
  Dim oDT As DataTable
  Dim oDR As DataRow
  Dim oDC As DataColumn
  Dim oTR As TableRow
  Dim oTHC As TableHeaderCell
  Dim oTC As TableCell

  oConn = New OleDbConnection("Provider=SQLOLEDB;Data
Source=(local);Initial Catalog=Music;User ID=music;Password=music")
  oConn.Open
```

Continued

Listing 21-2

Continued

```
oDA = New OleDbDataAdapter("SELECT * FROM t_bands", oConn)

oDS = New DataSet("Music")

oDA.Fill(oDS, "t_bands")

oDT = oDS.Tables("t_bands")

oTR = New TableRow
oTR.BackColor = System.Drawing.Color.LightGray
For Each oDC In oDT.Columns
        oTHC =  New TableHeaderCell
        oTHC.Text = oDC.ColumnName
        oTR.Cells.Add(oTHC)
Next
tblBands.Rows.Add(oTR)

For Each oDR In oDT.Rows
        oTR = New TableRow
        For Each oDC In oDT.Columns
            oTC = New TableCell
            oTC.Text = oDR.Item(oDC)
            oTR.Cells.Add(oTC)
        Next
        tblBands.Rows.Add(oTR)
    Next

    oTC.Dispose
    oTC = Nothing
    oTR.Dispose
    oTR = Nothing
    oDT.Dispose
    oDT = Nothing
    oDS.Dispose
    oDS = Nothing
    oDA.Dispose
    oDA = Nothing
    oConn.Close
    oConn = Nothing
End Sub
</SCRIPT>
<HTML>
<BODY>
<asp:Table id="tblBands" BorderWidth="1" GridLines="both" runat="server"/>
</BODY>
</HTML>
```

As you can see in Listing 21-2, you have constructed a DataSet object , oDS, using a OleDbDataAdapter object. You then created a reference to the t_bands table, oDT, through the DataSet's Tables property. Then you iterated through the columns in the t_bands table using a For . . . Next structure and added a header cell to the .NET TableRow object, oTR. The For structure is basically saying "For each column in t_bands, add a cell to the row." When you were done adding header cells, you added the row to the .NET Table control, tblBands. After you added your table header, you began iterating through the DataRow objects in oDT using another For . . . Next structure. For each row in t_bands, you then iterate through the columns and add a cell to a TableRow object as follows:

```
For Each oDC In oDT.Columns
    oTC = New TableCell
    oTC.Text = oDR.Item(oDC)
    oTR.Cells.Add(oTC)
Next
```

The key piece of code here is the line in which we obtain the data in our column using the syntax oDR.Item(oDC). All this is saying is "for this row, give me the data in column oDC." Pretty simple once you get the hang of it. Although you could have accomplished the same thing, with a lot less code, using DataBinding, this example illustrates some important concepts.

OK, those are all the properties we are going to cover for the DataTable object. The DataTable object also provides numerous methods, but to be quite honest you probably won't use most of them. We'll address only two of the methods, Dispose and NewRow, provided by the DataTable object. If you're interested in more, take a gander at your .NET documentation for a complete listing.

Dispose method

As usual it is good programming practice to dispose of all your objects after you are done using them in order to release valuable system resources. The DataTable object's Dispose method does this for you. Refer to Listing 21-2, to see the Dispose method in action. (Although there isn't too much to see.)

NewRow method

The NewRow method creates a new DataRow object with the same schema as the table through which it is being created. Once a row is created, you can add it to the table's DataRowCollection via the Rows property. Here's an example:

```
Dim oDR As DataRow
oDR = oDS.Tables(0).NewRow
oDR("band_title") = "Toad The Wet Sprocket"
' [ADD OTHER COLUMN INFORMATION HERE]
oDS.Tables(0).Rows.Add(oDR)
```

This example creates a new row in the first table (index of zero) in our DataSet, oDS.

Done!

REVIEW

Wow! We covered a ton of material in this session, including DataTable objects, DataRow objects, and DataColumn objects. All of these objects constitute a DataSet. Without them, a DataSet would be fairly useless. We could even say that the true power of the DataSet actually lies in its constituent objects. Although in this session, we were not able to cover all of the properties and methods of all of the objects that make up a DataSet, you gained a clearer understanding of the DataSet object model and how to work with it. The most important concept to take away from this session is that a DataSet object is effectively a set of objects, each with their own properties and methods, which are grouped together in a hierarchical fashion to provide you, as a developer, with a robust model through which you can access your data store.

QUIZ YOURSELF

1. What is a collection? (See "Tables property.")
2. How is a DataTable's Columns property related to a DataColumnCollection object? (See "Columns property.")
3. Through which DataTable properties can you gain access to the DataRows in that table? (See "Rows property.")

Introducing Data Binding

Session Checklist

✔ Understanding basic binding techniques

✔ Connecting ASP.NET Controls to data stores

✔ Binding the TreeView Control to an XML File

**30 Min.
To Go**

O
K, so you now understand all of the various ADO.NET objects, methods, and properties, which provide you a ton of flexibility in handling disconnected data; but now
you want to know how to bind all of those great ASP.NET controls to your data
objects, right? Well, this is the session you have been waiting for! We'll dive into the process
of connecting our data stores with the basic server controls, and explore how to bind an
XML file to the very useful Treeview control.

What Is Data Binding?

Data binding is the process of connecting a server control to a dataset. Data binding greatly
simplifies the amount and complexity of code required to generate basic output such as filling a drop-down list box with a set of names and values stored in a database, XML file,
array, hash table or even a custom object. By filtering criteria based upon previous selections, data binding enables you to provide user interfaces that are more intuitive. It also
assists in separating your code from your content.

If you have worked with ASP previously, then you probably are familiar with using the
RecordSet object to loop through a set of data and then manually build a dynamic drop-
down list or table using the result set. You may have even used Visual Interdev and the
Design Time Controls (DTC) to bind a RecordSet object to the Grid, Label, Checkbox, Option
Group, and other Visual Interdev DTCs. Most likely you also experienced the pain and frus-
tration of attempting to debug the DTCs once they were implemented. Even the simplest DTC

must have produced about 400 lines of code in your ASP Page, providing a painful and arduous debugging regime for even the most dedicated professional. With this complexity, you may have returned to the old Notepad build-it-yourself approach to reduce your late night troubleshooting sessions!

ASP.NET and ADO.NET now provide the flexibility of the build-it-yourself approach to connecting result sets to HTML objects without the headaches of the old DTC objects.

Binding to Arrays and Extended Object Types

The simplest example of data binding can be illustrated using array bound controls. Listing 22-1 demonstrates binding a simple combo-box control to an array. The first step is to establish an array structure. You can do this by declaring a new `ArrayList` and adding a list of values to it as follows.

Listing 22-1   *Example of binding arrays to server controls*

```
<%@ Page Language="VB" Debug="False" %>
<HTML>
    <SCRIPT LANGUAGE="VB" RUNAT="Server">
    Sub Page_Load(Sender as Object, E as EventArgs)
        If Not IsPostback Then
            'Dim and fill Array
            Dim aList as New ArrayList
            With aList
                .Add("Model 300 Skis")
                .Add("Model 1300 Skis")
                .Add("Model 2300 Skis")
                .Add("Model 3300 Skis")
            End With
            dbox1.DataSource = aList
            dbox1.DataBind()
        End If
    End Sub
    Sub dBox1_SelectedIndexChanged(sender As Object , e As System.EventArgs)
        Response.Write (dbox1.SelectedItem.Value.ToString())
    End Sub
    </SCRIPT>
    <BODY>
        <FORM RUNAT="Server" METHOD="post" ID="Form1">
            <ASP:DROPDOWNLIST ID="dBox1" RUNAT="Server" AUTOPOSTBACK="true"
ONSELECTEDINDEXCHANGED="dBox1_SelectedIndexChanged" />
        </FORM>
    </BODY>
</HTML>
```

Once the `ArrayList` is populated, you simply bind it to your selected control, in this example a `DropDownList` with an id of dBox1. You perform the binding by setting the `Control.DataSource()` method equal to the array and then using the `Control.DataBind()` method to bind the array to the control.

One of the issues with this approach is that both the value and the text are going to be the same. So, what if you want to establish an array that had a bound value and bound text that are different? You can also bind server controls to other objects such as custom classes, hash tables, and of course ADO.NET objects. Let's modify the code in Listing 22-1 so that we use a custom class called Ski that stores the product id and the product title for a set of skis. You can create an array of classes and then bind the control to the various properties of the class. This example illustrates how you can take just about any conforming class and bind its data to the server controls.

Building on the code in Listing 22-1, you simply create a new class called Ski that accepts a product id and product title when instantiated as shown in Listing 22-2. Additionally it supports ReadOnly properties to allow the return of the ProductId and ProductTitle values:

Listing 22-2 *Custom class for binding to Webserver controls*

```
Public Class Ski
    Private _ProductId as Integer
    Private _ProductTitle as String
    Public Sub New(ByVal i as Integer, ByVal s as String)
        _ProductId= i
        _ProductTitle = s
    End Sub

    Public Overridable ReadOnly Property ProductId()
        Get
            Return _ProductId
        End Get
    End Property
    Public Overridable ReadOnly Property ProductTitle()
        Get
            Return _ProductTitle
        End Get
    End Property
End Class
```

Then you simply modify the way in which you populate the array as shown in this example:

```
Sub Page_Load(Sender as Object, E as EventArgs)
If Not IsPostback Then
    Dim aList as New ArrayList()
    With aList
        .Add(new Ski(1001, "Model 300 Skis"))
        .Add(new Ski(1002, "Model 1300 Skis"))
        .Add(new Ski(1003, "Model 2300 Skis"))
        .Add(new Ski(1004, "Model 3300 Skis"))
    End With
    dbox1.DataSource = aList
    dbox1.DataBind()
End If
End Sub
```

Finally, add two new attributes, shown in bold below, to the DropDownList server control so that you can select which of the class properties provides the dataTextField and dataValueField attributes:

```
<ASP:DROPDOWNLIST ID="dBox1"
                  RUNAT="Server"
                  DATATEXTFIELD="ProductTitle"
                  DATAVALUEFIELD="ProductId"
                  ONSELECTEDINDEXCHANGED="dBox1_SelectedIndexChanged"
                  AUTOPOSTBACK="true"
/>
```

The full code for the classbinding example in this section can be found in the Session 22 folder on the CD-ROM, using the filename dropdownbindto-objectarray.aspx.

In the following sections, you will see how the data binding functionality can be extended to include database tables, views, stored procedures and XML datasets.

Binding to Database Data

20 Min. To Go

The examples in this section require that you have the pubs database installed and available.

Binding a control to a database table, view or stored procedure is very straightforward. First, you have to make sure you import the System.Data and System.Data.OleDb namespaces so that you have access to the ADO.NET objects as shown in Listing 22-3:

Listing 22-3 *Example of binding server controls to database*

```
<%@ Page Language="VB" Debug="False" %>
<%@ Import Namespace="System.Data" %>
<%@ Import Namespace="System.Data.OleDB" %>
```

Then implement a connection to the database in the Page_Load () event:

```
<HTML>
    <SCRIPT LANGUAGE="VB" RUNAT="Server">
    Sub Page_Load(Sender as Object, E as EventArgs)
        If Not IsPostback Then
            Dim connection as New OleDBConnection("provider=sqloledb;Data
Source=(local);Initial Catalog=pubs;User ID=sa;pwd=;")
```

In this case, we are connecting to the Pubs database on the local machine. Next, use the OleDBDataAdapter and DataSet objects you explored in earlier sessions to get the required dataset from the Authors table:

```
Dim myAdapter as New OleDBDataAdapter("SELECT * FROM Authors", connection)
Dim myDataset As New DataSet()
myAdapter.Fill(myDataset, "myDataset")
```

Then, just as we did in the array examples earlier, you need to set the DataSource properties on the server control and then call the DataBind() method.

```
            dbox1.DataSource = MyDataset.Tables(0).DefaultView
            dbox1.DataBind()
        End If
    End Sub
    </SCRIPT>
```

Finally, you make sure that you have set the appropriate dataTextField and dataValueField values on the server control:

```
    <BODY>
        <FORM RUNAT="Server" METHOD="post" ID="Form1">
            <ASP:DROPDOWNLIST ID="dBox1" RUNAT="Server" DATATEXTFIELD="au_lname"
DATAVALUEFIELD="au_id" AUTOPOSTBACK="true" />
        </FORM>
    </BODY>
</HTML>
```

You can use the same approach to bind server controls to stored procedures and views by modifying the DataAdapter properties as required.

Binding to XML

Binding server controls to an XML file is not any more complicated than binding using a standard database. Basically, you simply replace the Connection and DataAdapter objects with a FileStream object and a StreamReader object. The following example shows how to bind a simple XML dataset to a dropdown control.

You need to import the System.IO namespace in addition to System.Data so that you can open and read physical files. This will allow you to open and read an xml file stored in a local directory.

```
<%@ Page Language="VB" Debug="True" Trace="False"%>
<%@ Import Namespace="System.IO"%>
<%@ Import Namespace="System.Data" %>
<HTML>
    <SCRIPT LANGUAGE="VB" RUNAT="Server">
```

Next, you need to open the XML file. In this example, you have an XML representation of the Authors table from the Pubs database stored as pubs_authors.xml on your CD-ROM in the Session 22 folder.

```
Sub Page_Load(Sender as Object, E as EventArgs)
    Dim fs As New FileStream(Server.MapPath("pubs_authors.xml"), FileMode.Open,
FileAccess.Read)
```

Once you have the file open, you can store its contents in a StreamReader object.

```
    Dim xmlstream as New StreamReader(fs)
```

You then can fill your DataSet object using the DataSet.ReadXML() method and passing in your StreamReader. It is important that you remember to close the FileStream object when you are done, as it isn't closed automatically:

```
Dim ds as New DataSet
    If Not IsPostback Then
            ds.ReadXML(xmlStream)
            fs.Close
```

From here on out, you handle everything exactly as you did in the database example, setting the DataSource and calling the DataBind() method:

```
            dbox1.DataSource = ds.Tables(0)
            dbox1.DataBind()
        End If
End Sub
Sub dBox1_SelectedIndexChanged(sender As Object , e As System.EventArgs)
        Response.Write (dbox1.SelectedItem.Value.ToString())
End Sub
    </SCRIPT>
    <BODY>
        <FORM RUNAT="Server" METHOD="post" ID="Form1">
            <ASP:DROPDOWNLIST ID="dBox1" RUNAT="Server" DATATEXTFIELD="au_lname"
DATAVALUEFIELD="au_id" AUTOPOSTBACK="true"
ONSELECTEDINDEXCHANGED="dBox1_SelectedIndexChanged" />
        </FORM>
    </BODY>
</HTML>
```

The above code sample is stored in your Session 22 folder on the CD as dropdownbind-toxml.aspx. Next, we will look at what's required to bind one of the more advanced controls, the TreeView server control.

**10 Min.
To Go**

TreeView Control

The TreeView control is a supplemental control provided by Microsoft separately from the .NET Framework. It is one of four controls that are provided by Microsoft specifically for Web development purposes. The other ASP.NET Web controls include a Toolbar, TabControl and Multipage controls. These controls are made available at http://msdn.microsoft.com/downloads/samples/Internet/ASP_DOT_NET_ServerControls/WebControls/sample.asp. You will need to download and install these controls in order to run the samples in this section.

The TreeView control provides an excellent opportunity to illustrate how you can use the flexibility of XML combined with the TreeView control to support a robust navigational framework for your Web site. In Figure 22-1, you can see the use of the TreeView control to provide navigation for an online directory.

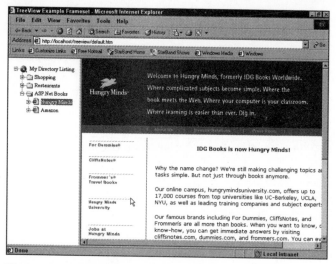

Figure 22-1   *TreeView control bound to an XML File*

The TreeView control enables you to develop a hierarchical navigational framework to represent any parent-child relationship. The hierarchical relationship shown in Figure 22-1 is stored in an xml file called treeview.xml.

Implement the TreeView server control

The data binding for the TreeView control is initiated through the TreeNodeSrc attribute. Here is an excerpt of Listing 22-4, showing the TreeNodeSrc attribute of the TreeView server control:

```
<IE:TREEVIEW RUNAT="server" AUTOPOSTBACK=true ID=tvw1 CHILDTYPE="Folder" SHOWPLUS="True"
TREENODESRC="treeview.xml">
```

This statement will bind the treeview control to the treeview.xml file. The treeview.xml file must support a specific hierarchical format as demonstrated below:

```
<TREENODES>
<TREENODE Text="Shopping">
    <TREENODE Text="The Gap" NavigateURL="http://www.gap.com" Target="main"/>
    <TREENODE Text="Brooks Brothers" Type="item"
NavigateURL="http://www.brooksbrothers.com" Target="main"/>
</TREENODE>
<TREENODE Text="Restaurants">
    <TREENODE Text="Chianti" Type="item"/>
    <TREENODE Text="Vinces" Type="treeview.xml"/>
</TREENODE>
<TREENODE Text="Books">
    <TREENODE Text="ASP.Net Books" Target=""/>
    <TREENODE Text="Hungry Minds" NavigateURL="http://www.hungryminds.com"
Target="main"/>
    <TREENODE Text="Amazon.com" NavigateURL="http://www.amazon.com" Target="main"/>
</TREENODE>
</TREENODES>
```

The TREENODESRC Attribute can be any relative or fixed URL pointer, so the xml file could reside anywhere on your intranet or the internet.

To obtain information on how to set up your Microsoft Internet Explorer WebControls visit http://msdn.microsoft.com/downloads/c-frame.htm?/ downloads/samples/internet/asp_dot_net_servercontrols/Webcontrols/ sample.asp

---

Listing 22-4 *Example of binding a TreeView control bound to an xml file*

```
<%@ Page Language="VB" Debug="true" Trace="False"%>
<%@ Import Namespace="Microsoft.Web.UI.WebControls"%>
<%@ Register TagPrefix="ie" Namespace="Microsoft.Web.UI.WebControls"
Assembly="Microsoft.Web.UI.WebControls"%>
<HTML>
<HEAD>
</HEAD>
<BODY ID="master">
<FORM ID="myform" RUNAT="server">
    <IE:TREEVIEW RUNAT="server" AUTOPOSTBACK=true ID=tvw1 CHILDTYPE="Folder"
SHOWPLUS="True" TREENODESRC="treeview.xml">
    <IE:TREENODETYPE TYPE="Root" EXPANDEDIMAGEURL="images/root.gif"
IMAGEURL="images/root.gif" CHILDTYPE="Folder" />
    <IE:TREENODETYPE TYPE="Folder" EXPANDEDIMAGEURL="images/folderopen.gif"
IMAGEURL="images/folder.gif" CHILDTYPE="Item"/>
    <IE:TREENODETYPE TYPE="Item" IMAGEURL="images/html.gif"/>
    </IE:TREEVIEW>
</FORM>
</BODY>
</HTML>
```

With this solution, we have illustrated the use of data binding to an XML stream, a powerful illustration of how we can easily leverage the ASP.NET framework to enhance the user experience.

The full source code for this example can be found in the Session 22 folder on the cd, under the filename treeveiwframeset.htm.

Done!

REVIEW

We have covered the basics of data binding in this session and illustrated its use in a wide range of controls to facilitate dynamic user interface components. The ability to bind your server controls against such a range of data sources — from hash tables to arrays to custom classes — provides a wide range of flexibility in handling your user interface elements.

QUIZ YOURSELF

1. Is it possible to bind server controls to each other? (See "Binding to Arrays and Extended Object Types.")

2. What are the major differences between binding to an XML file and an ADO.NET dataset? (See "Binding to Database Data" and "Binding to XML.")

3. List three elements that you can bind server controls to. (See "Binding to Arrays and Extended Object Types.")

Using the DataGrid Control with Bound Data

Session Checklist

✔ Binding controls to one another

✔ Implementing master-detail relationships

✔ Using DataBound columns with the DataGrid control

This session assumes you have SQL Server installed and have access to the Pubs database.

**30 Min.
To Go**

In this session we cover the basics of the DataGrid control. We start out by describing how to bind datasets to the DataGrid control, including how to format the output, and how to handle master/detail relationships. After completing this session, you should be able to understand how the DataGrid control can be used to eliminate much of the common scripting you did in ASP to handle the display of data in tables.

DataGrid Control Basics

ASP developers commonly face the problem of how to display a set of data in a table format. In ASP, you would typically open a RecordSet object and then use Response.Write to display the results in a dynamically generated table. In ASP.NET this task can be greatly simplified through the use of the DataGrid control.

Binding a set of data to a DataGrid control

In Listing 23-1, we have implemented a DataGrid by simply using the code:

```
<asp:datagrid id="datagrid" runat="server" />
```

Next, we created a function `BindData()` that opens a connection to the Pubs database, selects all the records in the `titles` table, and then fills a `DataSet` object with the results. Finally, we use the `datagrid.databind()` method to execute the binding. This binds the dataset to the `DataGrid` control. The `DataGrid` control handles all of the effort associated with formatting the results into a table and displaying the resulting output.

Listing 23-1   *Binding a Dataset to a DataGrid control*

```
<%@ Import Namespace="System.Data.OleDb" %>
<%@ Import Namespace="system.data" %>
<%@ Page Language="VB" Debug="False" Trace="False"%>
<HTML>
    <SCRIPT LANGUAGE="vb" RUNAT="server">
    DIM oConn as OleDbConnection
    DIM oCmd as OleDbDataAdapter
    DIM oDS as new dataset

    public sub page_load(sender as object,e as eventargs)
        if page.ispostback=false then
            BindData()
        end if
    end sub

    Function BindData()
        oConn=new OleDbConnection("provider=sqloledb;Data Source=(local);Initial
Catalog=pubs;User ID=sa;pwd=;")
        oCmd=new OleDbDataAdapter("select * from titles",oConn)
        oCmd.Fill(oDS,"titles")
        datagrid.datasource=oDS.tables("titles").defaultview
        datagrid.databind()
    End Function

    </SCRIPT>
    <BODY>
        <FORM ID="form1" RUNAT="server">
            <ASP:DATAGRID
                ID="datagrid"
                RUNAT="server"
                AUTOGENERATECOLUMNS="True"
                DATAKEYFIELD="title_id">
            </ASP:DATAGRID>
        </FORM>
    </BODY>
</HTML>
```

The `AutoGenerateColumns` property is what automatically generates the columns for the resulting dataset. The `DataKeyField` property specifies what data field should be used as a primary key for the table. This will be important later when we discuss editing and updating data with the `DataGrid` control. In this scenario, we did not have much control over which columns were displayed or how the output of the columns was formatted, it is clear that a lot of custom code can be eliminated through the use of the `DataGrid` control. In the next section we show how to overcome these issues.

Formatting the output of a DataGrid control

In the previous section, we let the DataGrid control handle all of the output properties by setting the AutoGenerateColumns attribute to True. In Listing 23-2, we have set this attribute to False and have instead used the Columns property combined with the ASP.NET BoundColumn control to select what fields are displayed and how they are formatted.

Listing 23-2 *Using the BoundColumn control and DataFormatString with the DataGrid control*

```
<ASP:DATAGRID ID="datagrid"
              RUNAT="server"
              AUTOGENERATECOLUMNS="False"
              DATAKEYFIELD="title_id">
    <COLUMNS>
        <ASP:BOUNDCOLUMN HEADERTEXT="YTD Sales"
                         DATAFIELD="ytd_sales"
                         READONLY="true"
                         DATAFORMATSTRING="{0:C}">
        </ASP:BOUNDCOLUMN>
    </COLUMNS>
    <ALTERNATINGITEMSTYLE BACKCOLOR="Gainsboro" />
    <FOOTERSTYLE FORECOLOR="White" BACKCOLOR="Silver" />
    <ITEMSTYLE BACKCOLOR="White" />
    <HEADERSTYLE FONT-BOLD="True" FORECOLOR="White" BACKCOLOR="Navy" />
</ASP:DATAGRID>
```

The DataField property determines what field in the dataset is displayed in the resulting output. In this case, we will display the ytd_sales field. Additionally, we have specified a specific formatting style for this data by using the DataFormatString property. The value for this property, {0:c}, will format the resulting output in the currency of the end user's locale.

The data format string consists of two parts separated by a colon in the form of {X:Yxx}, where X specifies the parameter number in a zero-based list of parameters. This value can only be 0 because there is only one value in each cell. Y specifies the format to display the value as shown in Table 23-1.

Table 23-1 *Formatting Styles Applied by the DataFormatString property*

Format Character	Description
C	Displays numeric values in currency format.
D	Displays numeric values in decimal format.
E	Displays numeric values in scientific (exponential) format.
F	Displays numeric values in fixed format.
G	Displays numeric values in general format.
N	Displays numeric values in number format.
X	Displays numeric values in hexadecimal format.

We can further specify the look and feel of the resulting table by using the `HeaderStyle`, `FooterStyle`, `ItemStyle`, and `AlternatingItemStyle` properties. These properties specify the look and feel of the final output. Use `HeaderStyle` to format the header row if you have established headings for any of the output columns. The `ItemStyle` provides the default formatting for each new row; and `AlternatingItemStyle` sets up a contrasting pattern when a long series of alternating data is to be displayed. The results of these formatting styles can be seen in Figure 23-1.

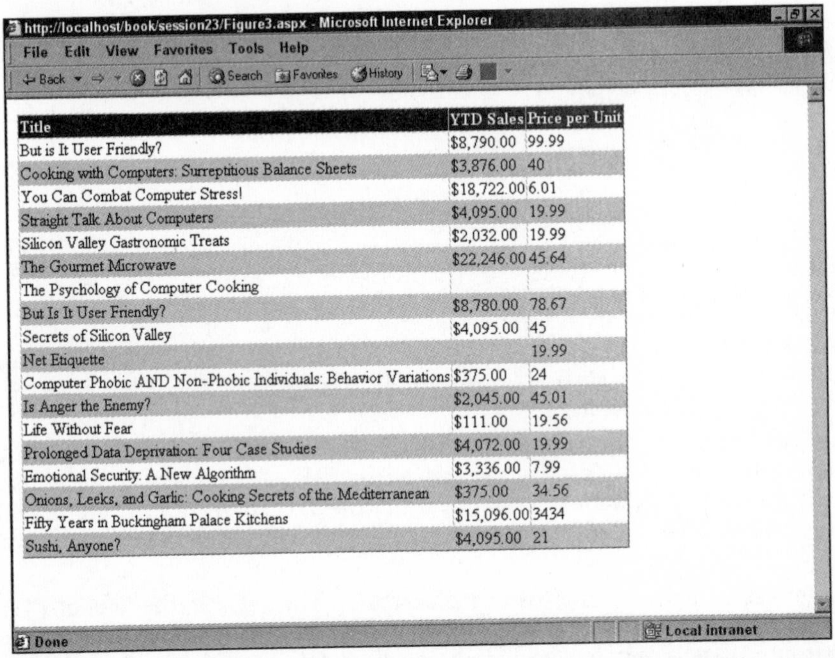

Title	YTD Sales	Price per Unit
But is It User Friendly?	$8,790.00	99.99
Cooking with Computers: Surreptitious Balance Sheets	$3,876.00	40
You Can Combat Computer Stress!	$18,722.00	6.01
Straight Talk About Computers	$4,095.00	19.99
Silicon Valley Gastronomic Treats	$2,032.00	19.99
The Gourmet Microwave	$22,246.00	45.64
The Psychology of Computer Cooking		
But Is It User Friendly?	$8,780.00	78.67
Secrets of Silicon Valley	$4,095.00	45
Net Etiquette		19.99
Computer Phobic AND Non-Phobic Individuals: Behavior Variations	$375.00	24
Is Anger the Enemy?	$2,045.00	45.01
Life Without Fear	$111.00	19.56
Prolonged Data Deprivation: Four Case Studies	$4,072.00	19.99
Emotional Security: A New Algorithm	$3,336.00	7.99
Onions, Leeks, and Garlic: Cooking Secrets of the Mediterranean	$375.00	34.56
Fifty Years in Buckingham Palace Kitchens	$15,096.00	3434
Sushi, Anyone?	$4,095.00	21

Figure 23-1 *Results of using various style properties of the DataGrid control*

Now that we understand how to control what fields to display and how to format the resulting output, lets move into a very common use for the `DataGrid` control, displaying master/detail relationships

Master/Detail Relationships with the DataGrid Control

When implementing user interfaces, a very common technique for navigating through sets of data is to utilize Master/Detail controls to facilitate data searching. For example, Figure 23-2 shows the data relationships that exist between the Authors table and the Titles Table in the Pubs database.

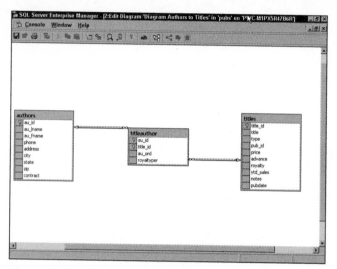

Figure 23-2 *Diagram of authors and titles relationship*

In Figure 23-2, there is a many-to-many relationship between authors and titles. The titleauthor table maintains these relationships. It is very likely that you may need to provide the user of this database a list of authors and provide a list of titles related to a specific author. You can quickly build such a Master/Detail relationship by using a bound dropdown list and a DataGrid control. You can load the dropdown list with the authors table and then filter the titles table by the selected author.

 The remainder of this session will refer to the masterdetail.aspx file located in the session 23 folder of the CD-ROM.

In the masterdetail.aspx file, you'll find three key functions that support the generation and binding of all data required to support the master/detail relationship shown in Listing 23-3.

Listing 23-3 *Partial Listing of masterdetail.aspx file illustrating core functions*

```
        Sub Page_Load(Src As Object, E as EventArgs)
            Dim connection as New OleDBConnection("provider=sqloledb;Data
Source=localhost;Initial Catalog=pubs;User ID=sa;pwd=")

        If Not IsPostback Then
            Connection.Open()
            Dim command as New OleDbCommand("SELECT * FROM Authors Order By au_lname,
au_fname", connection)
            Dim AuthorDataReader As OleDbDataReader = command.ExecuteReader()
            Dim sFullName as String
            While AuthorDataReader.Read()
                sFullName = AuthorDataReader.Item("au_fname") & " " &
AuthorDataReader.Item("au_lname")
```

Continued

Listing 23-3 *Continued*

```
                    authorlist.items.add(New ListItem(sFullName,
AuthorDataReader.Item("au_id")))
            End While
            AuthorDataReader.Close()
            Connection.Close()
            BindData()
        End If
        End Sub

    Function GetTitles(ByVal au_id As String) As DataView
        Try
            Dim connection as New OleDBConnection("provider=sqloledb;Data
Source=localhost;Initial Catalog=pubs;User ID=sa;pwd=")
            Dim command As New OleDBDataAdapter("SELECT titles.title_id, titles.title,
titles.price, titles.ytd_sales,titleauthor.au_ord,authors.au_id, titles.pub_id FROM
authors INNER JOIN titleauthor ON authors.au_id = titleauthor.au_id INNER JOIN titles ON
titleauthor.title_id = titles.title_id", connection)
            Dim dataset As New DataSet()
            Dim dataView1 as DataView
            command.Fill(dataset, "TitleAuthor")
            dataView1 = new DataView(dataset.Tables("TitleAuthor"))
            dataView1.RowFilter = "au_id='" & au_id &"'"
            Return dataview1
        Catch myException as Exception
            Message.Text = ("Exception: " + myException.ToString())
        End Try
    End Function

    Function BindData()
        Try
            Dim TitlesDataView As DataView = GetTitles(authorlist.SelectedItem.Value)
            titleGrid.DataSource = TitlesDataView
            titleGrid.DataBind()
        Catch myException as Exception
            Message.Text = ("Exception: " + myException.ToString())
        End Try
    End Function
```

Populating the Master control

In the Page_Load() function we establish a connection to the Pubs database, then proceed to fill an OleDbDataReader by connecting it to a OleDbCommand which has been attached to a SQL select statement. We have decided to use a OleDbDataReader object here as opposed to a DataSet object to simply illustrate how it can be used as easily as the DataSet object for this type of operation, forward reading a set of data.

We loop through the retrieved DataReader using the following control loop:

```
While AuthorDataReader.Read()
    sFullName = AuthorDataReader.Item("au_fname") & " " &
AuthorDataReader.Item("au_lname")
    authorlist.items.add(New ListItem(sFullName,
AuthorDataReader.Item("au_id")))
End While
```

This allows us to quickly loop through the records and populate the authorlist drop-down list. Finally we close the OleDbDataReader and the Connection Objects with

```
AuthorDataReader.Close()
Connection.Close()
```

It is important to remember that you need to close OleDbDataReader objects when you are completed with them, as they do not automatically go out of scope, closing the OleDbConnection the way that DataSet objects do.

General Rule on opening connections: If you explicitly open a connection, for instance by calling an Open() **method, then you will need to use a** Close() **method to avoid errors. When using** DataSet **objects, you never explicitly open a connection, so closing is not an issue.**

Now that we have a master list of authors populated, we need to filter the Titles table for the selected author and display the details in a DataGrid control. This is done by calling the BindData() function.

10 Min.
To Go

Filtering the detail listing

The BindData() function is the primary function, which initiates grabbing the authorid selected in the authorlist and then filtering the titles table by calling the GetTitles() function and passing the authorid value as shown below:

```
Function BindData()
    Try
        Dim TitlesDataView As DataView = GetTitles(authorlist.SelectedItem.Value)
        titleGrid.DataSource = TitlesDataView
        titleGrid.DataBind()
    Catch myException as Exception
        Message.Text = ("Exception: " + myException.ToString())
    End Try
End Function
```

The GetTitles() function accepts the authorid and does a multitable query of the authors, titleauthor, and titles tables to get a list of all titles, the price of each title, and the year to date revenue for the title. The following example illustrates the use of a DataView filter to filter the rows returned by the author id:

```
Function GetTitles(ByVal au_id As String) As DataView
    Try
        Dim connection as New OleDBConnection("provider=sqloledb;Data
Source=localhost;Initial Catalog=pubs;User ID=sa;pwd=")
        Dim command As New OleDBDataAdapter("SELECT titles.title_id, titles.title,
titles.price, titles.ytd_sales,titleauthor.au_ord,authors.au_id, titles.pub_id FROM
authors INNER JOIN titleauthor ON authors.au_id = titleauthor.au_id INNER JOIN titles ON
titleauthor.title_id = titles.title_id", connection)
        Dim dataset As New DataSet()
        Dim dataView1 as DataView
        command.Fill(dataset, "TitleAuthor")
        dataView1 = new DataView(dataset.Tables("TitleAuthor"))
        dataView1.RowFilter = "au_id='" & au_id &"'"
```

```
        Return dataview1
    Catch myException as Exception
        Message.Text = ("Exception: " + myException.ToString())
    End Try
End Function
```

Next, we bind the `DataGrid` control with the filtered `DataView` object. This is done with the final two statements of the `BindData()` function:

```
titleGrid.DataSource = TitlesDataView
titleGrid.DataBind()
```

First, you set the `DataSource` property of the `titleGrid` to the `Default View` of the `TitlesDataView`, and then you execute the `titleGrid.DataBind()` method to populate the `DataGrid` object. Figure 23-3 shows the results of your work.

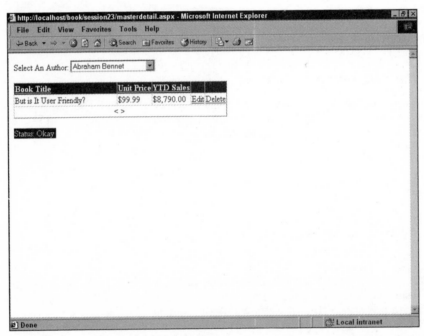

Figure 23-3 *Example of using the DataGrid control for master/detail relationships*

Done!

REVIEW

At this point you should be able to implement master/detail user interfaces in your applications. While the use of the `DataGrid` control has made your job much easier, the core part of the work continues to be understanding the use of ADO.NET objects in getting and filtering data.

Quiz Yourself

1. How do you control the formatted display of values in a `BoundColumn`? (See "Formatting the output of a DataGrid control.")

2. How can you control the ordering of values into columns of a `DataGrid`? (See Master/Detail Relationships with the DataGrid Control.")

3. Is a master/detail user interface more useful for a many-to-many relationship or a one-to-many relationship? (See "Master/Detail Relationships with the DataGrid Control.")

Beating the CRUD out of the DataGrid Control

Session Checklist

✔ Using the DataGrid control as a user interface for modifying data

✔ Using validation controls with template columns for data validation

✔ Sorting the columns of a DataGrid control

**30 Min.
To Go**

In Session 23, we illustrated how you can use the DataGrid control to support the display of data. However, just showing the data is useless if you can't provide updates or deletes. In this session we will build upon the examples used in Session 23 to illustrate how the DataGrid control can be used to update data. The DataGrid control comes with a whole host of built-in functionality that can be exposed to provide a highly customizable approach to building user interfaces to your database.

> **This session assumes you have SQL Server Installed and have access to the Pubs database.**

Updating Your Data

The DataGrid control provides the capability to support editing of bound data by using the EditCommandColumn. The EditCommandColumn handles the automatic generation of "Edit", "OK", and "Cancel" hyperlinks or images to facilitate the user interface elements of editing a DataGrid control. When the "Edit" hyperlink or alternatively an image is selected, the EditCommandColumn control will replace a DataGrid control read-only cell with an editable textbox. Figure 24-1 illustrates the resulting output of using the EditCommandColumn to build the "Edit" hyperlink.

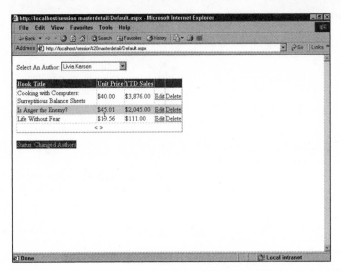

Figure 24-1   *Output of using the EditCommandColumn for editing a DataGrid control*

The property value that generates the `EditCommandColumn` is shown in the following code:

```
<asp:EditCommandColumn
  EditText="Edit"
  CancelText="Cancel"
  UpdateText="OK" >
</asp:EditCommandColumn>
```

Figure 24-2 illustrates the results of selecting the "Edit" hyperlink to edit a selected column.

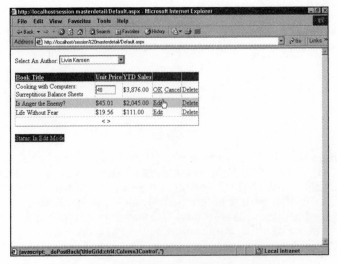

Figure 24-2   *Example of a data row being edited*

The DataGrid control will automatically display the appropriate hyperlinks — an "Edit" hyperlink when in standard mode, a "Cancel" and "Submit" hyperlink when in Edit mode. While the EditCommandColumn handles the generation of the GUI, you still have to provide all of the code to actually perform the edit, cancel and update functions. You attach the code modules to call when each of these events happen through the OnEditCommand, OnUpdateCommand, and OnCancel properties of the DataGrid control. For each of these properties you implement an appropriate function to handle the mechanics of the operation. Listing 24-1 illustrates the full HTML required to generate the DataGrid control and EditCommandColumn as discussed.

Listing 24-1 *HTML required to generate the DataGrid and EditCommandColumn*

```
<ASP:DATAGRID ID="titleGrid"
              RUNAT="SERVER"
              FORECOLOR="Black"
              AUTOGENERATECOLUMNS="false"
              DATAKEYFIELD="title_id"
              ONPAGEINDEXCHANGED="OnPageIndexChanged"
              ONEDITCOMMAND="OnEdit"
              ONCANCELCOMMAND="OnCancel"
              ONUPDATECOMMAND="OnUpdate"
              ONDELETECOMMAND="OnDelete"
              ONSORTCOMMAND="OnSorted"
              ALLOWSORTING="True"
              ALLOWPAGING="True"
              PAGESIZE="5"
              PAGERSTYLE-MODE="NextPrev"
              PAGERSTYLE-HORIZONTALALIGN="Center">
    <ALTERNATINGITEMSTYLE BACKCOLOR="Gainsboro" />
    <FOOTERSTYLE BACKCOLOR="Silver" FORECOLOR="White" />
    <ITEMSTYLE BACKCOLOR="White" />
    <HEADERSTYLE BACKCOLOR="Navy"
                 FORECOLOR="White"
                 FONT-BOLD="True" />
    <COLUMNS>
        <ASP:BOUNDCOLUMN HEADERTEXT="Title"
                         DATAFIELD="Title"
                         SORTEXPRESSION="Title">
        </ASP:BOUNDCOLUMN>
        <ASP:TEMPLATECOLUMN HEADERTEXT="Unit Price"
                            SORTEXPRESSION="Price">
            <ITEMTEMPLATE>
                <ASP:LABEL id="Label2"
                           RUNAT="server"
                           TEXT='<%# String.Format("{0:C}",
Container.DataItem("price"))%>'
                           WIDTH="50"
                           AUTOSIZE="True">
                </ASP:LABEL>
            </ITEMTEMPLATE>
            <EDITITEMTEMPLATE>
                <ASP:TEXTBOX id="editprice"
                             RUNAT="Server"
                             TEXT='<%# Container.DataItem("price")%>'
```

Continued

Listing 24-1 *Continued*

```
                                    WIDTH="50">
                   </ASP:TEXTBOX>
                   <BR>
                   <ASP:COMPAREVALIDATOR id="valeditprice" RUNAT="server"
CONTROLTOVALIDATE="editprice" ERRORMESSAGE="You must supply a positive currency value."
TYPE="Currency" OPERATOR="GreaterThan" VALUETOCOMPARE="0"
DISPLAY="dynamic"></ASP:COMPAREVALIDATOR>
                  </EDITITEMTEMPLATE>
               </ASP:TEMPLATECOLUMN>
               <ASP:BOUNDCOLUMN HEADERTEXT="YTD Sales"
                                 DATAFIELD="ytd_sales"
                                 SORTEXPRESSION="ytd_sales"
                                 DATAFORMATSTRING="{0:C}">
               </ASP:BOUNDCOLUMN>
               <ASP:EDITCOMMANDCOLUMN EDITTEXT="Edit"
                                       CANCELTEXT="Cancel"
                                       UPDATETEXT="OK">
               </ASP:EDITCOMMANDCOLUMN>
               <ASP:BUTTONCOLUMN TEXT="Delete"
                                  COMMANDNAME="Delete">
               </ASP:BUTTONCOLUMN>
            </COLUMNS>
         </ASP:DATAGRID>
```

In the following sections we will cover how to handle attaching functions to support the edit, cancel, update and delete events.

**20 Min.
To Go**

Handling the OnEditCommand Event

As illustrated in Listing 24-1, when a user selects the Edit hyperlink, the OnEditCommand event is fired, this event has been set to call the OnEdit subroutine. The following example displays the code contained in the OnEdit Sub:

```
Sub OnEdit(sender As Object, E As DataGridCommandEventArgs)
    Try
        'Set the Grid to Editable
        sender.EditItemIndex = E.Item.ItemIndex
        BindData()
        Message.Text = "Status: In Edit Mode"
    Catch myException as Exception
        Message.Text = ("Exception: " + myException.ToString())
    End Try
End Sub
```

This subroutine simply turns the editing mode of the DataGrid control on by setting its EditItemIndex to the value of the row the user was on when the Edit hyperlink was selected. This forces the DataGrid control to turn all fields in the selected row which are not set as ReadOnly to textboxes. When you wish to prevent a column from being edited, simply set the ReadOnly property of the column to True. In our example, the only column we are permitting the user to edit is the Unit Price column.

Next you must rebind the DataSet by calling the DataBind function. This will render the OK and Cancel hyperlinks that we established when building the EditCommandColumn. After the user has had the opportunity to edit the selected field, he or she can then select to process the update by selecting the OK hyperlink or to cancel the update with the Cancel hyperlink.

Handling the OnCancelCommand Event

Should the user choose to cancel the update then the OnCancelCommand event fires, which we have associated with the OnCanel subroutine. This routine simply sets the DataGrid control back to ReadOnly by setting the EditItemIndex to -1, then we simply rebind the data to the grid with the BindData function, as shown in the following example:

```
Sub OnCancel(sender As Object, E As DataGridCommandEventArgs)
    Try
        sender.EditItemIndex=-1
        BindData()
        Message.Text = "Status: Update Canceled"
    Catch myException as Exception
        Message.Text = ("Exception: " + myException.ToString())
    End Try
End Sub
```

Handling the OnUpdateCommand Event

When the user selects the OK hyperlink the OnUpdateCommand event fires. We have attached this event to the OnUpdate subroutine. In order to update the data, you need to have a way of effectively getting the user's updated values.

When we originally set up the TemplateColumn responsible for handling the display of the data, we set up an ItemTemplate that handles the formatting and display of values when the grid is in ReadOnly mode. At the same time, we set the EditItemTemplate to handle the display of values when the grid is in Edit mode.

```
<ASP:TEMPLATECOLUMN HEADERTEXT="Unit Price" SORTEXPRESSION="Price">
    <ITEMTEMPLATE>
        <ASP:LABEL id="Label2" RUNAT="server" TEXT='<%# String.Format("{0:C}",
Container.DataItem("price"))%>' WIDTH="50" AUTOSIZE="True"></ASP:LABEL>
    </ITEMTEMPLATE>
    <EDITITEMTEMPLATE>
        <ASP:TEXTBOX id="editprice" RUNAT="Server" TEXT='<%#
Container.DataItem("price")%>' WIDTH="50"></ASP:TEXTBOX>
        <BR>
        <ASP:COMPAREVALIDATOR id="valeditprice" RUNAT="server"
CONTROLTOVALIDATE="editprice" ERRORMESSAGE="You must supply a positive currency value."
TYPE="Currency" OPERATOR="GreaterThan" VALUETOCOMPARE="0"
DISPLAY="dynamic"></ASP:COMPAREVALIDATOR>
    </EDITITEMTEMPLATE>
</ASP:TEMPLATECOLUMN>
```

In the EditItemTemplate we set up a textbox to handle the display of editable data and gave it an id of editprice. Additionally we set up a validation control with an id of valeditprice to make sure that the user enters a positive currency value. Below we will cover how we use the validation control to validate the users input.

Checking that the user input has been validated

When the OnUpdate subroutine fires, the first thing to do is insure that the validator control, valeditprice is valid. If it is valid, you can then proceed with the update. We use the following code shown in Listing 24-2 to find the validation control and check that the values are within acceptable parameters. Assuming that the control is valid, you can then begin the update process.

Executing the update process

In our OnUpdate routine shown in Listing 24-2 we use the following line of code to find the editprice text box: txtBox = e.item.findcontrol("editprice").

Listing 24-2 *OnUpdate subroutine*

```
Sub OnUpdate(sender As Object, E As DataGridCommandEventArgs)
Try
    Dim sTitleId as String
    Dim dPrice as decimal
    Dim txtBox as TextBox
    Dim valCtrl as CompareValidator
    valCtrl = e.item.findcontrol("valeditprice")
    If valCtrl.isValid
        sTitleId = titlegrid.datakeys.item(e.item.itemindex)
        txtBox = e.item.findcontrol("editprice")
        dPrice =txtBox.Text
        UpdateTitles(dPrice, sTitleId)
        titleGrid.EditItemIndex=-1
        BindData()
        Message.Text ="Status: Update Completed"
    Else
        Message.Text ="Status: No Update, Validation Failed"
    End If
Catch myException as Exception
    Message.Text = ("Exception: " + myException.ToString())
End Try
End Sub
```

We then retrieve its contents with the following code:

```
dPrice =txtBox.Text
```

The last piece of information we need to call our `UpdateTitles` function is the Title Id, which can be found by looking at the bound `datakeys` collection and passing the edited rows `itemindex` value:

```
sTitleId = titlegrid.datakeys.item(e.item.itemindex)
```

Now that we have the Title Id and the updated price, we can call our `UpdateTitles` function and pass these values. Finally, before we finish we will need to set the `DataGrid` control back to ReadOnly and rebind the updated data to the grid so that the cell is set to a read-only status.

```
titleGrid.EditItemIndex=-1
BindData()
```

The following code provides a listing of the UpdateTitles subroutine, which actually performs the database update of the price:

```
Sub UpdateTitles(price As Decimal, title_id As String)
    Dim connection as New OleDBConnection("provider=sqloledb;Data
Source=localhost;Initial Catalog=pubs;User ID=sa;pwd=")
    Dim command as New OleDbCommand("UPDATE titles SET [price]=? WHERE [title_id] =?",
connection)
    Dim param0 as New OleDBParameter("price", OleDBType.Currency)
    param0.Value = price
    command.Parameters.Add(param0)
    Dim param1 as New OleDBParameter("title_id", OleDBType.VarChar)
    param1.Value = title_id
    command.Parameters.Add(param1)
    connection.Open()
    command.ExecuteNonQuery()
    connection.Close()
End Sub
```

Deleting Data with the OnDeleteCommand Event

**10 Min.
To Go**

Unfortunately, the `EditCommandColumn` doesn't provide an automated way to generate a Delete or Select hyperlink. However, you can use the `ButtonColumn` to implement a `Delete` method for the `DataGrid` control as shown in the following code:

```
<asp:ButtonColumn Text="Delete" CommandName="Delete">
</asp:ButtonColumn>
```

We attach a subroutine to execute when the hyperlink is selected as illustrated in Figure 24-2 with the following attribute of the `DataGrid` control:

```
OnDeleteCommand="OnDelete"
```

The following code illustrates the subroutine that fires when the hyperlink is selected:

```
Sub OnDelete(sender As Object, E As DataGridCommandEventArgs)
Try
    Dim sTitleId as String
```

```
    Dim sAuthorID as String
    sender.EditItemIndex=-1
    sTitleId = titlegrid.datakeys.item(e.item.itemindex)
    sAuthorID = AuthorList.SelectedItem.Value
    DeleteTitles(sTitleId, sAuthorId)
    BindData()
    Message.Text="Status: Delete Successful"
Catch myException as Exception
    Message.Text = ("Exception: " + myException.ToString())
End Try
End Sub
```

When the `OnDelete` subroutine is executed, we first set the `DataGrid` control to
ReadOnly to prevent any misplaced user interfaces once the selected row is deleted as illustrated in the following code segment.

```
sender.EditItemIndex=-1
```

Next, we obtain the Title Id and Author Id in the same way that we collected them in the
update scenarios earlier. Once we have the Title Id and Author Id we can call the
`DeleteTitles` subroutine to execute the actual delete as shown in the following example:

```
    Sub DeleteTitles(title_id as String, au_id as String)
        Dim connection as New OleDBConnection("provider=sqloledb;Data
Source=localhost;Initial Catalog=pubs;User ID=sa;pwd=")
        Dim command as New OleDbCommand("DELETE FROM TitleAuthor WHERE [title_id]=? And
[au_id]=?", connection)
        Dim param0 as New OleDBParameter("title_id", OleDBType.VarChar)
        param0.Value = title_id
        command.Parameters.Add(param0)
        Dim param1 as New OleDBParameter("au_id", OleDBType.VarChar)
        param1.Value = au_id
        command.Parameters.Add(param1)
        connection.Open()
        command.ExecuteNonQuery()
        connection.Close()
    End Sub
```

Finally, we call the `BindData` function to refresh the `DataGrid` control.

Sorting Columns with the DataGrid Control

Because the `DataGrid` control doesn't perform the actual sorting of the data but instead
handles the related events and methods, several steps must be taken in order to implement
sorting on the `DataGrid` control.

The first step is to set up the following two attributes on the `<ASP:DATAGRID>`:

```
OnSortCommand="OnSorted"
AllowSorting="True"
```

The `OnSortCommand` is the event that will be called when a user initiates a sort event.
The `OnSorted` subroutine builds the sorted `DataView` and rebinds the sorted information to

the `DataGrid` control. The `AllowSorting` attribute will turn the column headers of all template columns or bound columns that have implemented a `SortExpression` attribute into a hyperlink that users can click to initiate the `OnSortCommand`. An example of how to add the attribute to a `TemplateColumn` can be seen below:

```
<asp:TemplateColumn HeaderText="Unit Price" SortExpression="price" >
```

The `OnSorted` subroutine handles all of the heavy lifting associated with the sorting activity. The `OnSorted` subroutine used in our example can be reviewed in Listing 24-3.

Listing 24-3　*Example of implementing a sorting function for a DataGrid control*

```
Sub OnSorted(source As Object , e As DataGridSortCommandEventArgs)
    Try
        Dim sSortField as String
        Dim TitlesDataView As DataView =
GetTitles(authorlist.SelectedItem.Value)
        Dim bSortAsc as Integer
        sSortField = e.SortExpression.ToString()
        source.EditItemIndex=-1
        if Session("bsortAsc") = Nothing Then
            Session("bsortAsc") = 1
        Else
            bSortAsc= Session("bsortAsc")
        End If
        If bSortAsc = 1 Then
            Session("bSortAsc") = 0
            TitlesDataView.Sort= sSortField & " DESC"
            Message.Text ="Sort Descending on " & sSortField
        Elseif bSortAsc =0 Then
            Session("bSortAsc")= 1
            TitlesDataView.Sort= sSortField & " ASC"
            Message.Text ="Sort Ascending on " & sSortField
        Else
            Message.Text="bSortAsc fell through"
        End If
        titleGrid.DataSource = TitlesDataView
        titlegrid.databind()
    Catch myException as Exception
        Message.Text = ("Exception: " + myException.ToString())
    End Try
End Sub
```

To handle the sorting of a column on the `DataGrid` control, you need to first establish a `DataView` object that can be used to sort the information. In the `OnSorted` function, you call the `GetTitles` function and pass the appropriate Author Id:

```
Dim TitlesDataView As DataView = GetTitles(authorlist.SelectedItem.Value)
```

Next, you need to know what field the user selected for sorting; we can get the field name through the `SortExpression` property:

```
sSortField = e.SortExpression.ToString()
```

You also need to track whether the user desires the sort to be in ascending or descending order. In our example, we track this through the use of a session variable bSortAsc. When the value is equal to 1 then the sort is set for ascending, otherwise it is set for descending.

Once you know the field to sort on and the sorting direction, you can use the DataView to automatically sort the information using the Sort method of the DataView. You simply pass the name of the field to sort followed by the value ASC if you want the field sorted in ascending order or DESC if you want it sorted in descending order.

```
TitlesDataView.Sort= sSortField & " ASC"
```

Finally, we simply bind the DataView to the grid as follows:

```
titleGrid.DataSource = TitlesDataView
titlegrid.databind()
```

Figure 24-3 shows the resulting output of a user sorting the DataGrid control on the Unit Price field.

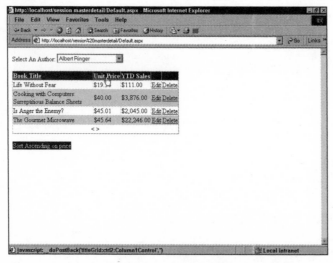

Figure 24-3 *Output after sorting the Unit Price field*

Done!

REVIEW

We have covered most of the major aspects of using the DataGrid control with ADO.NET and providing a user interface to support data updates, reads, and deletes. The examples provided for this session also demonstrate how to handle paging of data with the DataGrid control. You should explore these examples further to understand this technique.

QUIZ YOURSELF

1. How do you turn on the editing mode for a `DataGrid` control? (See "Updating Your Data.")

2. How can you use both a range and required field validator to validate user input? (See "Handling the OnUpdateCommand Event.")

3. How can you allow the user to better control how a column is sorted? For instance could you use an external dropdown list to sort columns in a specific manner? (See "Sorting Columns with the DataGrid Control.")

Data Shaping with ADO.NET

Session Checklist

✔ Introducing data shaping

✔ Handling hierarchical datasets

I n this session we will explore the ability of the `DataSet` object to support the use of parent-child relationships between tables.

**30 Min.
To Go**

What Is Data Shaping?

Data shaping is simply the process of reflecting the parent-child relationships that exist between data objects. For instance, let's look at demonstrating the parent-child relationship between two data objects: a set of stores and a set of titles sold by the stores. Figure 25-1 illustrates this relationship.

In ASP you could store these relationships in a hierarchical recordset by using the Shape Provider, and then produce a structured output representing the hierarchy to the user. The shaping syntax allowed you to build these parent-child relationships easily as illustrated in Listing 25-1.

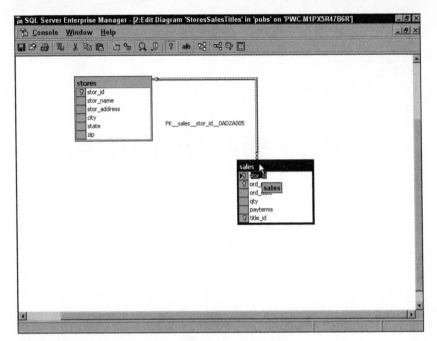

Figure 25-1   *Diagram of a parent child relationship*

Listing 25-1   *Example of Using the ADO Shape Provider*

```
<HTML>
    <HEAD>
        <SCRIPT LANGUAGE="VBScript" RUNAT="Server">
        Function DisplayShape()
        Dim myConnection
        Dim ShapeCommand
        Dim StoresRecordSet
        Dim SalesRecordSet
        Set myConnection=Server.CreateObject("ADODB.Connection")
        myConnection.Provider ="MSDataShape"
        myConnection.ConnectionString="DRIVER=SQL
Server;UID=sa;DATABASE=pubs;SERVER=(local);PWD=;"
        myConnection.Open

    'Constructing the Shape Command to Build RecordSet
        ShapeCommand = "SHAPE {SELECT stor_id, stor_name, stor_address FROM stores}"
        ShapeCommand = ShapeCommand &"APPEND ({select *, title from sales inner join
titles on sales.title_id=titles.title_id} AS Sales"
        ShapeCommand = ShapeCommand &" RELATE stor_id TO stor_id)"

        Set StoresRecordSet = Server.CreateObject("ADODB.Recordset")
        StoresRecordSet.Open ShapeCommand, myConnection

        Response.Write("<H2>List of Titles Sold By Store</H2>")
        Do While Not StoresRecordSet.EOF
            Response.Write("<BR><B><I>")
```

```
            Response.Write("Store Name: " & StoresRecordSet("stor_name"))
            Response.Write("</B></I>")
            Response.Write("<p>Address: " & StoresRecordSet("stor_address") & "</p>")
            Set SalesRecordSet= StoresRecordSet("Sales").Value
            Response.Write("<blockquote>")
            Response.Write("<p><i>List of Titles sold by " & StoresRecordSet("stor_name")
    &"</i></p>")
            Do While Not SalesRecordSet.EOF
                Response.Write("<p>Title = "& SalesRecordSet("title") & "</p>")
                SalesRecordSet.movenext
            Loop
            Response.Write("</blockquote>")
            StoresRecordSet.movenext
        Loop
        End Function
        </SCRIPT>
    </HEAD>
    <BODY>
        <%=DisplayShape%>
    </BODY>
</HTML>
```

Figure 25-2 shows the output from this code segment, producing the expected represen-tation of the parent-child relationships.

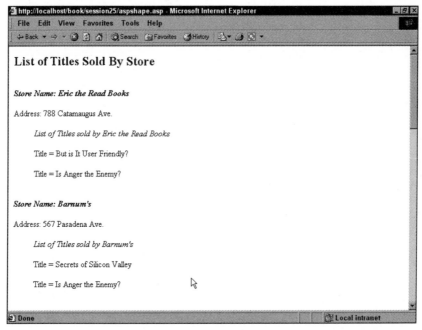

Figure 25-2 *Resulting output of using the hierarchical recordset in ASP*

ADO.NET does not support the use of the MSDataShape Provider or the shape syntax. Instead ADO.NET utilizes a method of the DataSet object, the Relations() method.

Why Shape Your Data?

The ability to display hierarchical or parent-child relationships is key to a wide variety of applications. You use these types of relationships whenever you need to list all orders associated with a product, all products associated with a category, all files contained in a folder, or customers located in all cities. Each of these examples can be represented in a parent-child relationship. Although we could set up a series of stored procedures or commands that query a set of data based upon a parent's unique key in order to return the filtered set of children, this method can create a tremendous amount of overhead.

In ADO.NET, we can use the Relations() method of the DataSet object to identify and enforce parent-child relationships between disparate sets of data, even if those data sets do not have an enforced relationship in the source database. As long as there is a way to connect to distinct data stores through a common key field, then we can enforce a parent-child relationship.

DataSet Object

20 Min.
To Go

If you are an ADO programmer, you may look at a DataSet object as a disconnected RecordSet object that contains one or more tables of data. In effect a DataSet is similar to a hierarchical RecordSet that is created using the MSDataShape ADO Provider and then building a SELECT command using the shape syntax as we discussed previously. If you are an XML developer, you're more likely to see the DataSet object as a specific Document Object Model (DOM), which is set to represent tables of data where each table contains a set of elements with a consistent strongly typed structure. Either of these views provides an accurate representation of the DataSet object.

The DataSet object in ADO.NET provides the ability to hold an unlimited number of data tables. We add data tables to the DataSet object by creating a DataAdapter and supplying a stored procedure or SQL syntax to fill the data table as shown in Listing 25-2:

Listing 25-2   *Example of using the DataAdapter and DataSet commands*

```
<%@ Import Namespace="System.Data.OleDB"%>
<%@ Import Namespace="System.Data" %>
<%@ Page Language="VB" Debug="true" %>
<HTML>
    <SCRIPT LANGUAGE="VB" RUNAT="server">

    Sub Page_Load()

        Dim myConnection as new OleDBConnection("provider=sqloledb;Data
Source=localhost;Initial Catalog=pubs;User ID=sa;pwd=")
        Dim myDataSet as New DataSet()
        Dim StoresDSCommand as new OleDBDataAdapter("select * from stores",
myConnection)

        StoresDSCommand.Fill(myDataSet,"Stores")

        Dim SalesDSCommand as OleDBDataAdapter
        SalesDSCommand = new OleDBDataAdapter("select *, title from sales inner join
titles on sales.title_id=titles.title_id", myConnection)
```

```
            SalesDSCommand.Fill(myDataSet,"Sales")


myDataSet.Relations.Add("StoreSale",myDataSet.Tables("Stores").Columns("stor_id"),myDataS
et.Tables("Sales").Columns("stor_id"))
            Dim Store as DataRow
            Dim Sale as DataRow

            Msg.Text=Msg.Text & "<H2>List of Titles Sold By Store</H2>"
            for each Store in myDataSet.Tables("Stores").Rows
                Msg.Text=Msg.Text & "<BR><B><I>"
                Msg.Text=Msg.Text & "Store Name: " & Store("stor_name").ToString()
                Msg.Text=Msg.Text & "</B></I>"
                Msg.Text=Msg.Text & "<p>Address: " & Store("stor_address") & "</p>"
                Msg.Text=Msg.Text & "<blockquote>"
                Msg.Text=Msg.Text & "<p><i>List of Titles sold by " & Store("stor_name")
&"</i></p>"
                for each Sale in Store.GetChildRows(myDataSet.Relations("StoreSale"))
                    Msg.Text=Msg.Text & "<p>Title = " & Sale("title").ToString() & "</p>"
                next

                Msg.Text=Msg.Text &"</blockquote>"
            next

        end sub

    </SCRIPT>
    <BODY>
        <ASP:LABEL ID="Msg" RUNAT="server" />
    </BODY>
</HTML>
```

This code fills the `myDataSet` object with the contents of the stores table.

```
SalesDSCommand.Fill(myDataSet,"Sales")
```

In order to describe relationships between these tables, so we can easily display or report on any hierarchical relationships that may exist, we need to use the `Relations()` method of the `DataSet` object. We will cover this in the next section.

Shaping Data with the Relations Method

10 Min. To Go

The `Relations` method enables you to set the parent-child relationship between two tables by supplying the name of the relation, the table and column, that should be the parent relation and the table and column that is the child relation. Looking at the code in Listing 25-2 from the previous section, we set up a relationship between the Stores table and the Sales table in `myDataSet` using the following code segment:

```
myDataSet.Relations.Add("StoreSale",myDataSet.Tables("Stores").Columns("stor_id"),myDataS
et.Tables("Sales").Columns("stor_id"))
```

This will establish a relationship where the Stores table represents the parent and is joined via the `stor_id` column to the Sales table. Using this relationship, you can quickly loop through each of the stores and provide a list of titles sold to each store. The following segment of Listing 25-2, illustrates how you can loop through each of the stores using a simple For...Next loop:

```
Dim Store as DataRow
Dim Sale as DataRow

Msg.Text=Msg.Text & "<H2>List of Titles Sold By Store</H2>"

for each Store in myDataSet.Tables("Stores").Rows
        Msg.Text=Msg.Text & "<BR><B><I>"
        Msg.Text=Msg.Text & "Store Name: " & Store("stor_name").ToString()
        Msg.Text=Msg.Text & "</B></I>"
        Msg.Text=Msg.Text & "<p>Address: " & Store("stor_address") & "</p>"
        Msg.Text=Msg.Text & "<blockquote>"
        Msg.Text=Msg.Text & "<p><i>List of Titles sold by " & Store("stor_name")
&"</i></p>"
```

In order to access each of the child records, we use the Relation method established earlier and a For...Next loop as illustrated in the following example:

```
        for each Sale in Store.GetChildRows(myDataSet.Relations("StoreSale"))
                Msg.Text=Msg.Text & "<p>Title = " & Sale("title").ToString() & "</p>"
        next
        Msg.Text=Msg.Text &"</blockquote>"
    next
end sub
```

The resulting output of Listing 25-2 can be seen in Figure 25-3.

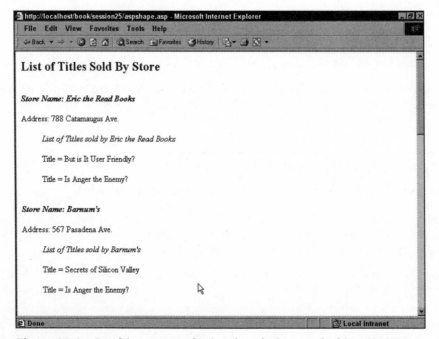

Figure 25-3 *Resulting output of using the relations method in ASP.NET*

Done!

REVIEW

The use of the Relations method enables you to quickly navigate hierarchical relationships between datasets. This common but powerful technique allows you as a developer to robustly handle complex relationships with ease.

QUIZ YOURSELF

1. How can parent-child relationships be established between data stores from different data sources? (See "Why Shape Your Data?")

2. Describe the differences between the ADO Shape Command and the ADO.Net Relations method. (See "What Is Data Shaping?" and "Why Shape Your Data?")

3. What limits are there in establishing tables and relationships for a specified DataSet object? (See "Shaping Data with the Relations Method.")

Handling ADO.NET Errors

Session Checklist

✔ Understanding the OLEDBException class and its interaction with the OLEDBError object

✔ Implementing custom OLEDBError handling in your application

✔ Implementing a generic event handler that writes errors to the Event Log

**30 Min.
To Go**

ADO.NET provides a framework similar to ADO for handling errors that occur when calling ADO.NET components. When the ADO.NET adapter encounters an error, it throws an Exception which can then be evaluated for any contained errors.

There are two types of exceptions that can be thrown: an OLEDBException and a a SQLException. An OLEDBException can be thrown by any OLE DB data source, while a SQLException is thrown by SQL Server. In this session, we will focus on handling the OLEDBException, however the approach for handling a SQLException is nearly identical except you have access to a broader range of properties to evaluate as shown in Table 26-1.

Table 26-1 *SQLException Properties not contained in* OLEDBException

SQLException Property	Description
Class	Gets the severity level of the error returned from the SQL Server .NET Data Provider.
LineNumber	Gets the line number within the Transact-SQL command batch or stored procedure that generated the error.
Number	Gets a number that identifies the type of error.

Continued

Table 26-1   *Continued*

SQLException Property	Description
Procedure	Gets the name of the stored procedure or remote procedure call (RPC) that generated the error.
Server	Gets the name of the computer running an instance of SQL Server that generated the error.
State	Gets the number modifying the error to provide additional information.

The Try . . . Catch . . . Finally error-handling functionality of ASP.NET is very useful for evaluating ADO.NET errors. Let's start by creating a function, GetRecords(). GetRecords() is a simple function that attempts to connect to a database, fill a dataset, and then return the dataset. In the next section we will implement OLEDBErrorHandler(), a generic error handler that will evaluate the errors that are established during calls in the GetRecords() function and then write those errors to the browser and to the System Event Log.

The code listings 26-1, 26-2, 26-3 are each segments of code extracted from the file errorhandle.aspx in the Session 26 folder of the CD.

Listing 26-1   *OLEDBError handling code segment from errorhandle.aspx*

```
<%@ Import Namespace="System.Diagnostics"%>
<%@ Import Namespace="System.Exception" %>
<%@ Import Namespace="System.Data.OleDB" %>
<%@ Import Namespace="System.Data" %>
<%@ Page Language="VB" Debug="False" Trace="False" %>
<HTML>
    <SCRIPT LANGUAGE="VB" RUNAT="server">

    Sub ExecuteDBCodeBtn_Click(Sender As Object, E as EventArgs)
        Try
          Dim MyDataset As DataSet = GetRecords()
          grid1.DataSource = MyDataset.Tables(0).DefaultView
          grid1.DataBind()
          Catch ex as Exception
                Dim oLabel as new Label()
                Dim sMess as String
                oLabel.Text=""
                oLabel.Id="ExecuteDBCodeBtn_ErrorLabel"
                Page.Controls.Add(oLabel)
                sMess = sMess & "<b><p>Code Error Occurred</p></b>"
                sMess = sMess & "<ul><li>" & ex.message & "</li></ul>"
                oLabel.Text = oLabel.Text & sMess
        End Try
```

```
        End Sub

    Function GetRecords() As DataSet
        Try
            Dim connection as New OleDBConnection(txtConnStr.Text)
            Dim command as New OleDBDataAdapter(txtSQLStr.Text, connection)
            Dim dataset As New DataSet()
            command.Fill(dataset, "dataset")
            Return dataset
        Catch myException as OLEDBException
            OLEDBErrorHandler(myException)
        End Try
    End Function
```

The GetRecords() function pulls the connection string from a textbox txtConnStr and the SQL statement from a textbox txtSQLstr. Next it attempts to fill the dataset and then return it. Whenever an error occurs in the ADO.NET Adapter, for instance if the password or server is invalid, or an incorrect statement is encountered in the SQL statement, then an exception is thrown. Using the Try . . . Catch statement, you can catch the OLEDBException and then begin the process of handling and evaluating the errors collection that it contains. This is a much more convenient solution than we had in ASP for capturing and passing a collection of errors. The ability for the OLEDBException class to act as a wrapper for the OLEDBErrors collection, makes passing the collection to a generic error handler much more simple.

In the next section, we will expand on the above code example and build an OLEDBErrorHandler() function in order to examine the ways that we can evaluate the errors collection.

OLEDBError Object Description

You can sort through the OLEDBException object to work with each of the OLEDBError objects it wraps. The OLEDBError class is created by the OleDBDataAdapter whenever an error occurs in connecting to or executing against a datasource. For each error encountered by the OleDBDataAdapter, a new OLEDBError object is instantiated and added to the OLEDBErrors collection, which is then wrapped by the OLEDBException class and instantiated as an object.

Listing 26-2, extends Listing 26-1 to illustrate how the OLEDBException object is passed to a generic error handler function OLEDBErrorHandler. The function can then process the errors collection. First, we dynamically add a label to the bottom of the page so that we can display the list of error messages. We will use the label to hold the text of our OLEDBException and OLEDBError properties.

Listing 26-2   *Passing an OLEDBException to an error handler*

```
    Function OLEDBErrorHandler(ByVal myException as OLEDBException)
        Dim sMess As String
        Dim oLabel as new Label()
        Dim eItem as OLEDBError

        'Add a label to the page dynamically to show errors
```

Continued

Listing 26-2 *Continued*

```
                oLabel.Text = ""
                oLabel.Id="OleDBLabel"
                Page.Controls.Add(new LiteralControl("<hr>"))
                Page.Controls.Add(oLabel)

                'Loop throught the Errors in OLEDBException
                sMess=sMess & "<p><b>Database Error" & myException.ErrorCode.ToString()
&" Occurred: " & myException.Message &"</b></p>"
                sMess=sMess & "<p>StackTrace: " & myException.StackTrace.ToString()
&"</p>"
                sMess=sMess & "<p>TargetSite: " & myException.TargetSite.ToString()
&"</p>"
                For each eItem in myException.Errors
                        sMess=sMess & "<ul>"
                        sMess = sMess &"<li>Error Message: " & eItem.Message & "</li>"
                        sMess = sMess &"<li>Source of Error: " & eItem.Source & "</li>"
                        sMess = sMess &"<li>Native Error Id: " &
eItem.NativeError.ToString() & "</li>"
                        sMess = sMess &"<li>SQL State: " & eItem.SQLState & "</li>"
                        sMess=sMess & "</ul>"
                        oLabel.Text = oLabel.Text & sMess
                Next
                WriteEvent(myException)
        End Function
```

This function works by defining a variable, eItem as an OLEDBError object. You can then use a For . . . Each . . . Next loop to iterate through the collection, and process each error respectively. The results of this process can be seen in Figure 26-1.

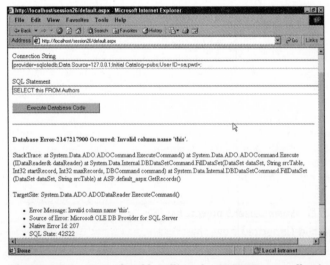

Figure 26-1 *Example of handling the OLEDBErrors collection*

Now the OLEDBError object properties can be accessed and displayed. We will cover these properties in the next section.

20 Min.
To Go

OLEDBError Object Properties

In Listing 26-1, we displayed each of the OLEDBError properties on the label by adding them consecutively to the sMess string variable. We then displayed the results on the run-time generated label control. Let's take a quick review of each of these properties and see what type of information that they provide:

- The Message property provides a short description of the error that was generated. In Figure 26-1 you can see that we attempted to include an invalid column create_error in the SQL Statement. The Message property generates a clear description of the error, Invalid column name 'create_error'.

- The NativeError property enables you to obtain the database-specific error information typically in the form of a code that you can utilize to reference the database technical manuals. Only as a last resort do you want to be utilizing these codes for troubleshooting!

- The Source property retrieves the name of the object that generated the error. In Figure 26-1 you can determine that we were using the OLEDB provider and connecting to a SQL Server Database.

- The SQLState property gets the five-character error code following the ANSI SQL standard for the database. The character string value returned for an SQLSTATE consists of a two-character class value followed by a three-character subclass value. A class value of 01 indicates a warning and is accompanied by a return code of SQL_SUCCESS_WITH_INFO. Class values other than 01, except for the class IM, indicate an error and are accompanied by a return value of SQL_ERROR. The class IM is specific to warnings and errors that derive from the implementation of ODBC itself. The subclass value 000 in any class indicates that there is no subclass for that SQLSTATE. The assignment of class and subclass values is defined by SQL-92. The specific references and descriptions for these values can be identified by referencing the provider documentation. In Figure 26-1, we were provided a SQLState code of 42S22, which maps to an error description of Column not found.

OLEDBError Object Methods

The methods of the OLEDBError object are the same as the other ASP.NET equivalents.

- The Equals() method (inherited from object) determines whether the specified object is the same instance as the current object.

- The GetHashCode() method (inherited from object) serves as a hash function for a particular type, suitable for use in hashing algorithms and data structures like a hash table.

- The GetType() method (inherited from object) gets the type of the object.

- The ToString() method provides a conversion to string method.

- The Finalize() method (inherited from object) enables the object to attempt to free resources and perform other cleanup operations before the object is reclaimed by the Garbage Collector (GC). This method may be ignored by the Common Language Runtime; therefore, necessary cleanup operations should be done elsewhere.

- MemberwiseClone (inherited from object) creates a shallow copy of the current object.

OLEDBException Properties

The OLEDBException class wraps the OLEDBErrors collection, and as such draws much of the values for its properties from the underlying collection of OLEDBError objects. For instance, the values stored in the Source and Message properties are exactly the same as that of the first OLEDBError object stored in the OLEDBErrors collection. Let's look at each property to evaluate how it can be used to garner additional information about the error.

- The ErrorCode property (inherited from ExternalException) provides the error identification number (HResult) of the error generated by the first OLEDBError object, the property is read-only, and can be useful for researching the cause of the error.

- The Errors property contains the OLEDBErrors collection and captures all errors generated by the OleDB data adapter. This is the most frequently used property, and the one that allows you to cycle through all the errors generated by the OleDB data adapter.

- The HelpLink property (inherited from Exception) indicates a link to the help file associated with this exception, and is read-only. Typically in the case of the OLEDBErrors collection, this property will be emptied; it is more commonly used with the generic Exception object when errors are raised specifically by the application.

- The InnerException property (inherited from Exception) retrieves a reference to an inner (that may be nested) exception.

- The Message property is simply a copy of the message contained in the first OLEDBError of the Errors collection.

- The Source property is simply a copy of the source property contained in the first OLEDBError of the Errors collection.

- The StackTrace property (inherited from Exception) indicates the stack trace as a text string, which is valuable for determining where the error occurred. This property allows you to follow from the lowest child in the hierarchy to the originating function, which initiated the call that established the error. Figure 26-1 shows that by reviewing the StackTrace property you can identify that the original call that created the error was in ASP.default_aspx.GetRecords(), indicating the default.aspx page and the GetRecords() function.

- The TargetSite property (inherited from Exception) indicates the method that threw this exception. This property is read-only.

**10 Min.
To Go**

Writing Errors to the Event Log

Now that you understand how to capture each of the OleDB errors, let's look at how you might log these errors to the System Event Log as well as display them to the user. Why would you want to write errors to the System Event Log? One reason is that whenever you are dealing with errors in the handling of data, you should provide multiple methods for identifying, troubleshooting, and resolving the issue. One method you can use to help identify certain errors is to write errors to the Event Log. This is especially useful in capturing issues that occur infrequently and may be difficult to track down.

In Listing 26-1 the last statement calls the `WriteEvent()` function. This function accepts as a parameter an exception and then goes through the process of writing the error summary to the Event Log. In order to use this function, you need to import the `System.Diagnostics` namespace using:

```
<%@ Import Namespace="System.Diagnostics"%>
```

Then you can implement the generic event log handler as shown in Listing 26-3 which completes Listing 26-2 discussed earlier in this session:

Listing 26-3 *Writing error events to the system event log*

```
Function WriteEvent(ByVal myException as Exception)
        Dim sPage as String = Request.Path
        Dim Message As String = "Url " & sPage
        Dim sLogName As String = "myLogFile"
        Dim oLog as New EventLog

        Message = Message  & " Error: "
        Message = Message  & myexception.message
        If (Not EventLog.SourceExists(sLogName)) Then
                    EventLog.CreateEventSource(sLogName,sLogName)
        End if
        oLog.Source = sLogName
        oLog.WriteEntry(Message, EventLogEntryType.Error)
    End Function
 </SCRIPT>
 <BODY>
    <FORM RUNAT="server" ID="Form1">
        <H1>
            ASP.NET OleDB Exception Handling
        </H1>
        <P>
            This example is useful for testing some of the typical errors that may
occur
            while connecting to OleDB datasources. Try creating errors in the
            connection string and sql statements to see how error handling is
reported.
        </P>
        <P>
            <ASP:LABEL RUNAT="Server" ID="Label1">Connection String</ASP:LABEL>
```

Continued

Listing 26-3 *Continued*

```
                <ASP:TEXTBOX ID="txtConnStr" RUNAT="server" WRAP="False"
WIDTH="800">provider=sqloledb;Data Source=127.0.0.1;Initial Catalog=pubs;User
ID=sa;pwd=;</ASP:TEXTBOX>
            </P>
            <P>
                <ASP:LABEL RUNAT="Server" ID="Label2">SQL Statement</ASP:LABEL>
                <ASP:TEXTBOX ID="txtSQLStr" RUNAT="server" WRAP="False"
WIDTH="800">SELECT * FROM
GENERATE ERROR IN SQL</ASP:TEXTBOX>
            </P>
            <P>
                <ASP:BUTTON TEXT="Execute Database Code" ONCLICK="ExecuteDBCodeBtn_Click"
RUNAT="server" ID="Button1" />
            </P>
            <P>
                <ASP:DATAGRID ID="grid1" RUNAT="server" />
            </P>
        </FORM>
    </BODY>
</HTML>
```

With this function, you are simply capturing the page that generated the error and, creating a new log file called myLogFile, or opening it if it already exists, then writing the
message summary to the log file. That's it! Now you can open the Event Viewer from your
Control Panel ⇨ Administrative Tools ⇨ Event Viewer icon and review the log file, as illustrated in Figure 26-2, providing a way for remote administrators and local administrators to
troubleshoot issues.

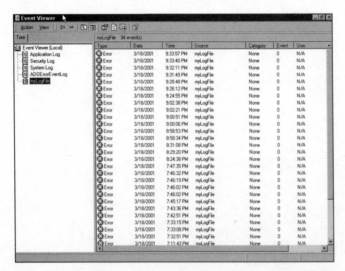

Figure 26-2 *Using the Event Viewer to view errors in the Event Log*

Done!

REVIEW

You should now understand how to use the OLEDBException class and the OLEDBErrors collection to retrieve the errors that are produced by the OleDBDataAdapter. As the previous examples have shown, capturing these errors is straightforward — the real difficulty is resolving them!

QUIZ YOURSELF

1. How many OleDB errors can be handled by the OLEDBException class? (See "OLEDBError Object Description.")

2. How could you implement a global generic OleDB error handler for use across your application? (See "OLEDBError Object Description.")

3. If the first OleDB error in an OLEDBErrors collection contained the value Invalid column name 'this' in its Message property, then what would be the value of the OLEDBException.Message property wrapping this collection? (See "OLEDBError Object Properties.")

PART

V

Sunday Morning Part Review

The following set of questions is designed to provide you feedback on how well you understood the topics covered during this part of the book. Please refer to Appendix A for the answers to each question.

1. A DataSet object can be created without the use of the (SQL or ADO) DataAdapter's Fill method.

    True/False

2. The DataSet is a container class.

    True/False

3. *Fill in the blank:* The _____ property, which is read-only, returns the number of DataTables in a DataTableCollection object.

4. *Fill in the blank:* The _____ property gets a specified DataTable from a DataTableCollection object.

5. *Fill in the blank:* _____ is the process of connecting a server control to a DataSet.

6. You can bind server controls to an array of custom classes.

    True/False

7. Setting the attribute AutoPostBack="true" on a server control forces the reposting of the page to the server.

    True/False

8. DTC objects are part of the ASP.NET Framework.

    True/False

9. *Fill in the blank:* The property _____ is what automatically generates the columns for a DataGrid control.

10. Using the following property/value combination, DataFormatString="{0:C}" for a field will format the contents as what format type.

    a. Decimal

    b. Currency

    c. Date

    d. Fixed

11. To format alternating rows of data in a datagrid, manipulate which property?

    a. HeaderStyle

    b. FooterStyle

    c. ItemStyle

    d. AlternatingItemStyle

12. The DataReader control should be closed with the Close method.
    True/False

13. The U in CRUD stands for what?

    a. Understand

    b. Update

    c. Unique

    d. Undo

14. You must code your own modules to provide update, delete, and create functionality.
    True/False

15. *Fill in the blank:* To set the number of records on each page, the _____ property should be set.

16. The RangeValidator Control cannot be used with the DataGrid when in Edit mode.
    True/False

17. Data shaping is simply the process of:
    a. Reflecting the parent child relationships
    b. Manipulating data values
    c. Updating a DataSet
    d. None of the above

18. A parent-child relationship is a type of hierarchy.
    True/False

19. The `DataSet` object can hold no more than 10 data tables.
    True/False

20. A special provider must be used to shape data with ADO.NET.
    True/False

21. `Try...Catch...Finally` is a type of structured error handling.
    True/False

22. The `ADOException` class acts as a _____ for the `ADOErrors` collection.
    a. Wrapper
    b. Object
    c. Holding point
    d. None of the above

23. What property provides a short description of the error that was generated?
    a. `Message`
    b. `NativeError`
    c. `Source`
    d. None of the above

24. What property retrieves the name of the object that generated the error?
    a. `Message`
    b. `NativeError`
    c. `Source`
    d. None of the above

PART

VI

Sunday Afternoon

SOAP It Up!

Session Checklist

✔ Using SOAP in the .NET Platform

✔ Using SOAP in a heterogeneous computing environment

**30 Min.
To Go**

I n this session, we discuss how the ASP.NET platform is incorporating at its core the adoption of open Internet standards to support interoperability across distributed heterogeneous computing environments. With ASP.NET you can implement Web Services, which enable you to build distributed applications that expose your business logic to any application client regardless of the operating system, programming language, or object model it is built on. A key standard that is critical to this approach is the SOAP specification, which supports the invocation of business objects across the Internet or an intranet regardless of the client or the server's operating platform and without requiring any proprietary software on either side of the communication.

Introducing SOAP

SOAP (Simple Object Access Protocol) is a wire protocol specification for invoking methods, on servers, services, components, and objects. As the Internet expands to deliver an ever-increasing set of services and applications, communication between numerous different platforms, such as CORBA and COM, is critical to support the evolving needs of application-to-application communication in Business-to-Business (B2B), Business-to-Commerce (B2C), and Business-to-Everyone (B2E) environments.

Before SOAP, if you had a business component written as a Java Servlet that supported the lookup and publication of data, it was basically impossible to instantiate that object with a COM-based business component running on the opposite side of a firewall. The Java servlet built on the CORBA platform would typically require the use of the Object Management Group's Internet Inter-ORB Protocol (IIOP) to facilitate distributed application interaction, whereas the COM component would use COM Internet Services (CIS) plus

Distributed Component Object Model (DCOM), Remote Data Services (RDS), or Remote Scripting to communicate with distributed objects, thus providing no simple or efficient way for consumer or provider applications to communicate easily across the Internet through proxy servers and firewalls.

SOAP was submitted to the W3C by Microsoft, IBM, DevelopMentor, and UserLand among others to address these issues. There are two major stated goals of the SOAP specification:

- Provide a standard object invocation protocol built on Internet standards, using HTTP as the transport protocol and XML for the data encoding.
- Create an extensible protocol and payload format that can evolve over time.

SOAP eliminates a lot of the complexity associated with the other distributed object invocation solutions, such as DCOM and IIOP, by simply not specifying how issues such as garbage collection, type safety, versioning, object by reference, and other similar communication issues should be handled. Instead it focuses on simply defining the mechanism to pass commands and parameters between HTTP clients and servers regardless of the operating system, programming language, or object model used on either side of the communication.

Early product implementations of SOAP illustrate the broad diversity of object models, platforms, and programming languages. These include:

- Nouveau ORB by Rogue Wave
- Orbix 2000 by Iona
- Voyager by ObjectSpace
- Frontier Groupware by UserLand
- Windows DNA by Microsoft

Accessing Remote Data with SOAP

**20 Min.
To Go**

Let's look at an example of how the SOAP specification allows two applications to operate across firewalls to provide services to one another. We will examine a theoretical Web site, www.soapitup.com, which provides personalized portal pages for its customers. The site runs on a Sun Solaris platform using Java Servlets to support the delivery of customized stock quotes and research to its customers.

Another site, www.stockquoteserver.com, is a service that provides realtime stock quotes, volume and trade data, and other information as a B2B service. This site operates on a Windows 2000-based architecture using an ASP.NET solution to provide its service.

www.soapitup.com would like to access the GetQuote method of the StockQuote Service on the www.stockquoteserver.com site, and then return the results of the service to www.soapitup.com end users.

Prior to the SOAP application this type of communication for anything but the most simplistic of calls would have been extremely difficult and time consuming to develop as the applications are operating on two distinct object models, CORBA and COM.

With SOAP, however, this heterogeneous environment can communicate easily, allowing the Java Servlets to activate the COM objects on www.stockquoteserver.com with ease.

Figure 27-1 illustrates how a www.soapitup.com customer would access the www.soapitup.com Web site and be provided with a stock quote that was retrieved by www.soapitup.com from www.stockquoteserver.com.

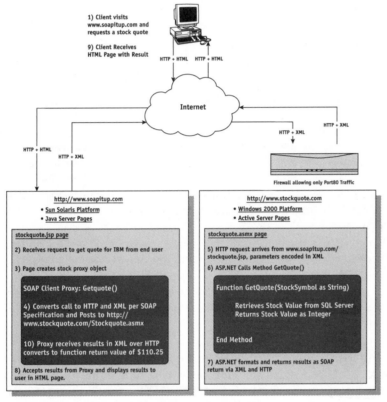

Figure 27-1 *Illustration of SOAP request in heterogeneous environment*

Figure 27-1 illustrates each of the steps that occur in a SOAP Communication. Lets look at each step below:

1. First, a customer opens the stockquote.jsp page on the www.soapitup.com WebWeb site. The user requests a stock quote by entering a stock name and hitting the submit button.

2. Next, the stockquote.jsp page captures the stock symbol from the user.

3. The stockquote.jsp page then invokes a client proxy for the www.stockquote-server.com GetQuote object.

4. This proxy will generate a SOAP client request and encapsulate it in an HTTP POST as follows:

```
POST /StockQuote.asmx HTTP/1.1
Host: www.stockquoteserver.com
Content-Type: text/xml; charset="utf-8"
```

```
Content-Length: nnn
<SOAP-ENV:Envelope>
    <SOAP-ENV:Body>
        <m:GetQuote xmlns:m="Some-Namespace-URI">
                <symbol>IBM</symbol>
        </m:GetQuote>
    </SOAP-ENV:Body>
</SOAP-ENV:Envelope>
```

The first four lines are standard HTTP, indicating a posting of the content to http://www.stockquoteserver.com/StockQuote.asmx. The content type is defined as text/xml, which lets the server know that the payload is going to be sent as an XML message.

SOAP defines two types of messages, Call and Response, in order to allow clients to invoke a remote procedure and allow the called procedure on the server to respond with appropriate values.

The Call example above defines the envelope and body in a standard XML structure that clearly indicates we are accessing the GetQuote method and passing the value IBM as the parameter.

5. Because this request is a standard HTTP POST that embeds XML, there are no issues passing this request across the firewall protecting the www.stockquoteserver.com site.

6. Once the stockquote.asmx page receives the request, it can quickly decipher the XML structure of the request and call the GetQuote method and pass the value IBM as the parameter.

Because the SOAP specification doesn't describe how the provider service should call its respective methods, the only constraint on the provider's choice of language or operating system is that it support the SOAP wire protocol.

7. Once the value is retrieved, a SOAP response message is created as follows:

```
HTTP/1.1 200 OK
Content-Type: text/xml; charset="utf-8"
Content-Length: nnnn
<SOAP-ENV:Envelope>
    <SOAP-ENV:Body>
        <m:GetQuoteResponse xmlns:m="Some-Namespace-URI">
                <result>110</result>
        </m:GetQuoteResponse>
    </SOAP-ENV:Body>
</SOAP-ENV:Envelope>
```

8. The proxy called on the www.soapitup.com/stockquote.jsp page now can accept the SOAP response packet above and pass the results back to the calling function.

9. The user then receives the HTML page formatted by the stockquote.jsp page.

SOAP Discovery (DISCO)

**10 Min.
To Go**

The SOAP discovery specification allows a consumer or client to automatically determine what services and methods a Web Service provides. Through SOAP discovery, the provider can report this information to the application consumer so that a dialogue can be established. Discovery of Web Services (DISCO) is a specification that defines a document format based on XML and a protocol for getting the discovery document through a known URL. Through DISCO, a developer can explore the published services available at a specific URL. In effect, it allows potential client applications of your Web Service to shop around and explore what is available.

Web Service Description Language (WSDL)

The Services Description Language provides developers of Web Service client applications the detailed information needed to create proxies for accessing the Web service. The WSDL will describe the public functions provided by the Web Service, the required and optional parameters, the ordering of those parameters, as well as the data types. The WSDL also will specify the format, type, and structure of the returned data so that the consumer can appropriately handle the response.

Let's look at a portion of the WSDL for the StockQuote Service that describes those requests submitted via a HTTP POST request:

```
...
<httppost xmlns="urn:schemas-xmlsoap-org:post-sdl-2000-01-25">
  <service>
    <requestResponse name="GetQuote"
href="http://www.stockquoteserver.com/StockQuote.asmx/GetQuote">
      <request>
        <form>
          <input name="Symbol"/>
        </form>
      </request>
      <response>
        <mimeXml ref="s0:double"/>
      </response>
    </requestResponse>
  </service>
</httppost>
...
```

In this example the <request> tags enclose a description of the input parameter <symbol> and the <response> tags enclose the format of the response that can be expected from this service, in this case a value type of double. There is little else required by a consumer of this service in order to begin using the provider.

Using SOAP with ASP.NET

SOAP is the standard wire transmission protocol used when building Web Services with ASP.NET. This provides you as a developer the ability to ignore the details of implementing the specific XML code required to provide the required requests. Additionally, ASP.NET provides built-in facilities for exposing the WSDL of a document by simply appending an ?WSDL to the end of any *.asmx file.

In Session 28, we will examine ASP.NET Web Services in detail so that you can better understand how ASP.NET utilizes these published open standards to implement a distributed computing environment.

Done!

REVIEW

By using the power of the SOAP specification, you can easily build distributed applications that have the capability to marshal other resources regardless of location, platform, or programming language. Exposing public methods on your business objects in such a manner greatly enhances reusability, scalability, and integration effectiveness with other applications.

QUIZ YOURSELF

1. If you wanted to find the format of return values supported by a Web Service that was published by a provider what would you refer to? (See "Web Service Description Language (WSDL).")

2. What existing standards and protocols are used in the SOAP specification? (See "Introducing SOAP.")

3. What two types of messages are supported by the SOAP specification? (See "Accessing Remote Data with SOAP.")

Web Services

**30 Min.
To Go**

The Internet is currently comprised of an enormous number of heterogeneous entities: servers, operating systems, databases, and so on. Diversity in and of itself isn't bad, but when it comes to communication between these heterogeneous entities, diversity can be a problem.

One way to solve these problems is to develop a set of standards that everyone can use to communicate. However, when everyone is attached to their own personal set of standards or protocols, agreeing upon a universal standard becomes nearly impossible. So, what to do? Well, you take "something" (or "somethings") that everyone uses, combine them, and turn them into a standard. These "somethings" are HTTP and XML. HTTP, Hypertext Transfer Protocol, is the protocol that essentially all Web browsers and servers use to request and serve Web pages, respectively. XML, Extensible Markup Language, is a cross-platform method for encoding information transferred over HTTP.

Microsoft has, in the .NET Framework, rolled HTTP and XML into something it calls Web Services. A *Web Service* is a seamless way for objects on a server to accept incoming requests from a client via HTTP and return an XML-based response. Because Web Services are built on HTTP and XML, they can be used by practically everyone on the Internet. In this session, we will demonstrate how to build a Web Service and how to discover and use someone else's Web Service.

Developing a Web Service

In this example, you will write a Web Service that exposes the data in the Music database, which you have used periodically throughout this book.

You can use any text editor or Visual Studio to build a Web Service. Although the process is simplified tremendously by using Visual Studio, we will use good ol' Notepad to write our Music Web Service, because we know just about everyone has access to Notepad.

Unlike ASP.NET pages, which have a file extension of .aspx, Web Services have a file extension of .asmx. So, the first thing you need to do is create a file named music.asmx.

Now open the music.asmx file and start it off with the following line of code:

```
<%@ WebService Language="VB" class="Music" %>
```

This line of code defines your file as a Web Service and indicates that you will be using VB.NET to write the service. The class attribute represents the class that the Web Service will expose.

The next thing you need to do, as with an ASP.NET page, is import the namespaces necessary to implement your Web Service. Because you'll be accessing the Music database you built in Session 4 with SQL Server, we'll need to import the System.Data and System.Data.SqlClient namespaces. Additionally, when writing a Web Service you need to import the System.Web.Services namespace. Add the following Imports statements to the music.asmx file:

```
Imports System
Imports System.Web.Services
Imports System.Data
Imports System.Data.SqlClient
```

Now that you have imported the appropriate namespaces and thereby have access to the classes necessary for your implementation, you need to declare your class, Music. To define a VB.NET class, we use the following structure:

```
Class [Class Name]
    ' Properties and Methods go here
End Class
```

So our Music class declaration will look like this:

```
Class Music
    ' Properties and Method go here
End Class
```

Since we are using a Web Service-enabled class, the class should be derived from the Web Service class. In order to accomplish this, our class declaration should be modified as follows:

```
Class Music Inherits : WebService
    ' Properties and Method go here
End Class
```

Deriving your class from the `WebService` **class is optional, but we recommend that you do so to improve readability.**

**20 Min.
To Go**

Your Web Service has to actually do something, so you need to add a method to the `Music` class. Your method, call it `GetBandInfo` for now, will simply return a DataSet containing two DataTables, one with a band's members and one with a band's albums when passed the band's name as a parameter. To add a public method to a class, use the following VB.NET syntax:

```
Public Function [Function Name]([Parameter Name] As [Data Type], . . .])
    ' Implementation Code
End Function
```

In order to make a method callable via a Web Service you need to add the `<WebMethod()>` attribute to your function definition. So, your `GetBandInfo` method will look like this before you add implementation code:

```
<WebMethod()> Public Function GetBandInfo(sBandName As String) As DataSet
    ' Implementation code
End Function
```

Listing 28-1 shows the complete code for the `Music` class.

Listing 28-1   *A Music class example*

```
<%@ WebService Language="VB" class="Music" %>
Imports System
Imports System.Web.Services
Imports System.Data
Imports System.Data.SqlClient

Class Music : Inherits WebService
  <WebMethod()> Public Function GetBandInfo(sBandName As String) As
DataSet
    Dim oConn As SqlConnection
    Dim oCmd As SqlCommand
    Dim oDA As SqlDataAdapter
    Dim oParam As SqlParameter
    Dim oDataSet As New DataSet

    oConn = New SqlConnection
    With oConn
      .ConnectionString = "Data Source=jbutler014a; Initial Catalog=Music;
User ID=music; Password=music"
      .Open
    End With

    oParam = New SqlParameter("@sBandName", SqlDbType.VarChar, 100)
```

Continued

Listing 28-1 *Continued*

```
        oParam.Value  = sBandName

        oCmd = New SqlCommand
        With oCmd
          .CommandType = CommandType.StoredProcedure
          .CommandText = "prAlbumInfo"
          .Parameters.Add(oParam)
          .Connection = oConn
        End With

        oDA = New SqlDataAdapter
        With oDA
          .SelectCommand = oCmd
          .Fill(oDataSet, "Albums")
        End With

        oCmd.CommandText = "prMemberInfo"
        oDA.Fill(oDataSet, "Members")

        oDA.Dispose
        oDA = Nothing
        oCmd = Nothing
        oConn.Dispose
        oConn = Nothing

        return oDataSet
    End Function
End Class
```

At this point, you should understand all of the implementation code. What you've done here is add two tables to the DataSet your Web Service will return.

And that's it! You have successfully written your first Web Service. Now you must deploy the Web Service. Deploying a Web Service is very simple. If you have your own Web server, create a virtual directory named "Music" and then copy the music.asmx file into this directory. That's it! To call the Web Service, in your Web browser, simply type in the path to the Web Service. If you actually created the Music virtual directory, the path would look like this:

```
http://localhost/Music/music.asmx
```

Figure 28-1 shows the response you should get from the Web Service.

Music WebService

No additional reference information about the Music web service is available at this time.

The Music WebService exposes the following web methods:

- GetBandInfo

For a formal XML definition of the Music WebService, please review its: SDL Contract.

Web Method Reference

GetBandInfo Web Method

No additional reference information about the GetBandInfo web method is available at this time.

Request parameters:
- sBandName

Response type:
- DataSet

Invoke the GetBandInfo Web Method:

Enter parameter values and then click the 'Invoke' button to invoke the GetBandInfo web method.

Parameter	Value
sBandName:	

Invoke

Figure 28-1   *music.asmx response*

The Music Web Service's response represented in Figure 28-1 is automatically generated by the Web Services runtime. You'll notice that this response contains several valuable pieces of information including the name of the Web Service, the methods implemented by the Web Service, the required parameters, the return data type and the protocols (such as SOAP, HTTP GET, or HTTP POST) you can use to invoke the Web Service's methods. You are also provided a facility with which to test the Web Service. Type the name of your favorite band in the sBandName textbox and click the Invoke button. A new browser should open for you with the Web Service's XML response to your request. Pretty cool, huh?

Consuming a Web Service

There are basically two ways to use a Web Service. You can either call the Web Service directly from your browser, as you just did, or you can use some application to programmatically call the service. Making a direct browser request is easy, but programmatically accessing a Web Service can be a little more difficult especially if you don't know anything about the particular Web Service you'd like to use. In order to communicate with a Web Service, you need to know what methods it supports, what the input parameters are, and what each method returns. In other words, you need to establish a communication contract with Web Service. So how do you get this information? Luckily, Web Services are able to describe themselves. .NET Web Services automatically produce an XML-formatted Web Service Description Language (WSDL) document that describes the Service. Appending ?WSDL to a Web Service's URL returns an WSDL document that a client application can use to *discover* a Web Service. To obtain the WSDL document for your Music Web Service, use the following URL:

```
http://localhost/music/music.asmx?SDL
```

You should get an XML document in your browser window. This XML-formatted WSDL document is effectively your "communication contract" that describes the Web Service. The WSDL, as you'll see, details the protocols supported by the Web Service — for example, HTTP GET, HTTP POST, or SOAP — as well as the semantics for calling the services and returning values. Here is a small sample of the music.asmx WSDL document:

```
<soap xmlns="urn:schemas-xmlsoap-org:soap-sdl-2000-01-25">
  <service>
    <addresses>
      <address uri="http://localhost/music/music.asmx" />
    </addresses>
    <requestResponse name="GetBandInfo"
soapAction="http://tempuri.org/GetBandInfo">
      <request ref="s0:GetBandInfo" />
      <response ref="s0:GetBandInfoResult" />
    </requestResponse>
  </service>
</soap>
```

This section of the WSDL document defines how SOAP (refer to the first line) calls should be made to the Music Web Service. The WSDL also gives the URI (line 4) to use in order to access the Web Service. Perhaps most importantly, the Music SDL described the method it implements. On line 7, you can see that we can request the GetBand Info method.

OK, so now that you know where the Web Service is located and what method(s) it supports, you're ready to go, right? Well not quite. You now need to build a proxy class through which to access the Web Service from an application, in this case an ASP.NET page.

10 Min. To Go

A *proxy* is essentially a class that behaves like a local object, but it is actually just a mechanism for communicating with the Web Service. The proxy serializes, sends, receives, and deserializes the method requests. (These activities are commonly referred to as marshaling and transport activities.) There are three ways to create a Web Service proxy:

- Using Visual Studio.NET
- Using command line tools
- Using Internet Explorer 5.5 behaviors

Creating a proxy via VS.NET is simple. It's essentially the same as adding a reference to a Visual Basic project. IE behaviors are neat, but they're outside the scope of this book. So, you're going to build a proxy using a command line tool, WSDL.exe. WSDL.exe is a command line utility that creates a stub or proxy class based on a WSDL document. Once you have created your proxy class, you can then compile the proxy class into an assembly and use it to call a Web Service without needing to write any of the aforementioned marshaling or transport logic.

To create a proxy class based on your Music Web Service, go to your computer's command prompt and type the following:

```
WSDL http://localhost/Music/music.asmx?sdl /l:VB /n:myMusic
```

If all went well, you should have received a message that looks like this:

```
.\Music.vb
```

The WebServiceUtil utility accepts many different parameters. The /c[ommand]: switch indicates that you want to create a proxy class. The /pa[th]: switch denotes the location of the SDL upon which you want to base your proxy class. The /l[anguage]: switch denotes in which language the proxy class will be created. You can just as easily create a C# proxy class by changing the language switch to /l:CSharp. Finally, the /n[amespace]: switch indicates the namespace to create the code in. The default is the global namespace. We used myMusic for demonstration purposes.

 If you can't find the proxy class Music.vb, **it was created in the directory from which WSDL.exe was executed. This is the default behavior. You could have specified a physical path in which to create the proxy using the** /o[ut]: **switch. For example,** /o:C:\.

Now that you have the proxy class, let's compile it into an assembly. If you haven't already done so, create a physical directory named bin in your Music virtual directory's physical path. OK, now run the following command:

```
vbc /out:bin\Music.dll /t:library /r:System.dll /r:System.Xml.dll
/r:System.Web.Services.dll /r:System.Data.dll music.vb
```

This command simply creates an assembly, music.dll, based on the Music.vb proxy class and puts it in our /bin directory. The /r[eference]: switch tells the compiler to include a specified assembly. When compiling a Web Service, you must always include System.XML.dll and System.Web.Services.dll. The System.Data.dll is included because you used ADO.NET in the Music Web Service.

That's it! You're done. Now that the music.dll component has been deployed to your /bin directory, you can call the Music Web Service from an ASP.NET page. Here's an example:

```
<%@ Page Language="VB" debug="true" %>
<%@ Import Namespace="System.Data" %>
<script language="VB" runat="server">
Sub Page_Load(Sender As Object, E As EventArgs)
  Dim oDS As DataSet
  Dim wsMusic As New myMusic.Music

  oDS = wsMusic.GetBandInfo("Hootie & The Blowfish")

  dgMembers.DataSource = oDS.Tables(0).DefaultView
  dgMembers.DataBind
End Sub
</script>
<html>
<body>
<asp:DataGrid id="dgMembers" BorderWidth="1" GridLines="both"
runat="server"/>
</body>
</html>
```

This is a simple example, but you get the point. You'll notice that when you declared the variable wsMusic, you used the following line of code:

```
Dim wsMusic As New myMusic.Music
```

In this line, you are creating a new object based on the `Music` class in the `myMusic` namespace. If you hadn't specified `myMusic` as the namespace in which to create the `Music` proxy class when you executed the WebServiceUtil utility, but rather used the default, you could write:

```
Dim wsMusic As Music
```

Once you create the `wsMusic` object, you can call its methods. In the following line of code, you call the `GetBandInfo` method and pass it a string, `Hootie & The Blowfish`:

```
oDS = wsMusic.GetBandInfo("Hootie & The Blowfish")
```

Because we know the method returns a DataSet, we bound its first table to a `DataGrid` control, dgMembers.

Done!

REVIEW

Web Services are an exciting piece of the .NET Framework that, with the help of XML and HTTP, enable you to easily encapsulate your business logic in .NET components and provide a service to any Web clients that speak HTTP and XML. An XML-based WSDL file, which is generated by the Web Service's infrastructure, provides a machine-readable description of the functionality available through the Web Service.

QUIZ YOURSELF

1. What is Web Service? (See session introduction.)
2. On which two Internet protocols are Web Services based? (See session introduction.)
3. What methods can be used to access a Web Service? (See "Consuming a Web Service.")

Migrating from ASP to ASP.NET

Session Checklist

✔ Understanding the major changes in syntax and function for ASP.NET

✔ Identifying major areas of risk in migrating your applications

✔ Understanding how ASP and ASP.NET can coexist

This session provides an overview of the challenges you will face as you migrate your applications from ASP to ASP.NET.

**30 Min.
To Go**

ASP and ASP.NET Compatibility

After installing the .NET Framework in your existing ASP environment, you will find that you are able to continue running your ASP pages without modification. Additionally, as you begin to write your own ASP.NET pages you will find that they operate nicely side by side with your existing ASP pages. However, as you begin to migrate code from your ASP pages to ASP.NET you will find that there are at least four major areas of differences in how you coded in ASP versus how you will code in ASP.NET:

- You can only script in one language per page or user control.
- Page rendering your content through function calls is no longer supported.
- You must define your functions as script blocks.
- There are syntax differences and language modifications.

Scripting language limitations

When creating ASP pages, developers will commonly use VBScript, JScript, PerlScript, or even Python. While the use of scripting languages is fine given their ease of use, they do have several disadvantages over compilable languages such as C#, VB .NET, or C++. The primary disadvantage is performance. Every time an ASP page is requested, the page is interpreted by the relevant scripting engine and cached to increase performance. This is done through an in-memory cache, so at any time only a relatively small number of ASP pages can be effectively cached. The second major disadvantage is that scripting languages are often designed for accomplishing procedurally oriented tasks in a quick and effective manner. This often means that they lack the full functionality and extensibility that a C# or VB .NET language would support.

In ASP.NET, pages are generated with languages such as VB .NET, C++, and C#. ASP.NET is not limited to these languages, however, as ASP.NET pages can be created with any compiler that can generate .NET Common Language Runtime (CLR)-compliant code. Additionally once this code is compiled, regardless of the language, it is stored as Microsoft Intermediate Language (MSIL) in the form of an executable (.exe) or dynamic-link library (.dll) file. When the code is executed on a client system, it undergoes a final round of Just In Time (JIT) compilation to transform it into machine-specific instructions. Theoretically, this means that there are no performance differences between language selections in terms of final delivered performance! Code written for the .NET platform runs under the control of the CLR. Language selection under ASP.NET is thus a lifestyle choice rather than a decision based upon expected performance, integration with the API, or other factors. All languages have access to and support the same base set of classes and functionality, and all execute to the same performance standards.

 The CLR has been designed to replace the existing runtime layers of COM, Microsoft Transaction Services (MTS), and COM+.

In ASP, you could readily mingle VBScript- and JScript-coded functions in the same page. In ASP.NET, VBScript has been replaced by VB .NET, which provides a range of syntax modifications that you will need to address. Although JScript is still supported, most JScript developers will prefer to use C#. So, from a core code migration perspective, you should examine any of your existing ASP pages that incorporate more than one language on the server side.

 While you can no longer mix languages on the server side, you can include a client-side scripting language that is interpreted by the client browser and is different from what is used on the server side. For instance, you could have all of your business logic written in VB .NET and compiled on the server side, and have client-side code written in JavaScript.

Rendering HTML page elements

In order to manipulate the display properties of an HTML control in ASP, you would inter-mingle scripting values with the HTML of the control to modify font sizes, colors, and other properties of the HTML element — the final code would then be rendered appropriately and sent to the end user's browser. In ASP.NET, although you can render directly to the browser, you should focus instead on using object-oriented techniques to modify the property values and execute the methods of the ASP.NET server controls.

Listing 29-1 shows an example of an ASP page written to display a textbox with a black background, gray text, 20pt font, and a defined text value.

Listing 29-1 *Using ASP to render an HTML control*

```
<%@Language = "VBScript"%>
<%
Sub DisplayTextBox(forecolor, backcolor, value, fontsize)
    Response.Write("<input type='text' name='txtDisplay' value='" & value & "'")
    Response.Write("style=color:" & forecolor & ";background-color:"& backcolor &
";font-size:" &
        fontsize & "pt;>")
    Response.Write("</textbox>")
End Sub
%>
<HTML>
    <BODY>
        <%DisplayTextBox "gray","black", "Hello World","20" %>
    </BODY>
</HTML>
```

The `DisplayTextBox` function is called after the `<body>` tag has been rendered, and the subroutine accepts the `forecolor`, `backcolor`, `value`, and `fontsize` attributes passed in the function call. The `DisplayTextBox` then effectively generates a series of strings that are subsequently rendered in the browser.

In ASP.NET, you will need to establish script blocks, and implement structured functions, which can then manipulate the control directly through the control's inherent properties and methods. This is illustrated in Listing 29-2.

Listing 29-2 *Using ASP.NET to render an HTML control*

```
<HTML>
    <%@ Page Language="VB" Debug="False" Trace="False" %>
    <HEAD>
        <SCRIPT LANGUAGE="vb" RUNAT="server">
        Sub Page_Load(sender as Object, e as EventArgs)
            Dim oColor as System.Drawing.Color
            UpdateTextBox(oColor.gray,oColor.black,"Hello World", 20)
        End Sub

        Function UpdateTextBox(forecolor, backcolor, value, fontsize)
            Dim oColor as System.Drawing.Color
```

Continued

Listing 29-2 *Continued*

```
            txtDisplay.Text = value
            txtDisplay.ForeColor = forecolor
            txtDisplay.BackColor = backcolor
            txtDisplay.Font.Size = FontUnit.Point(fontsize)
        End Function

        </SCRIPT>
    </HEAD>
    <BODY>
        <FORM RUNAT="server" ID="Form1">
            <ASP:TEXTBOX ID="txtDisplay" RUNAT="server" />
        </FORM>
    </BODY>
</HTML>
```

In this example, the `UpdateTextBox` function is called each time the page is rendered and passes the requisite parameters similar to what occurred in the ASP example. The `UpdateTextBox` function, however, operates very differently — instead of the developer modifying the output stream rendered in the browser directly, the developer works with the properties and methods of the TextBox to obtain the desired results.

In both the ASP and the ASP.NET examples, the formatted output and the rendered HTML are nearly identical, both generating a similar looking HTML 3.2-compliant rendered output.

```
<input name="txtDisplay" type="text" value="Hello World" id="txtDisplay"
style="color:Gray;background-color:Black;font-size:20pt;" />
```

Using script blocks

In ASP.NET, there is a radical shift away from supporting the unstructured, interpreted script code that was typically written in procedural terms. In ASP, during each page execution, the code begins processing the first line of code and then works its way down. This encouraged ASP developers to intermingle HTML code with the scripting logic to produce a mess of spaghetti code without good separation of logic and presentation layers.

The impact of the move to script blocks means that the code segment shown in Listing 29-3 will no longer work.

Listing 29-3 *Mixing VBScript and HTML in ASP*

```
<%@Language = "VBScript"%>
<HTML>
    <HEAD>
        <%Function CreateTable()%>
        <TABLE>
            <%For x = 1 to 10%>
            <TR>
                <TD>
                    <%Response.Write "Cell Number" & x%>
                </TD>
```

```
        </TR>
        <%Next%>
    </TABLE>
    <%End Function%>
    </HEAD>
    <BODY>
        <%=CreateTable()%>
    </BODY>
</HTML>
```

Instead, the code must be moved to a consolidated script block as shown in Listing 29-4, and Response.Write statements must be used to properly display the table.

Listing 29-4   *Using script blocks in ASP.NET*

```
<%@ Page Language="VB" Debug="False" Trace="False" %>
<HTML>
    <HEAD>
        <SCRIPT LANGUAGE="vb" RUNAT="Server">
        Function CreateTable()
        Dim x as Integer
        Response.Write("<table>")
        For x = 1 to 10
            Response.Write("<tr>")
            Response.Write("<td>")
            Response.Write("Cell Number" & x)
            Response.Write("</td>")
            Response.Write("</tr>")
        Next
        Response.Write("</table>")
        End Function
        </SCRIPT>
    </HEAD>
    <BODY>
        <%=CreateTable()%>
    </BODY>
</HTML>
```

If you have not used script block based rendering using Response.Write() statements in your existing ASP applications, you will be in for some long nights migrating your application logic to ASP.NET. In fact, you will probably want to go ahead and perform a redesign, rather than simply performing a line-by-line conversion.

Syntax differences and language modifications

There are a ton of syntax modifications — mostly attached to the switch in supported languages — that you will need to become familiar with in ASP.NET. For the majority of you who have been coding primarily in VBScript, you will need to ramp up on the syntax differences in VB .NET.

**10 Min.
To Go**

For a full listing of syntax changes that you will need to understand when using VB .NET in ASP.NET be sure to reference `http://msdn.microsoft.com/vbasic/technical/upgrade/language.asp`.

Enclosing function/subroutine calls in parentheses

In the previous examples, we illustrated how in ASP you can call functions or subroutines without using parentheses to encase the passed parameters. In VB .NET, you must encase all parameters in parentheses.

Strongly typed variables

ASP supported variant-oriented languages, meaning that you must declare objects as Variants and then at runtime assign them to objects, integers or any other data type desired. Since you now are using compiled languages, you must declare variables as a specific type and then convert them as needed. Table 29-1 shows some of the differences in variable declaration.

Table 29-1   *Declaring Variables*

VBScript in ASP	VB .NET in ASP.NET
Dim i	Dim i As Integer
Dim s	Dim s As String
Dim s1,s2	Dim s1, s2 As String
Dim o	
Set o = CreateObject("")	Dim o As New Object()

Error handling

Using VB .NET or C#, you have access to the power of the `Try...Catch...Finally` statement to handle your errors. This provides significantly more control than is available using VBScript under ASP. Table 29-2 illustrates how errors are handled in VBScript and how they are handled in VB .NET.

Table 29-2   *Handling Errors*

VBScript in ASP	VB .NET in ASP.NET
Function WriteFile()	Function WriteFile()
On Error Resume Next	Try

VBScript in ASP	VB .NET in ASP.NET
'Do Something	'Do Something
'Raise a Fake Error	'Raise a Fake Error
Err.Raise(1000)	Err.Raise(1000)
if Err.Number=0 Then	Catch
WriteFile="No Errors"	Return "Error Number " & Err.Number &" was raised."
Else	
WriteFile= Err.Number & " was raised."	
End If	End Try
End Function	End Function

No more set

In VBScript, you often declare a variable as an object, then use the Set statement to assign it to an instance of a COM object. Neither the use of Set in this fashion nor the use of Let statements are supported in VB .NET.

Arguments are now passed ByVal as default

A subtle change that is going to cause a lot of headaches for you is that most parameters are passed by value as the default. This is the exact opposite of VB6. For example, take a procedure such as:

```
Function add(A As Int, B As Int)
    A=A+B
    Return A
End Function
```

When you use it in VB .NET as add(C, D) you will discover that neither of the input variables C or D is modified by the procedure.

Running ASP Pages under Microsoft.NET

As we mentioned earlier, you can operate your ASP pages side by side with your ASP.NET pages. You should consider several other factors when operating a portion of your application in ASP and the other portion on ASP.NET:

- Session variables are not natively shared between ASP and ASP.NET pages.
- You will not have access to the ADO.NET components from ASP.

- You should maintain your security framework in ASP.
- Avoid mixing ASP and ASP.NET if you are building .NET applications for distribution.

Assuming that you are not making extensive use of session variables and are not planning on redistributing the application, then mixing your ASP and ASP.NET pages should be fairly straightforward.

Using VB6 Components with ASP.NET

In the next session, we will examine how you can use VB6 components — or for that matter any unmanaged code — in your ASP.NET applications. Additionally we will show how you can use these components via early binding using the TlbImp.exe utility.

The type library importer utility (TlbImp.exe) is responsible for converting the type definitions found within a COM type library into equivalent definition in .NET runtime metadata format. A detailed documentation of the utility can be found in the .NET documentation.

Done!

REVIEW

We have covered at a high level the major differences in ASP and ASP.NET. Overall you probably have the feeling that there is quite a bit of rework to perform in order to successfully migrate to ASP.NET. We hope, however, that you do appreciate the significant benefits that can be obtained through this migration effort.

QUIZ YOURSELF

1. How is the rendering of HTML objects handled in ASP.NET? (See "Rendering HTML page elements.")
2. What is a script block? (See "Using script blocks.")
3. Can you early bind VB6 components in ASP.NET? (See "Using VB6 Components with ASP.NET.")

Migrating from ADO to ADO.NET

Session Checklist

✔ Modifying code to run ADO under ASP.NET

✔ Early binding ADO COM objects in ASP.NET

✔ Understanding performance issues of using ADO under the .NET Framework

**30 Min.
To Go**

I n this session, we look at what is required to begin the migration of your existing ADO
code to the .NET Framework. These options range from straight code migration to
employing early binding to full migration of your ADO business objects to ADO.NET.

Preparing a Migration Path

ADO.NET is a very different animal from ADO. Migrating to ADO.NET from ADO is not a path
well traveled at this point, nor is it one that should be taken lightly. But ADO.NET is a critical piece of the ASP.NET Framework; and, like ADO itself, ADO.NET is likely to become a
common data access footprint. If you are choosing the ASP.NET platform as your development platform, then you should plan on adopting ADO.NET to support your data handling
code.

Because the ADO.NET platform is significantly different from the ADO solution, do not
underestimate the time required to perform a migration. Unlike ASP code, which can be
ported to ASP.NET with relatively few modifications, ADO.NET provides no such luxury. In
fact, it is possible that you will first begin your migration to ASP.NET by migrating your ASP
VBScript or JScript to ASP.NET and continuing to run your ADO code as is. So, yes, it is possible to execute your ADO code in an ASP.NET page, with some limitations.

When you are comfortable operating in the .NET Framework, then you should begin the
process of looking at how to transform your ADO code to ADO.NET. A few things should
guide your thinking when preparing for this task:

- Forget about how your ADO code operates and remove any preconceptions about how it should translate into ADO.NET.

- Go back to the design of your data access components and begin mapping the design to the new ADO.NET model. Look at the features provided and determine if the cost in relation to the benefit is worth the migration.

- As you migrate data tier objects, focus first on those objects providing the lowest risk and highest benefit. Because you can operate ASP and ASP.NET as well as ADO and ADO.NET in the same environment, you don't have to force yourself into a big bang migration step. Instead, you can make the migration incrementally.

In the next sections, we look at how you can migrate your ADO code to the ASP.NET Framework.

ADO and ADO.NET Compatibility

We have covered much of the new functionality offered in the ADO.NET object model and its advantages and disadvantages in the .NET Framework. Table 30-1 offers a useful summary of some of the essential compatibility differences that you should be aware of when attempting to decide when and how you will begin the migration of your ADO code to ADO.NET. The table provides a description of the key differences in major features of the two data access frameworks to help guide your thinking when deciding what to upgrade.

Table 30-1   *Comparing Features of ADO and ADO.NET*

Feature	ADO	ADO.NET
Data storage and presentation	Uses the RecordSet object, which may contain multiple result sets to store the results for multiple tables	DataSet object may consist of collections of one or more Database Tables, Relationships, and Constraints that form a memory-resident database
Relationships between multiple tables	Supports the use of the SHAPE provider to build hierarchical RecordSet, or requires the use of a JOIN query to create a view from multiple database tables in a single result table	Supports the DataRelation object to associate rows in one DataTable object with rows in another DataTable object
Access to individual rows of a data set	Scans rows sequentially	Uses a navigation approach for nonsequential access to each row in a table. Has the capability to follow hierarchical relationships to navigate from rows in one table to related rows in another table

Feature	ADO	ADO.NET
Support for server-side cursors	Provided by the `RecordSet` object through setting the `Connection` Object	Supported for forward-only execution via the `DataReader`. `DataReader` can also execute SQL commands directly and handle the return of data rows
Support for Disconnected Data Access	Supported in the `RecordSet` object but typically supports connected access, represented by the `Connection` object. Communication to a database occurs through the OLE DB provider	The `DataSet` object supports disconnected data access by storing data in XML
Support for passing data between providers and consumers, tiers or components	By default uses COM marshaling to transmit a disconnected record set, effectively limiting this capability to COM environments. Limited capability to store data as an XML file and then use manual programmatic tasks to transport to non COM oriented consumers	All transports occur with an XML file, and provide ability to transport schemas via XSD
Support for transferring data across firewalls.	Not natively supported in the RecordSet object. Transport can occur through the use of COM Internet Services (CIS) plus Distributed Component Object Model (DCOM), Remote Data Services (RDS), use of the SOAP Toolkit or remote scripting, all of which provide their own complications in terms of requirements on the consumer side of the transaction or complexity of support on the server side	Fully supported with WebServices leveraging SOAP and XML as the envelope and HTTP as the transport

Continued

Table 30-1 *Continued*

Feature	ADO	ADO.NET
Scalability	ADO typically incurs extensive database locks that, when combined with lengthy active database connections, tend to compete for limited database resources and thus limit scalability	ADO.NET supports disconnected access to database data, thus removing much of the competition for limited database resources and providing a much more scalable solution

Running ADO under ASP.NET

*20 Min.
To Go*

Here's an example illustrating the various methods that can be used to run your existing ADO code in the .NET Framework. First let's look at a typical ASP page that retrieves a list of authors from the Pubs database using ASP and ADO, shown in Listing 30-1.

Listing 30-1 *A typical ASP page for retrieving data from a database*

```
<%@ LANGUAGE = "VBSCRIPT" %>
<HTML>
    <BODY>
        <%
    DIM oConn, oRS
    Set oConn = Server.CreateObject("ADODB.Connection")
    Set oRS = Server.CreateObject("ADODB.RecordSet")
    oConn.Open "provider=sqloledb;Data Source=(local);Initial Catalog=pubs;User
ID=sa;pwd="
    Set oRS = oConn.execute("SELECT * FROM Authors;")
    Response.Write("<H1>ADO Running Under ASP</H1>")
    Response.Write("<H2>Using Late Binding</H2>")
    if oRS.BOF and oRS.EOF then
       Response.Write("No Records")
    else
       oRS.MoveFirst
       Do While Not oRS.EOF
          Response.Write(oRS("au_fname") _
             & " " & oRS("au_lname") & "<br>")
          oRS.MoveNext
       Loop
       Response.Write("<p>End of RecordSet</p>")
    end if
    oRS.close
    Set oRS = nothing
%>
    </BODY>
</HTML>
```

This code will not run as it is under ASP.NET, primarily due to syntax differences in the languages. To test this, change the file extension of the previous code from *.asp to *.aspx and see what error messages are displayed. In order to migrate this code to the .NET Framework using VB as the programming language, you would need to eliminate the Set statement from your code. Next, you need to fully qualify your object references, so in Listing 30-1 you must append a .value to each of your RecordSet value references. You must enclose your method parameters in parentheses, and you must set the page directive ASPCOMPAT="True". Listing 30-2 shows the required modifications (shown in bold) made to Listing 30-1 to make the ASP code using ADO operational under ASP.NET.

Listing 30-2   *A migrated ASP page that runs under ASP.NET using unmanaged ADO code*

```
<%@ LANGUAGE = "VB" ASPCOMPAT="True"%>
<HTML>
    <BODY>
        <%
    DIM oConn, oRS
    'We removed Set statement
    oConn = Server.CreateObject("ADODB.Connection")
    'We removed Set statement
    oRS = Server.CreateObject("ADODB.RecordSet")
    'We Added Parentheses
    oConn.Open("provider=sqloledb;Data Source=(local);Initial Catalog=pubs;User
ID=sa;pwd=")
    'We Removed Set statement
    oRS = oConn.execute("SELECT * FROM Authors;")
    Response.Write("<H1>ADO Running Under ASP.NET</H1>")
    Response.Write("<H2>Using Late Binding</H2>")
    if oRS.BOF and oRS.EOF then
       Response.Write("No Records")
    else
       oRS.MoveFirst
       Do While Not oRS.EOF
          ' Added .Value
          Response.Write(oRS("au_fname").Value _
             & " " & oRS("au_lname").Value & "<br>")
          oRS.MoveNext
       Loop
       Response.Write("<p>End of RecordSet</p>")
    end if
    oRS.close
    'Removed the Set statement
    oRS = nothing %>
    </BODY>
</HTML>
```

This approach enables you to migrate much of your existing ADO code to ASP.NET by simply handling the syntax differences between VBScript and VB .NET.

However, this approach requires that you utilize late binding. When handling COM objects under the .NET Framework, early binding is the preferred method. Early binding allows your application to bind directly to the address of the function being called and thus avoids the extra overhead in doing a runtime lookup. This generally provides a twofold performance increase over late binding in terms of execution speed. Additionally early binding provides you with type safety. Early binding also provides compile time warnings if the data type of a parameter or return value is incorrect, saving a lot of time when writing and debugging code.

 For details on the advantages of early versus late binding refer to Microsoft Knowledge Base Article ID: Q245115, "Using Early Binding and Late Binding in Automation."

We can perform early binding of ADO COM objects through the use of a .NET Framework utility called Tlbimp.exe. We cover this in the following section.

Early Binding ADO COM Objects in ASP.NET

The .NET Framework introduces two new classifications for object activation:

- Managed objects
- Unmanaged objects

Managed objects are objects created with .NET-compliant compilers such as C# and VB .NET. *Unmanaged objects* are the current generation of COM objects including the ADO objects. Managed objects take full advantage of the .NET Framework. For instance, managed objects can be changed without unloading the DLL. Managed objects don't need to be registered using regsvr32; you can simply copy them from system to system without the headaches associated with DLL hell.

When you are using a managed object, it's simple to make that object available within your application. All you have to do is import the objects into your code using the @ Import page directive:

```
<%@ Import namespace="Myobject">
```

To activate the object with VB you instantiate the object as follows.

```
Dim thisObject as New MyObject()
```

Working with unmanaged objects is slightly more complicated, as the .NET Framework cannot just access the object as it normally would with managed code objects. In order to use unmanaged objects such as ADO, you need to use Runtime Callable Wrappers (RCW). RCW act as a proxy for the unmanaged object. These wrappers work just like any other managed class in the .NET runtime client, but they just marshal calls between managed and unmanaged code.

 In order to use this approach and support early binding of ADO COM objects in an *.aspx page you will need to do the following:

**10 Min.
To Go**

1. Create the RCW for the ADO object, in this case **msado15.dll**.
2. Add the managed wrapper of the object to the bin directory.
3. Use the object as a normal managed code object.

The type library importer utility (TlbImp.exe) is responsible for converting the type definitions found within a COM type library into equivalent definitions in the .NET runtime metadata format. (A full detailed documentation of the utility can be found in the .NET documentation.) In order to use this utility so that you can incorporate your ADO library elements for use in your ASP.NET pages you have to do the following:

1. Locate the ADO objects, typically located at C:\Program Files\Common Files\ system\ado\msado15.dll.

2. Locate the TlbImp.exe file, typically located at C:\Program Files\Microsoft.Net\FrameworkSDK\Bin.

3. Run the TlbImp.Exe import utility as follows:

```
[Insert Path]\TlbImp [Insert Path]\msado15.dll /out: [Destination
Path]\ADODB.dll
```

This will create a DLL named ADODB.dll with the RCW wrapper for use in your .NET applications. Now that the wrapper is created, the next thing to do is to copy the ADODB.dll to the bin directory of your ASP.NET application. If you do not have a bin directory, you should create one under your application root.

Once the previous steps are carried out, instantiating the object is the same as using any normal managed object. You set up the namespace and the assembly to reflect the ADODB.dll we created earlier.

```
<%@ Import Namespace="ADODB"%>
<%@ Assembly Name = "ADODB"%>
<%@ Page Language="VB"%>
```

Then you can just access the ADO COM object as you would any managed COM component and get the benefits associated with early binding as illustrated in Listing 30-3.

Listing 30-3 *Accessing an ADO.COM object with early binding*

```
<%@ Import Namespace="ADODB"%>
<%@ Assembly Name = "ADODB"%>
<%@ Page Language="VB"%>
<HTML>
<HEAD>
   <TITLE>ADO Access from ASP.NET with Early Binding</TITLE>
</HEAD>

<BODY>
<%
   DIM oConn as New ADODB.Connection
   DIM oRS as New ADODB.RecordSet
   DIM oCmd as New ADODB.Command

   oConn.Open ("provider=sqloledb;Data Source=(local);Initial Catalog=pubs;User
ID=sa;pwd=")

   oRS.CursorType=ADODB.CursorTypeEnum.adOpenKeyset
```

Continued

Listing 30-3   *Continued*

```
oRS.LockType= ADODB.LockTypeEnum.adLockOptimistic
oRS.Open ("Authors",oConn,,, ADODB.CommandTypeEnum.adCmdTable)

If (oRS.BOF OR oRS.EOF) Then
    Response.Write("No records found")
End If

Response.Write("<H2>Using Early Binding</H2>")
if oRS.BOF and oRS.EOF then
        Response.Write("No Records")
    else
        oRS.MoveFirst
        Do While Not oRS.EOF
            Response.Write(oRS("au_fname").Value _
        & " " & oRS("au_lname").Value & "<br>")
    oRS.MoveNext
        Loop
Response.Write("<p>End of RecordSet</p>")
        end if
%>
</BODY>
</HTML>
```

Done!

REVIEW

We covered how to adapt your existing ADO code to operate in ASP.NET, summarized the key differences between the features of ADO and ADO.NET, and discussed how to take advantage of early binding of COM objects. These are some of the major alternatives you should consider when you start migrating code to the .NET Framework.

QUIZ YOURSELF

1. What utility provides the ability to early bind COM objects in the .NET Framework? (See "Early Binding ADO COM Objects in ASP.NET.")

2. What are two major advantages of early binding? (See "Running ADO under ASP.NET.")

3. List two syntax differences between ASP and ASP.NET. (See "Running ADO under ASP.NET.")

Sunday Afternoon Part Review

The following set of questions is designed to provide you with feedback on how well you understood the topics covered during this part of the book. Please refer to Appendix A for the answers to each question.

1. SOAP is a Microsoft proprietary standard.
   True/False

2. SOAP-encapsulated data can freely transport across corporate firewalls.
   True/False

3. List two examples of commercial applications implementing SOAP.

   _____

   _____

4. Which language can support SOAP?
   a. VB
   b. Java
   c. COBOL
   d. All of the above

5. Microsoft's Web Services are based on HTTP and HTML.
   True/False

6. Which of the following file extensions is used for a Web Service?

   a. .aspx

   b. .ascx

   c. .asmx

   d. .ws

7. *Fill in the blank:* The _____ attribute needs to be added to VB method to make it Web-callable.

8. *Fill in the blank:* A _____ document is a "communication contract" that describes a Web Service.

9. In ASP.NET you can combine VB .NET and C# on the same page.
   True/False

10. Theoretically, VB .NET performs less efficiently than C# in ASP.NET.
    True/False

11. The CLR has been designed to replace the existing runtime layers of COM, Microsoft Transaction Services (MTS), and COM+.
    True/False

12. `Set` statements are supported in VB .NET.
    True/False

13. Multiple `DataTable` objects can be stored in one DataSet.
    True/False

14. Late binding provides better overall compiled performance than early binding.
    True/False

15. It is possible to execute unmanaged ADO under ASP.NET.
    True/False

16. The tlbimp.exe utility must be used to support early binding of unmanaged code.
    True/False

APPENDIX

A

Answers to Part Reviews

This appendix provides the answers for the Part Review questions.

Friday Evening Review Answers

1. A
2. False. A Web server's primary responsibility is to handle HTTP requests.
3. False. The two primary protocols for Internet client/server communications are TCP/IP and HTTP.
4. D
5. False. Windows 3.1 is not a supported .NET platform. However, Windows 98, ME, NT, 2000, and XP can run .NET applications. ASP.NET Server Side Applications are, however, limited to 2000 and XP Platforms for development and production.
6. IIS 4.0
7. No. Installing the final release of the .NET SDK over the Beta Releases is not recommended.
8. No. Installing the .NET SDK side by side with your Visual Studio 6.0 or other applications is supported.
9. True. A database in the most general terms can be thought of as a collection of tables. A database can also contain many other objects such as the relationships between tables, stored procedures, triggers, and views.
10. C
11. True
12. False. Database tables are composed of rows and columns.
13. C
14. True. Either Query Analyzer or Enterprise Manager can be used to manage a SQL Server database and its constituent objects.

15. B
16. False. SQL Server is a software application, not hardware.
17. False. The T-SQL statement used to create a new database is CREATE DATABASE.

Saturday Morning Review Answers

1. True
2. Create, Retrieve, Update, Delete
3. C. The SQL INSERT statement is used to add data to a table.
4. False. The field value needs be enclosed in single quotes since it is a string. The correct SQL statement is INSERT INTO t_bands (band_title) VALUES ('Hootie & The Blowfish').
5. True
6. Hierarchical
7. True. XML is actually a subset of SGML.
8. False. XML was designed to work with any application.
9. False. ASP.NET pages are event-based. When an ASP.Net page is loaded a series of events, including Page_Load, are fired.
10. Events
11. Page_Load, Page_Unload
12. C
13. True. HTML controls maintain their state between client requests by utilizing the hidden "VIEWSTATE" form field.
14. False. HTML controls generate HTML code specific to the requesting browser type.
15. A
16. C
17. False
18. False. Web controls can be bound to many types of data stores including XML, arrays or COM objects.
19. False. ASP.NET Controls can be programmatically added to a page at run-time.
20. C
21. False. ASP.NET User controls have an .ascx file extension.
22. True. You can modularize the design of your application by encapsulating frequently used presentation logic in User controls.
23. False. <html>, <body>, and <form> tags should not be included in User controls. By excluding these HTML tags from User controls, you will be less limited in where you can use the controls.
24. A

Saturday Afternoon Review Answers

1. False. The required field validator can be used with controls supporting user input.

2. ^([a-zA-Z0-9_\-\.]+)@((\[[0-9]{1,3}\.[0-9]{1,3}\.[0-9]{1,3})|([a-zA-Z0-9\-\.]+))\.([a-zA-Z]{2,3}|[0-9]{1,3})(\]?)$, which will validate a series of letters or numbers regardless of capitalization, including "_" and "-", ^([a-zA-Z0-9_\-\.]+), followed by a literal @ character, followed by either an IP address or alternately a domain name using a valid extension such as COM, BIZ, and so on.

3. True. Multiple Validation controls can be used to validate a single control.

4. A

5. A

6. Out-of-process

7. Stores session state out-of-process, allowing you to run your application across multiple servers; Supports request-based load balancing; Provides adequate redundancy, reliability, and uptime when used in conjunction with clustering and hardware or software load balancing; Provides ability to support periodic "code rot" purges; Provides ability to partition an application across multiple worker processes.

8. Stores session state out-of-process, allowing you to run your application across multiple servers; Supports request-based load balancing; Provides extensive redundancy, reliability, and uptime when used in conjunction with clustering and hardware or software load balancing; Provides ability to support periodic "code rot" purges; Provides ability to partition an application across multiple worker processes; Provides ability to partition an application across multiple Web farm machines, Additionally the use of SQL Server provides the use of the Enterprise series of features in terms of memory optimization, clustering, database mirroring, failover and scalability that is less easily achieved using the State Server approach.

9. Authentication

10. Impersonation

11. A

12. <authorization>

13. A

14. C

15. TimeSpan.Zero provides an absolute expiration.

16. When you first insert an object into the cache.

17. False. The Recordset object is a traditional ADO object. .NET uses a series of objects, including DataReader and DataSet objects, to mimic the Recordset object's functionality.

18. True

19. True. The DataSet object can contain multiple tables, in the form of DataTable objects, as well the relationships between the tables.

20. True
21. False. An object is an instance of a class.
22. Object Oriented Programming or OOP
23. True
24. New

Saturday Evening Review Answers

1. D
2. A
3. False. A Connection object, either a SQLConnection or an OLEDBConnection, can be created through a Command object.
4. C
5. True
6. False. The ADO.NET Command objects provide several constructors.
7. C
8. CommandType
9. True. You can only move forward through a DataReader object.
10. OLEDBCommand
11. False. A DataReader can only be created through a Command object.
12. False. You can only move forward through a DataReader object.
13. False. The DataSet object can contain multiple tables, in the form of DataTable objects, as well the relationships between the tables.
14. True.
15. SelectCommand
16. Fill

Sunday Morning Review Answers

1. True. A DataSet can be created explicitly through a variety of constructors.
2. True. A DataSet can contain numerous constituent objects, most notably DataTable objects.
3. Count
4. Item
5. Data binding
6. True
7. True. Setting a control's AutoPostBack property to "true" forces the page in which it contained to repost when its state is changed.

8. False
9. `AutoGenerateColumns`
10. B
11. D
12. True. You should close all objects when you are done using them. Doing so releases valuable server resources.
13. B. Update.
14. True. The `DataAdapter` objects provide methods to manage data updates, deletes, or inserts.
15. `PageSize`
16. False
17. A
18. True
19. False. There is no set limit to the number of tables a `DataSet` object can contain.
20. False. A DataSet is an ideal object to implement data shaping.
21. True VB.NET now impements the `Try...Catch...Finally` construct for error handling.
22. A
23. A
24. C

Sunday Afternoon Review Answers

1. False. SOAP is the proposed Internet standard that is currently being evaluted by the World Wide Web Consortium.
2. True. Since SOAP utilizes HTTP as its transport mechanism, and assuming the firewall supports HTTP requests, SOAP traffic can be handled just as easily as simple Web requests.
3. Rogue Wave's Nouveau ORB, Iona's Orbix 2000, ObjectSpace's Voyager, Userland's Frontier Groupware Product, Microsoft's Windows DNA
4. D
5. False. Microsoft's Web Services are based on HTTP and XML.
6. C
7. `<WebMethod()>`
8. Web Service Description Language or WSDL
9. False When authoring an ASP.NET page, you must use only one language.
10. False All ASP.NET pages are translated into the same Intermediate Langauge that is then compiled at run-time. So, there is no performance benefit to using one language over another.
11. True

12. False
13. True
14. False
15. True. You can either turn ASP Compatibility on, or implement a Runtime Callable Wrapper with the type library importer utility (TlbImp.exe).
16. True

APPENDIX

What's on the CD-ROM

This appendix provides you with information on the contents of the CD that accompanies this book. For the latest and greatest information, please refer to the ReadMe file located at the root of the CD. Here is what you will find:

- System Requirements
- Using the CD with Windows, Linux, and Macintosh
- What's on the CD
- Troubleshooting

System Requirements

Make sure that your computer meets the minimum system requirements listed in this section. If your computer doesn't match up to most of these requirements, you may have a problem using the contents of the CD.

For Windows 9x, Windows 2000, Windows NT4 (with SP 4 or later), Windows Me, or Windows XP:

The following are the system requirements for running the CD-ROM:

- A PC with a 133 MHz or higher Pentium-compatible CPU
- 128MB of RAM minimum; 256MB recommended, because more memory generally improves responsiveness
- A minimum of 850MB of disk storage space to install the .NET Framework and the sample programs on the CD
- A CD-ROM drive
- A Windows-compatible monitor with at least 256 colors
- Windows (Service Pack 6) 2000 or Windows XP
- Internet Explorer 5.5
- Data Access Components 2.6
- .NET Framework SDK
- IIS 4.0, or IIS 5.0

The software provided with this book is not compatible for installation on the Mac OS, Linux, or other operating systems or non-PC hardware.

Using the CD with Windows

To install the items from the CD to your hard drive, follow these steps:

1. Insert the CD into your computer's CD-ROM drive.
2. A window will appear with the following options: Install, Explore, eBook, Links, and Exit.

    Install: Gives you the option to install the supplied software and/or the author-created samples on the CD-ROM.

    Explore: Allows you to view the contents of the CD-ROM in its directory structure.

    eBook: Allows you to view an electronic version of the book.

    Links: Opens a hyperlinked page of web sites.

    Exit: Closes the autorun window.

If you do not have autorun enabled or if the autorun window does not appear, follow the steps below to access the CD.

1. Click Start ⇨ Run.
2. In the dialog box that appears, type ***d:\setup.exe***, where *d* is the letter of your CD-ROM drive. This will bring up the autorun window described above.
3. Choose the Install, Explore, eBook, Links, or Exit option from the menu. (See Step 2 in the preceding list for a description of these options.)

What's on the CD

The following sections provide a summary of the software and other materials you'll find on the CD.

Author-created materials

All author-created material from the book, including code listings and samples, are on the CD in the folder named "Author".

- The sample programs developed or discussed in the text
- SQL scripts to create the Music database discussed in the text

The Software Directory

The Software directory contains the self-assessment test and evaluation or trial applications that may assist you in your ASP.NET development.

The installation files for each application can be found in their respective subdirectories.

The HMI Test directory contains test software and data files. Their purposes are to help you determine how much you have learned from this book and to help you identify sessions you may need to study more, as well as those you can skip.

Applications

The following evaluation or trial products are on the CD:

- **Adobe Acrobat Reader**
- **BrowserHawk**

  BrowserHawk allows developers to accurately recognize Web browsers and their capabilities. This tool allows you to easily create dynamic Web sites which support a wide variety of browsers. BrowserHawk frees you from all the hassles and complexities involved in detecting and accounting for browser differences. It allows you to easily produce sites with a consistent look, feel, and level of operation for all visitors to your site, regardless of the browser used, with graceful degradation for older browsers. For more information, visit www.cyscape.com.

- **ASPUpload**

  ASPUpload is an Active Server component which enables an ASP application to accept, save and manipulate files uploaded with a browser. For more information, visit www.aspupload.com.

- **Brinkster.com Web Hosting Service**

  Brinkster is a Web hosting company focused on providing Microsoft active server pages (ASP) hosting services to the small and mid-market web developer. Services offered allow unconstrained creativity in the design of fully functional and interactive Web sites. For more information, visit www.brinkster.com

- **.NET Compression Library**

  This tool is filled with components which extend the .NET class library. Xceed developers have created a new object-oriented, transactional design that is a radical departure from traditional ActiveX Zip component architectures. For more information, visit www.exceedsoft.com.

- **Infragistics UltraSuite**

  Infragistics UltraSuite offers a huge array of ActiveX controls for Windows development, giving developers everything necessary to create solutions that look great and run efficiently, faster than ever before. For more information visit www.infragistics.com.

Shareware programs are fully functional, trial versions of copyrighted programs. If you like particular programs, register with their authors for a nominal fee and receive licenses, enhanced versions, and technical support. *Freeware programs* are copyrighted games, applications, and utilities that are free for personal use. Unlike shareware, these programs do not require a fee or provide technical support. *GNU software* is governed by its own license, which is included inside the folder of the GNU product. See the GNU license for more details.

Trial, demo, or evaluation versions are usually limited either by time or functionality (such as being unable to save projects). Some trial versions are very sensitive to system date changes. If you alter your computer's date, the programs will "time out" and will no longer be functional.

eBook version of ASP.NET Database Programming Weekend Crash Course

The complete text of this book is on the CD in Adobe's Portable Document Format (PDF). You can read and search through the file with the Adobe Acrobat Reader (also included on the CD). For more information on Adobe Acrobat Reader, go to www.adobe.com.

Troubleshooting

If you have difficulty installing or using any of the materials on the companion CD, try the following solutions:

- **Turn off any anti-virus software that you may have running.** Installers sometimes mimic virus activity and can make your computer incorrectly believe that it is being infected by a virus. (Be sure to turn the anti-virus software back on later.)
- **Close all running programs.** The more programs you're running, the less memory is available to other programs. Installers also typically update files and programs; if you keep other programs running, installation may not work properly.
- **Reference the ReadMe:** Please refer to the ReadMe file located at the root of the CD-ROM for the latest product information at the time of publication.

If you still have trouble with the CD, please call the Hungry Minds Customer Care phone number: (800) 762-2974. Outside the United States, call 1 (317) 572-3994. You can also contact Hungry Minds Customer Service by e-mail at techsupdum@hungryminds.com. Hungry Minds will provide technical support only for installation and other general quality control items; for technical support on the applications themselves, consult the program's vendor or author.

ADO.NET Class Descriptions

OleDbConnection Class

Properties

ConnectionString	Gets or sets the string used to open a data store.
ConnectionTimeout	Gets or sets the time to wait while establishing a connection before terminating the attempt and generating an error.
Container	Returns the Container that contains the component. The Container is an interface to the component's container.
Database	Gets the name of the current database or the database to be used once a connection is open.
DataSource	Gets the location and filename of the data source.
Provider	Gets the name of OLE DB provider.
ServerVerison	Gets a string containing the version of the server to which the client is connected.
Site	Gets or sets the site of the component. A site binds a component to a container and enables communication between them, as well as provides a way for the container to manage its components.
State	Gets the current state of the connection.

Methods

BeginTransaction	Begins a database transaction.
ChangeDatabase	Changes the current database for an open OleDbConnection.

Continued

OleDbConnection Class   *Continued*

Methods

`Close`	Closes the connection to the datasource. This is the preferred method.
`CreateCommand`	Creates and returns an `OleDbCommand` object associates with the `OleDbConnection`.
`Dispose`	Disposes of the `OleDbConnection` object.
`Equals`	Determines whether the specified object is the same instance as the current object.
`GetHashCode`	Serves as a hash function for a particular type, suitable for use in hashing algorithms and data structures such as a hash table.
`GetLifeTimeService`	Retrieves a lifetime service object that controls the lifetime policy for this instance. For the default Lifetime service this will be an object of type ILease.
`GetOleDbSchemaTable`	Returns the schema table and associated restriction columns of the specified schema.
`GetType`	Gets the type of the object.
`InitializeLifeTimeService`	Objects can provide their own lease and so control their own lifetime. They do this by overriding the `InitializeLifetimeService` method provided on `MarshalByRefObject`.
`Open`	Opens a database connection with the current property settings specified by the `ConnectionString`.
`ToString`	Returns a string that represents the current object.

OleDbCommand Class

Properties

`CommandText`	Gets or sets the SQL command text or stored procedure to execute at the data source.
`CommandTimeout`	Gets or sets the time to wait while executing the command before terminating the attempt and generating an error.
`CommandType`	Gets or sets how the `CommandText` property is interpreted.
`Connection`	Gets or sets the `OleDbConnection` used by this instance of the `OleDbCommand`.

Container	Returns the IContainer that contains the component.
DesignTimeVisible	Gets or sets a value indicating whether the command object should be visible in a customized Windows Forms Designer control.
Parameters	Gets the collection of OleDbParameterCollection.
Site	Gets or sets the site of the component.
Transaction	Gets or sets the transaction in which the OleDbCommand executes.
UpdatedRowSource	Gets or sets how command results are applied to the DataRow when used by the Update method of a DBDataAdapter.

Methods

Cancel	Cancels the execution of a command.
CreateParameter	Create an instance of an OleDbParameter object.
Dispose	Releases the resources used by the component.
Equals	Determines whether the specified object is the same instance as the current object.
ExecuteNonQuery	Executes a SQL statement against the Connection and returns the number of rows affected.
ExecuteReader	Overloaded. Send the CommandText to the Connection and builds an OldDbDataReader.
ExecuteScalar	Executes the query, and returns the first column of the first row in the resultset returned by the query. Extra columns or rows are ignored.
GetHashCode	Serves as a hash function for a particular type, suitable for use in hashing algorithms and data structures such as a hash table.
GetLifeTimeService	Retrieves a lifetime service object that controls the lifetime policy for this instance. For the default Lifetime service this will be an object of type ILease.
GetType	Gets the type of the object.
InitializeLifeTimeService	Objects can provide their own lease and so control their own lifetime. They do this by overriding the InitializeLifetimeService method provided on MarshalByRefObject.

Continued

OleDbConnection Class *Continued*

Methods

Prepare	Creates a prepared (or compiled) version of the command on the data source.
ResetCommandTimeout	Resets the CommandTimeout property to the default value.
ToString	Returns a string that represents the current object.

OleDbDataReader Class

Properties

Depth	Gets a value indicating the depth of the nesting for current row.
FieldCount	Indicates the number of fields within the current record. This property is read-only.
IsClosed	Indicates whether the DataReader is closed.
Item	Overloaded. Gets the value a column in its native format.
RecordsAffected	Gets the number of rows changed, inserted, or deleted by the execution of the SQL statement.

Methods

Close	Closes the OleDbDataReader object.
Equals	Determines whether the specified object is the same instance as the current object.
GetBoolean	Returns the value of the specified column as a Boolean.
GetByte	Returns the value of the specified column as a byte.
GetBytes	Returns the value of the specified column as a byte array.
GetChar	Returns the value of the specified column as a character.
GetChars	Returns the value of the specified column as a character array.
GetDataTypeName	Returns the name of the back-end data type.
GetDateTime	Returns the value of the specified column as a DateTime object.
GetDecimal	Returns the value of the specified column as a Decimal object.

GetDouble	Returns the value of the specified column as a double-precision floating-point number.
GetFieldType	Returns the type that is the data type of the object.
GetFloat	Returns the value of the specified column as a single-precision floating-point number.
GetGuid	Returns the value of the specified column as a globally unique identifier.
GetHashCode	Serves as a hash function for a particular type, suitable for use in hashing algorithms and data structures such as a hash table.
GetInt16	Returns the value of the specified column as a 16-bit signed integer.
GetInt32	Returns the value of the specified column as a 32-bit signed integer.
GetInt64	Returns the value of the specified column as a 64-bit signed integer.
GetLifeTimeService	Retrieves a lifetime service object that controls the lifetime policy for this instance. For the default Lifetime service this will be an object of type ILease.
GetName	Returns the name of the specified column.
GetOrdinal	Gets the column ordinal, given the name of the column.
GetSchemaTable	Returns a DataTable that describes the column metadata of the OleDbDataReader.
GetString	Returns the value of the specified column as a string.
GetTimeSpan	Returns the value of the specified column as a TimeSpan object.
GetType	Gets the type of the object.
GetValue	Gets the value of the column at the specified ordinal in its native format.
GetValues	Gets all the attribute columns in the current row.
InitializeLifetimeService	Objects can provide their own lease and so control their own lifetime. They do this by overriding the InitializeLifetimeService method provided on MarshalByRefObject.

Continued

OleDbDataReader Class   *Continued*

Methods

IsDBNull	Advances the data reader to the next result, when reading the results of batch SQL statements.
NextResult	Advances the data reader to the next result, when reading the results of batch SQL statements.
Read	Advances the OleDbDataReader to the next record.
ToString	Returns a string that represents the current object.

OleDbDataAdapter Class

Properties

AcceptChangesDuringFill	Gets or sets a value indicating whether AcceptChanges is called on a DataRow after it is added to the DataTable.
Container	Returns the IContainer that contains the component.
DeleteCommand	Gets or sets a command for deleting records from the data set.
InsertCommand	Gets or sets a command used to insert new records into the data source.
MissingMappingAction	Determines the action to take when incoming data does not have a matching table or column.
MissingSchemaAction	Determines the action to take when existing DataSet schema does not match incoming data.
SelectCommand	Gets or sets a command used to select records in the data source.
Site	Gets or sets the site of the component. A site binds a component to a container and enables communication between them, as well as provides a way for the container to manage its components.
TableMappings	Gets a collection that provides the master mapping between a source table and a DataTable.
UpdateCommand	Gets or sets a command used to update records in the data source.

Methods

Dispose	Releases the resources used by the component.

Equals	Determines whether the specified object is the same instance as the current object.
Fill	Overloaded. Adds or refreshes rows in the DataSet to match those in an ADO Recordset or Record object.
FillSchema	Overloaded. Adds a DataTable to a DataSet and configures the schema to match that in the data source.
GetFillParameters	Gets the parameters set by the user when executing an SQL SELECT statement.
GetHashCode	Serves as a hash function for a particular type, suitable for use in hashing algorithms and data structures such as a hash table.
GetLifeTimeService	Retrieves a lifetime service object that controls the lifetime policy for this instance. For the default Lifetime service this will be an object of type ILease.
GetType	Gets the type of the object.
InitializeLifetimeService	Objects can provide their own lease and so control their own lifetime. They do this by overriding the InitializeLifetimeService method provided on MarshalByRefObject.
ToString	Returns a string that represents the current object.
Update	Overloaded. Calls the respective INSERT, UPDATE, or DELETE statements for each inserted, updated, or deleted row in the DataSet from a DataTable named "Table."

OleDbParameterCollection Class

Properties

Count	Gets the number of OleDbParameter objects in the collection.
Item	Overloaded. Gets or sets the OleDbParameter with a specified attribute. Overloading is the practice of supplying more than one definition for a given a property or method within the scope of a class.

Methods

Add	Overloaded. Adds an OleDbParameter to the OleDbCommand.

Continued

OleDbParameterCollection Class   *Continued*

Properties

`Clear`	Removes all items from the collection.
`Contains`	Overloaded. Indicates whether an `OleDbParameter` exists in the collection.
`CopyTo`	Copies `OleDbParameter` objects from the `OleDbParameterCollection` to the specified array.
`Equals`	Overloaded. Determines whether two object instances are equal.
`GetHashCode`	Serves as a hash function for a particular type, suitable for use in hashing algorithms and data structures such as a hash table.
`GetLifeTimeService`	Retrieves a lifetime service object that controls the lifetime policy for this instance. For the default Lifetime service this will be an object of type ILease.
`GetType`	Gets the type of the current instance.
`IndexOf`	Overloaded. Gets the location of the `OleDbParameter` in the collection.
`InitializeLifetimeService`	Objects can provide their own lease and so control their own lifetime. They do this by overriding the `InitializeLifetimeService` method provided on `MarshalByRefObject`.
`Insert`	Inserts an `OleDbParameter` in the collection at the specified index.
`Remove`	Removes the specified `OleDbParameter` from the collection.
`RemoveAt`	Overloaded. Removes the specified `OleDbParameter` from the collection.
`ToString`	Returns a string that represents the current object.

OleDbParameter Class

Properties

`DBType`	Gets or sets the `DBType` of the parameter.
`Direction`	Gets or sets a value indicating whether the parameter is input-only, output-only, bidirectional, or a stored procedure return value parameter.

isNullable	Gets or sets a value indicating whether the parameter accepts null values.
OleDbType	Gets or sets the OleDbType of the parameter.
ParameterName	Gets or sets the name of the OleDbParameter.
Precision	Gets or sets the maximum number of digits used to represent the Value property.
Scale	Gets or sets the number of decimal places to which Value is resolved.
Size	Gets or sets the maximum size, in bytes, of the data within the column.
SourceColumn	Gets or sets the name of the source column mapped to the DataSet and used for loading or returning the Value.
SourceVersion	Gets or sets the DataRowVersion to use when loading Value.
Value	Gets or sets the value of the parameter.

Methods

Equals	Overloaded. Determines whether two objects instances are equal.
GetHashCode	Serves as a hash function for a particular type, suitable for use in hashing algorithms and data structures such as a hash table.
GetLifeTimeService	Retrieves a lifetime service object that controls the lifetime policy for this instance. For the default Lifetime service this will be an object of type ILease.
GetType	Gets the type of the current instance.
InitializeLifetimeService	Objects can provide their own lease and so control their own lifetime. They do this by overriding the InitializeLifetimeService method provided on MarshalByRefObject.
ToString	Gets a string containing the ParameterName.

SqlConnection Class

Properties

ConnectionString	Gets or sets the string used to open a SQL Server database.

Continued

SqlConnection Class *Continued*

Properties

ConnectionTimeout	Gets or sets the time to wait while establishing a connection before terminating the attempt and generating an error.
Container	Returns the IContainer that contains the component.
Database	Gets the name of the current database or the database to be used once a connection is open.
DataSource	Gets the name of the instance of SQL Server to which to connect.
PacketSize	Gets the size (in bytes) of network packets used to communicate with an instance of SQL Server.
ServerVerison	Gets a string containing the version of the instance of SQL Server to which the client is connected.
Site	Gets or sets the site of the component.
State	Gets the current state of the connection.
WorkStationID	Gets a string that identifies the database client.

Methods

BeginTransaction	Begins a database transaction.
ChangeDatabase	Changes the current database for an open SqlConnection.
Close	Closes the connection to the datasource. This is the preferred method.
CreateCommand	Creates and returns an SqlCommand object associates with the SqlConnection.
Dispose	Disposes of the SqlConnection object.
Equals	Determines whether the specified object is the same instance as the current object.
GetHashCode	Serves as a hash function for a particular type, suitable for use in hashing algorithms and data structures such as a hash table.
GetLifeTimeService	Retrieves a lifetime service object that controls the lifetime policy for this instance. For the default Lifetime service this will be an object of type ILease.
GetType	Gets the type of the object.

InitializeLifeTimeService	Objects can provide their own lease and so control their own lifetime. They do this by overriding the InitializeLifetimeService method provided on MarshalByRefObject.
Open	Opens a database connection with the current property settings specified by the ConnectionString.
ToString	Returns a string that represents the current object.

SqlCommand Class

Properties

CommandText	Gets or sets the Transact-SQL command text or stored procedure to execute at the data source.
CommandTimeout	Gets or sets the time to wait while executing the command before terminating the attempt and generating an error.
CommandType	Gets or sets how the CommandText property is interpreted.
Connection	Gets or sets the SqlConnection used by this instance of the SqlCommand.
Container	Returns the IContainer that contains the component.
DesignTimeVisible	Gets or sets a value indicating whether the command object should be visible in a customized Windows Forms Designer control.
Parameters	Gets the collection of SqlParameterCollection.
Site	Gets or sets the site of the component.
Transaction	Gets or sets the transaction in which the SqlCommand executes.
UpdatedRowSource	Gets or sets how command results are applied to the DataRow when used by the Update method of a DBDataAdapter.

Methods

Cancel	Cancels the execution of a command.
CreateParameter	Creates an instance of an SqlParameter object.
Dispose	Releases the resources used by the component.

Continued

Methods

`Equals`	Determines whether the specified object is the same instance as the current object.
`ExecuteNonQuery`	Executes a SQL statement against the Connection and returns the number of rows affected.
`ExecuteReader`	Overloaded. Send the `CommandText` to the Connection and builds an `OldDbDataReader`.
`ExecuteScalar`	Executes the query, and returns the first column of the first row in the resultset returned by the query. Extra columns or rows are ignored.
`ExecuteXMLReader`	Sends the `CommandText` to the `SqlConnection` and builds an `XmlReader` object.
`GetHashCode`	Serves as a hash function for a particular type, suitable for use in hashing algorithms and data structures such as a hash table.
`GetLifeTimeService`	Retrieves a lifetime service object that controls the lifetime policy for this instance. For the default Lifetime service this will be an object of type ILease.
`GetType`	Gets the type of the object.
`InitializeLifeTimeService`	Objects can provide their own lease and so control their own lifetime. They do this by overriding the `InitializeLifetimeService` method provided on `MarshalByRefObject`.
`Prepare`	Creates a prepared (or compiled) version of the command on the data source.
`ResetCommandTimeout`	Resets the `CommandTimeout` property to the default value.
`ToString`	Returns a string that represents the current object.

SqlDataReader Class

Properties

`Depth`	Gets a value indicating the depth of the nesting for current row.
`FieldCount`	Indicates the number of fields within the current record. This property is read-only.
`IsClosed`	Indicates whether the DataReader is closed.

Item	Overloaded. Gets the value of a column in its native format.
RecordsAffected	Gets the number of rows changed, inserted, or deleted by the execution of the SQL statement.

Methods

Close	Closes the SqlDataReader object.
Equals	Determines whether the specified object is the same instance as the current object.
GetBoolean	Returns the value of the specified column as a Boolean.
GetByte	Returns the value of the specified column as a byte.
GetBytes	Returns the value of the specified column as a byte array.
GetChar	Returns the value of the specified column as a character.
GetChars	Returns the value of the specified column as a character array.
GetDataTypeName	Returns the name of the back-end data type.
GetDateTime	Returns the value of the specified column as a DateTime object.
GetDecimal	Returns the value of the specified column as a Decimal object.
GetDouble	Returns the value of the specified column as a double-precision floating-point number.
GetFieldType	Returns the type that is the data type of the object.
GetFloat	Returns the value of the specified column as a single-precision floating-point number.
GetGuid	Returns the value of the specified column as a globally unique identifier.
GetHashCode	Serves as a hash function for a particular type, suitable for use in hashing algorithms and data structures such as a hash table.
GetInt16	Returns the value of the specified column as a 16-bit signed integer.
GetInt32	Returns the value of the specified column as a 32-bit signed integer.

Continued

SqlDataReader Class   *Continued*

Methods

GetInt64	Returns the value of the specified column as a 64-bit signed integer.
GetLifeTimeService	Retrieves a lifetime service object that controls the lifetime policy for this instance. For the default Lifetime service this will be an object of type ILease.
GetName	Returns the name of the specified column.
GetOrdinal	Gets the column ordinal, given the name of the column.
GetSchemaTable	Returns a DataTable that describes the column metadata of the SqlDataReader.
GetSqlBinary	Gets the value of the specified column as a SqlBinary.
GetSqlBoolean	Gets the value of the specified column as a SqlBoolean.
GetSqlByte	Gets the value of the specified column as a SqlByte.
GetSqlDataTime	Gets the value of the specified column as a SqlDateTime.
GetSqlDecimal	Gets the value of the specified column as a SqlDecimal.
GetSqlDouble	Gets the value of the specified column as a SqlDouble.
GetSqlGuid	Gets the value of the specified column as a SqlGuid.
GetSqlInt16	Gets the value of the specified column as a SqlInt16.
GetSqlInt32	Gets the value of the specified column as a SqlInt32.
GetSqlInt64	Gets the value of the specified column as a SqlInt64.
GetSqlMoney	Gets the value of the specified column as a SqlMoney.
GetSqlSingle	Gets the value of the specified column as a SqlSingle.
GetSqlString	Gets the value of the specified column as a SqlString.
GetSqlValue	Gets an object that is a representation of the underlying SqlDbType variant.
GetSqlValues	Gets all the attribute columns in the current row.
GetString	Returns the value of the specified column as a string.
GetTimeSpan	Returns the value of the specified column as a TimeSpan object.
GetType	Gets the type of the object.

GetValue	Gets the value of the column at the specified ordinal in its native format.
GetValues	Gets all the attribute columns in the current row.
InitializeLifetimeService	Objects can provide their own lease and so control their own lifetime. They do this by overriding the InitializeLifetimeService method provided on MarshalByRefObject.
IsDBNull	Advances the data reader to the next result, when reading the results of batch SQL statements.
NextResult	Advances the data reader to the next result, when reading the results of batch SQL statements.
Read	Advances the SqlDataReader to the next record.
ToString	Returns a string that represents the current object.

SqlDataAdapter Class

Properties

AcceptChangesDuringFill	Gets or sets a value indicating whether AcceptChanges is called on a DataRow after it is added to the DataTable.
Container	Returns the IContainer that contains the component.
DeleteCommand	Gets or sets a command for deleting records from the data set.
InsertCommand	Gets or sets a command used to insert new records into the data source.
MissingMappingAction	Determines the action to take when incoming data does not have a matching table or column.
MissingSchemaAction	Determines the action to take when existing DataSet schema does not match incoming data.
SelectCommand	Gets or sets a command used to select records in the data source.
Site	Gets or sets the site of the component.
TableMappings	Gets a collection that provides the master mapping between a source table and a DataTable.
UpdateCommand	Gets or sets a command used to update records in the data source.

Continued

SqlDataAdapter Class   *Continued*

Methods

Dispose	Releases the resources used by the component.
Equals	Determines whether the specified object is the same instance as the current object.
Fill	Overloaded. Adds or refreshes rows in the DataSet to match those in an ADO Recordset or Record object.
FillSchema	Overloaded. Adds a DataTable to a DataSet and configures the schema to match that in the data source.
GetFillParameters	Gets the parameters set by the user when executing an SQL SELECT statement.
GetHashCode	Serves as a hash function for a particular type, suitable for use in hashing algorithms and data structures such as a hash table.
GetLifeTimeService	Retrieves a lifetime service object that controls the lifetime policy for this instance. For the default Lifetime service this will be an object of type ILease.
GetType	Gets the type of the object.
InitializeLifetimeService	Objects can provide their own lease and so control their own lifetime. They do this by overriding the InitializeLifetimeService method provided on MarshalByRefObject.
ToString	Returns a string that represents the current object.
Update	Overloaded. Calls the respective INSERT, UPDATE, or DELETE statements for each inserted, updated, or deleted row in the DataSet from a DataTable named "Table."

SqlParameterCollection Class

Properties

Count	Gets the number of SqlParameter objects in the collection.
Item	Overloaded. Gets or sets the SqlParameter with a specified attribute.

Methods

Add	Overloaded. Adds an SqlParameter to the SqlCommand.
Clear	Removes all items from the collection.

Contains	Overloaded. Indicates whether an SqlParameter exists in the collection.
CopyTo	Copies SqlParameter objects from the SqlParameterCollection to the specified array.
Equals	Overloaded. Determines whether two object instances are equal.
GetHashCode	Serves as a hash function for a particular type, suitable for use in hashing algorithms and data structures such as a hash table.
GetLifeTimeService	Retrieves a lifetime service object that controls the lifetime policy for this instance. For the default Lifetime service this will be an object of type ILease.
GetType	Gets the type of the current instance.
IndexOf	Overloaded. Gets the location of the SqlParameter in the collection.
InitializeLifetimeService	Objects can provide their own lease and so control their own lifetime. They do this by overriding the InitializeLifetimeService method provided on MarshalByRefObject.
Insert	Inserts an SqlParameter in the collection at the specified index.
Remove	Removes the specified SqlParameter from the collection.
RemoveAt	Overloaded. Removes the specified SqlParameter from the collection.
ToString	Returns a string that represents the current object.

SqlParameter Class

Properties

DBType	Gets or sets the DBType of the parameter.
Direction	Gets or sets a value indicating whether the parameter is input-only, output-only, bidirectional, or a stored procedure return value parameter.
IsNullable	Gets or sets a value indicating whether the parameter accepts null values.

Continued

SqlParameter Class *Continued*

Properties

Offset	Gets or sets the offset of the Value property.
ParameterName	Gets or sets the name of the SqlParameter.
Precision	Gets or sets the maximum number of digits used to represent the Value property.
Scale	Gets or sets the number of decimal places to which Value is resolved.
Size	Gets or sets the maximum size, in bytes, of the data within the column.
SourceColumn	Gets or sets the name of the source column mapped to the DataSet and used for loading or returning the Value.
SourceVersion	Gets or sets the DataRowVersion to use when loading Value.
SqlDbType	Gets or sets the SqlDbType of the parameter.
Value	Gets or sets the value of the parameter.

Methods

Equals	Overloaded. Determines whether two objects instances are equal.
GetHashCode	Serves as a hash function for a particular type, suitable for use in hashing algorithms and data structures such as a hash table.
GetLifeTimeService	Retrieves a lifetime service object that controls the lifetime policy for this instance. For the default Lifetime service, this will be an object of type ILease.
GetType	Gets the type of the current instance.
InitializeLifetimeService	Objects can provide their own lease and so control their own lifetime. They do this by overriding the InitializeLifetimeService method provided on MarshalByRefObject.
ToString	Gets a string containing the ParameterName.

DataSet Class

Properties

CaseSensitive	Gets or sets a value indicating whether string comparisons within DataTable objects are case-sensitive.
Container	Gets the container for the component.
DataSetName	Gets or sets the name of this DataSet.
DefaultViewManager	Gets a custom view of the data contained by the DataSet that allows filtering, searching, and navigating using a custom DataViewManager.
DesignMode	Gets a value indicating whether the component is currently in design mode.
EnforceConstraints	Gets or sets a value indicating whether constraint rules are followed when attempting any update operation.
ExtendedProperties	Gets the collection of custom user information.
HasErrors	Gets a value indicating whether there are errors in any of the rows in any of the tables of this DataSet.
Locale	Gets or sets the locale information used to compare strings within the table.
Namespace	Gets or sets the namespace of the DataSet.
Prefix	Gets or sets an XML prefix that aliases the namespace of the DataSet.
Relations	Get the collection of relations that link tables and allow navigation from parent tables to child tables.
Site	Gets or sets a System.ComponentModel.ISite for the DataSet.
Tables	Gets the collection of tables contained in the DataSet.

Methods

AcceptChanges	Commits all the changes made to this DataSet since it was loaded or the last time AcceptChanges was called.
BeginInit	Begins the initialization of a DataSet that is used on a form or used by another component. The initialization occurs at runtime.

Continued

DataSet Class *Continued*

Methods

Clear	Clears the DataSet of any data by removing all rows in all tables.
Clone	Clones the structure of the DataSet, including all DataTable schemas, relations, and constraints.
Copy	Copies both the structure and data for this DataSet.
Dispose	Disposes of the component.
End Init	Ends the initialization of a DataSet that is used on a form or used by another component. The initialization occurs at runtime.
Equals	Determines whether the specified object is the same instance as the current object.
GetChanges	Overloaded. Returns a copy of the DataSet containing all changes made to it since it was last loaded, or since AcceptChanges was called.
GetHashCode	Serves as a hash function for a particular type, suitable for use in hashing algorithms and data structures such as a hash table.
GetService	Gets the implementer of the IServiceProvider.
GetType	Gets the type of the current instance.
GetXml	Returns the XML representation of the data stored in the DataSet.
GetXmlSchema	Returns the XSD schema for the XML representation of the data stored in the DataSet.
HasChanges	Overloaded. Gets a value indicating whether the DataSet has changes, including new, deleted, or modified rows.
InferXmlSchema	Returns the XSD schema for the XML representation of the data stored in the DataSet.
Merge	Overloaded. Merges this DataSet with a specified DataSet.
ReadXml	Overloaded. Reads XML schema and data into the DataSet.
ReadXmlSchema	Overloaded. Reads an XML schema into the DataSet.

RejectChanges	Rolls back all the changes made to this DataSet since it was created, or the last time DataSet.AcceptChanges was called.
Reset	Resets the DataSet to its original state. Subclasses should override Reset to restore a DataSet to its original state.
ToString	Returns a string that represents the current object.
WriteXml	Overloaded. Writes XML schema and data from the DataSet.
WriteXmlSchema	Overloaded. Writes the DataSet structure as an XML schema.

DataView Class

Properties

AllowDelete	Sets or gets a value indicating whether deletes are allowed.
AllowEdit	Gets or sets a value indicating whether edits are allowed.
AllowNew	Gets or sets a value indicating whether the new rows can be added using the AddNew method.
ApplyDefaultSort	Gets or sets a value indicating whether to use the default sort.
Container	Gets the container for the component.
Count	Gets the number of records in the DataView after RowFilter and RowStateFilter have been applied.
DataViewManager	Gets the DataView associated with this view.
DesignMode	Gets the value indicating whether the component is currently in design mode.
Item	Gets a row of data from a specified table. In C#, this property is the indexer for the DataView class.
RowFilter	Gets or sets the expression used to filter which rows are viewed in the DataView.
RowStateFilter	Gets or sets the row state filter used in the DataView.
Site	Gets or sets the site of the component.
Sort	Gets or sets the sort column or columns, and sort order for the table.
Table	Gets or sets the source DataTable.

Continued

DataView Class   *Continued*

Methods

AddNew	Adds a new row to the DataView.
BeginInit	Begins the initialization of a DataView that is used on a form or used by another component. The initialization occurs at runtime.
Delete	Deletes a row at the specified index.
Dispose	Disposes of the DataView object.
EndInit	Ends the initialization of a DataView that is used on a form or used by another component. The initialization occurs at runtime.
Equals	Determines whether the specified object is the same instance as the current object.
Find	Overloaded. Finds a row in the DataView.
GetEnumerator	Gets the enumerator for the DataView.
GetHashCode	Serves as a hash function for a particular type, suitable for use in hashing algorithms and data structures such as a hash table.
GetService	Gets the implementer of the IServiceProvider.
GetType	Gets the type of the object.
ToString	Returns a string that represents the current object.

DataTableCollection Class

Properties

Count	Gets the total number of elements in a collection.
IsReadOnly	Indicates whether the BaseCollection is read-only. This property is read-only.
IsSynchronized	Indicates whether the BaseCollection is synchronized. This property is read-only.
Item	Overloaded. Gets the specified table from the collection.
SyncRoot	Gets an object that can be used to synchronize the collection.

Methods

Add	Overloaded. Adds a DataTable to the collection.
AddRange	Copies the elements of the specified DataTable array to the end of the collection.
CanRemove	Verifies if a DataTable can be removed from the collection.
Clear	Clears the collection of any tables.
Contains	Overloaded. Verifies whether the collection contains a specific table.
CopyTo	Copies all the elements of the current InternalDataCollectionBase to a one-dimensional Array, starting at the specified InternalDataCollectionBase index.
Equals	Determines whether the specified object is the same instance as the current object.
GetEnumerator	Gets an IEnumerator for the collection.
GetHashCode	Serves as a hash function for a particular type, suitable for use in hashing algorithms and data structures such as a hash table.
GetType	Gets the type of the object.
IndexOf	Overloaded. Returns the index of a specified table.
Remove	Overloaded. Removes a table from the collection.
RemoveAt	Removes the table at the given index from the collection.
ToString	Returns a string that represents the current object.

DataTable Class

Properties

CaseSensitive	Indicates whether string comparisons within the table are case-sensitive.
ChildRelations	Gets the collection of child relations for this DataTable.
Columns	Gets the collection of columns that belong to this table.
Constraints	Gets the collection of constraints maintained by this table.
Container	Gets the container for the component.

Continued

Properties

DataSet	Gets the DataSet that this table belongs to.
DefaultView	Gets a customized view of the table that may include a filtered view, or a cursor position.
DesignMode	Gets a value indicating whether the component is currently in design mode.
DisplayExpression	Gets or sets the expression that will return a value used to represent this table in UI.
ExtendedProperties	Gets the collection of customized user information.
HasErrors	Gets a value indicating whether there are errors in any of the rows in any of the tables of the DataSet to which the table belongs.
Locale	Gets or sets the locale information used to compare strings within the table.
MinimumCapacity	Gets or sets the initial starting size for this table.
Namespace	Gets or sets the namespace for the DataTable.
ParentRelations	Gets the collection of parent relations for this DataTable.
Prefix	Gets or sets an XML prefix that aliases the namespace of the DataTable.
PrimaryKey	Gets or sets an array of columns that function as primary keys for the DataTable.
Rows	Gets the collection of rows that belong to this table.
Site	Gets or sets an System.ComponentModel.ISite for the DataTable.
TableName	Gets or sets the name of the DataTable.

Methods

AcceptChanges	Commits all the changes made to this table since the last time AcceptChanges was called.
BeginInit	Begins the initialization of a DataTable that is used on a form or used by another component. The initialization occurs at runtime.
Clear	Clears the table of all data.

Clone	Clones the structure of the DataTable, including all DataTable schemas, relations, and constraints.
Compute	Executes a command against the DataTable object's DataRowCollection ad returns the computed value.
Copy	Copies both the structure and data for this DataTable.
Dispose	Overloaded. Releases the resources used by the MarshalByValueComponent.
EndInit	Ends the initialization of a DataTable that is used on a form or used by another component. The initialization occurs at runtime.
EndLoadData	Turns off notifications, index maintenance, and constraints while loading data.
Equals	Determines whether the specified object is the same instance as the current object.
GetChanges	Overloaded. Gets a copy of the DataTable containing all changes made to it since it was last loaded, or since AcceptChanges was called.
GetErrors	Returns an array of DataRow objects that contain errors.
GetHashCode	Serves as a hash function for a particular type, suitable for use in hashing algorithms and data structures such as a hash table.
GetService	Gets the implementer of the IServiceProvider.
GetType	Gets the type of the object.
ImportRow	Copies a DataRow, including original and current values, DataRowState values, and errors, into a DataTable.
NewRow	Creates a new DataRow with the same schema as the table.
RejectChanges	Rolls back all changes that have been made to the table since it was loaded, or the last time AcceptChanges was called.
Select	Overloaded. Returns an array of DataRow objects.
ToString	Returns the TableName and DisplayExpression, if there is one, as a concatenated string.

DataColumnCollection Class

Properties

Count	Gets the total number of elements in a collection.
IsReadOnly	Indicates whether the InternalDataBaseCollection is read-only. This property is read-only.
IsSynchronized	Indicates whether the InternalDataBaseCollection is synchronized. This property is read-only.
Item	Overloaded. Gets the specified DataColumn from the collection. In C#, this property is the indexer for the ColumnsCollection class.
SyncRoot	Gets an object that can be used to synchronize the collection.

Methods

Add	Overloaded. Adds a DataColumn to the columns collection.
AddRange	Copies the elements of the specified DataColumn array to the end of the collection.
CanRemove	Checks if a given column can be removed from the collection.
Clear	Clears the collection of any columns.
Contains	Overloaded. Checks whether the collection contains a specified column.
CopyTo	Copies all the elements of the current InternalDataCollectionBase to a one-dimensional Array, starting at the specified InternalDataCollectionBase index.
Equals	Determines whether the specified object is the same instance as the current object.
GetEnumerator	Gets an IEnumerator for the collection.
GetHashCode	Serves as a hash function for a particular type, suitable for use in hashing algorithms and data structures such as a hash table.
GetType	Gets the type of the object.
IndexOf	Returns the index of a column specified by name.
Remove	Overloaded. Removes a column from the collection.

RemoveAt	Removes the column at the specified index from the collection.
ToString	Returns a string that represents the current object.

DataColumn Class

Properties

AllowDBNull	Gets or sets a value indicating whether NULL values are allowed in this column for rows belonging to the table.
AutoIncrement	Gets or sets a value indicating whether the column automatically increments the value of the column for new rows added to the table.
AutoIncrementSeed	Gets or sets the starting value for a column that has its AutoIncrement property set to true.
AutoIncrementStep	Gets or sets the increment used by a column with its AutoIncrement property set to true.
Caption	Gets or sets the caption for this column.
ColumnMapping	Gets or sets the MappingType of the column.
ColumnName	Gets or sets the name of the column within the DataColumnCollection.
Container	Gets the container for the component.
DataType	The type of data stored in the column.
DefaultValue	Gets or sets the default value for the column when creating new rows.
DesignMode	Gets a value indicating whether the component is currently in design mode.
Expression	Gets or sets the expression used either to filter rows, calculate the column's value, or create an aggregate column.
ExtendedProperties	Gets the collection of custom user information.
MaxLength	Gets or sets the maximum length of a text column.
Namespace	Gets or sets the namespace of the DataColumn.
Ordinal	Gets the position of the column in the DataColumnCollection collection.

Continued

DataColumn Class *Continued*

Properties

Prefix	Gets or sets an XML prefix that aliases the namespace of the DataTable.
ReadOnly	Gets or sets a value indicating whether the column allows changes once a row has been added to the table.
Site	Gets or sets the site of the component.
Sparse	Gets or sets a value indicating whether the column should store data in a fashion optimized for sparse data patterns.
Table	Gets the DataTable to which the column belongs to.
Unique	Gets or sets a value indicating whether the values in each row of the column must be unique.

Methods

Dispose	Disposes of the component by releasing all resources used by the component.
Equals	Determines whether the specified object is the same instance as the current object.
GetHashCode	Serves as a hash function for a particular type, suitable for use in hashing algorithms and data structures such as a hash table.
GetService	Gets the implementer of the IServiceProvider.
GetType	Gets the type of the object.
ToString	Returns the expression of the column, if one exists.

DataRowCollection Class

Properties

Count	Gets the count of the rows in DataRowCollection.
IsReadOnly	Indicates whether the InternalDataBaseCollection is read-only. This property is read-only.
IsSynchronized	Indicates whether the InternalDataBaseCollection is synchronized. This property is read-only.

Item	Gets the row at the specified index. In C#, this property is the indexer for the `DataRowCollection` class.
SyncRoot	Gets an object that can be used to synchronize the collection.

Methods

Add	Overloaded. Adds a DataRow to the `DataRowCollection`.
Clear	Clears the collection of all rows.
Contains	Overloaded. Gets a value indicating whether any row in the collection contains a specified value in the primary key or keys column.
CopyTo	Copies all the elements of the current `InternalDataBaseCollection` to a one-dimensional Array, starting at the specified `InternalDataBaseCollection` index.
Equals	Determines whether the specified object is the same instance as the current object.
Find	Overloaded. Gets a specified `DataRow`.
GetEnumerator	Gets an `IEnumerator` for the collection.
GetHashCode	Serves as a hash function for a particular type, suitable for use in hashing algorithms and data structures such as a hash table.
GetType	Gets the type of the object.
Remove	Overloaded. Removes a specific row from the `DataRowCollection`.
RemoveAt	Removes the row with the specified index from the collection.
ToString	Returns a string that represents the current object.

DataRow Class

Properties

HasErrors	Gets a value indicating whether there are errors in a column's collection.

Continued

Properties

Item	Overloaded. Gets or sets data stored in a specified column. In C#, this property is the indexer for the DataRow class.
ItemArray	Gets or sets all of the values for this row through an array.
RowError	Gets or sets the custom error description for a row.
RowState	Gets the current state of the row in regards to its relationship to the DataRowCollection.
Table	Gets the DataTable for which this row has a schema.

Methods

AcceptChanges	Commits all the changes made to this row since the last time AcceptChanges was called.
BeginEdit	Begins an edit operation on a DataRow object.
CancelEdit	Cancels the current edit on the row.
ClearErrors	Clears the errors for the row, including the RowError and errors set with SetColumnError.
Delete	Deletes the row.
EndEdit	Ends the edit occurring on the row.
Equals	Determines whether the specified object is the same instance as the current object.
GetChildRows	Overloaded. Gets the child rows of this DataRow.
GetColumnError	Overloaded. Gets the error description for a column.
GetColumnsInError	Gets an array of columns that have errors.
GetHashCode	Serves as a hash function for a particular type, suitable for use in hashing algorithms and data structures such as a hash table.
GetParentRow	Overloaded. Gets the parent row of a DataRow.
GetParentRows	Overloaded. Gets the parent rows of this DataRow.
GetType	Gets the type of the object.
HasVersion	Gets a value indicating whether a specified version exists.
IsNull	Overloaded. Gets a value indicating whether the specified column contains a NULL value.

RejectChanges	Rejects all changes made to the row since AcceptChanges was last called.
SetColumnError	Overloaded. Sets the error description for a column.
SetParentRow	Overloaded. Sets the parent row of a DataRow.
SetUnspecified	Sets the value of a DataColumn with the specified name to unspecified.
ToString	Returns a string that represents the current object.

DataRelationCollection Class

Properties

Count	Gets the total number of elements in a collection.
IsReadOnly	Indicates whether the InternalDataCollectionBase is read-only. This property is read-only.
IsSynchronized	Indicates whether the InternalDataCollectionBase is synchronized. This property is read-only.
Item	Overloaded. Get the specified DataRelation from the collection. In C#, this property is the indexer for the ataRelationCollection class.
SyncRoot	Gets an object that can be used to synchronize the collection.

Methods

Add	Overloaded. Adds a DataRelation to the DataRelationCollection.
AddRange	Copies the elements of the specified DataRelation array to the end of the collection.
Clear	Clears the collection of any relations.
Contains	Gets a value of true if this collection has a relation with the given name (case insensitive), false otherwise.
CopyTo	Copies all the elements of the current InternalDataCollectionBase to a one-dimensional Array, starting at the specified InternalDataCollectionBase index.
Equals	Determines whether the specified object is the same instance as the current object.

Continued

DataRelationConnection Class Continued

Methods

GetEnumerator	Gets an IEnumerator for the collection.
GetHashCode	Serves as a hash function for a particular type, suitable for use in hashing algorithms and data structures such as a hash table.
GetType	Gets the type of the object.
Remove	Removes a DataRelation from the collection.
RemoveAt	Removes the relation at the specified index from the collection. An IndexOutOfRangeException is generated if this collection doesn't have a relation at this index. The CollectionChanged event is fired if it succeeds.
ToString	Returns a string that represents the current object.

DataRelation Class

Properties

ChildColumns	Gets the child columns of this relation.
ChildKeyConstraint	Gets the ForeignKeyConstraint for the relation.
ChildTable	Gets the child table of this relation.
DataSet	Gets the DataSet to which the relation's collection belongs to.
Nested	Gets or sets a value indicating whether relations are nested.
ParentColumns	Gets the parent columns of this relation.
ParentKeyConstraint	Gets the constraint that ensures values in a column are unique.
ParentTable	Gets the parent table of this relation.
RelationName	Gets or sets the name used to retrieve a DataRelation from the DataRelationColleciton.

Methods

Equals	Determines whether the specified object is the same instance as the current object.
GetHashCode	Serves as a hash function for a particular type, suitable for use in hashing algorithms and data structures such as a hash table.

GetType	Gets the type of the object.
ToString	Gets the RelationName, if one exists.

ConstraintCollection Class

Properties

Count	Gets the total number of elements in a collection.
IsReadOnly	Indicates whether the InternalDataCollectionBase is read-only. This property is read-only.
IsSynchronized	Indicates whether the InternalDataCollectionBase is synchronized with the data source. This property is read-only.
Item	Overloaded. Get the specified Constraint from the collection. In C#, this property is the indexer for the ConstraintCollection class.
SyncRoot	Gets an object that can be used to synchronize the collection.

Methods

Add	Overloaded. Adds a Constraint to the ConstraintCollection.
AddRange	Copies the elements of the specified Constraint array to the end of the collection.
CanRemove	Indicates if a Constraint can be removed.
Clear	Clears the collection of any relations.
Contains	Gets a value of true if this collection has a relation with the given name (case insensitive), false otherwise.
CopyTo	Copies all the elements of the current InternalDataCollectionBase to a one-dimensional Array, starting at the specified InternalDataCollectionBase index.
Equals	Determines whether the specified object is the same instance as the current object.
GetEnumerator	Gets an IEnumerator for the collection.

Continued

Constraint Class *Continued*

Properties

GetHashCode	Serves as a hash function for a particular type, suitable for use in hashing algorithms and data structures such as a hash table.
GetType	Gets the type of the object.
Remove	Removes a Constraint from the collection.
RemoveAt	Removes the constraint at the specified index from the collection.
ToString	Returns a string that represents the current object.

Constraint Class

Properties

ConstraintName	The name of a constraint in the ConstraintCollection.
Table	Gets the DataTable to which the constraint applies.

Methods

Equals	Determines whether the specified object is the same instance as the current object.
GetHashCode	Serves as a hash function for a particular type, suitable for use in hashing algorithms and data structures such as a hash table.
GetType	Gets the type of the object.
ToString	Gets the ConstraintName, if there is one, as a string.

DataTableMappingCollectionClass

Properties

Count	Gets the total number of elements in a collection.
Item	Overloaded. Get the specified DataTableMapping from the collection. In C#, this property is the indexer for the DataTableMappingCollection class.

Methods

Add	Overloaded. Adds a DataTableMapping to the DataTableMappingCollection.
AddRange	Copies the elements of the specified DataTableMapping array to the end of the collection.
Clear	Clears the collection of any relations.
Contains	Gets a value of true if this collection has a relation with the given name (case insensitive), false otherwise.
CopyTo	Copies the elements of the DataTableMappingCollection to the specified array.
GetByDataSetTitle	Gets the DataTableMapping object with the specified DataSet table name.
GetHashCode	Serves as a hash function for a particular type, suitable for use in hashing algorithms and data structures such as a hash table.
GetLifetimeService	Retrieves a lifetime service object that controls the lifetime policy for this instance. For the default Lifetime service this will be an object of type ILease.
GetType	Gets the type of the object.
IndexOf	Overloaded. Gets the location of the specified DataTableMapping object within the collection.
IndexOfDataSetTitle	Gets the location of the DataTableMapping object with the specified DataSet table name.
InitializeLifetimeService	Objects can provide their own lease and so control their own lifetime. They do this by overriding the InitializeLifetimeService method provided on MarshalByRefObject.
Insert	Inserts a DataTableMapping object into the DataTableMappingCollection at the specified index.
Remove	Removes a DataTableMapping from the collection.
RemoveAt	Removes the DataTableMapping at the specified index from the collection.
ToString	Returns a string that represents the current object.

DataTableMapping Class

Properties

ColumnMappings	Gets the DataColumnMappingCollection for the DataTable.
DataSetTable	Gets or sets the table name from a DataSet.
SourceTable	Gets or sets the case-sensitive source table name from a data source.

Methods

Equals	Determines whether the specified object is the same instance as the current object.
GetDataTableBySchemaAction	Returns the current DataTable for a given DataSet using the specified MissingSchemaAction.
GetHashCode	Serves as a hash function for a particular type, suitable for use in hashing algorithms and data structures such as a hash table.
GetLifetimeService	Retrieves a lifetime service object that controls the lifetime policy for this instance. For the default Lifetime service this will be an object of type ILease.
GetType	Gets the type of the object.
InitializeLifeTimeService	Objects can provide their own lease and so control their own lifetime. They do this by overriding the InitializeLifetimeService method provided on MarshalByRefObject.
ToString	Converts the current SourceTable name to a string.

Coding Differences in ASP and ASP.NET

Retrieving a Table from a Database

How you did it with VBScript in ASP

```
Function GetStores(stor_id)
    Dim oRS, oConn, oCmd, oParam
    OConn = "provider=sqloledb;Data Source=(local);Initial Catalog=pubs;User
ID=sa;pwd=;"
    Set oCmd = Server.CreateObject("ADODB.Command")
    OCmd.CommandText = "SELECT * FROM Stores WHERE [stor_id]=?"
    OCmd.ActiveConnection = oConn
    Set oParam = oCmd.CreateParameter("stor_id",3,1,,stor_id)
    OCmd.Parameters.Append oParam
    Set oRS = Server.CreateObject("ADODB.Recordset")
    ORS.Open oCmd
    Set GetStores = oRS
End Function
```

How you do it with VB .NET in ASP.NET

```
Function GetStores(stor_id As Integer) As DataSet
    Dim oConn as New OLEDBConnection("provider=sqloledb;Data Source=(local);Initial
Catalog=pubs;User ID=sa;pwd=;")
    Dim oCmd as New OLEDBDataAdapter("SELECT * FROM Stores WHERE [stor_id]=?", oConn)
    Dim oParam as New OLEDBParameter("stor_id",OLEDBType.Integer)
    oParam.Value = stor_id
    oCmd.SelectCommand.Parameters.Add(oParam)
    Dim oDS As New DataSet()
    oCmd.Fill(oDS, "stores")
    Return oDS
End Function
```

How you do it with C# in ASP.NET

```
DataSet GetStores(int stor_id) {
     OleDbConnection oConn = new OleDbConnection("provider=sqloledb;Data
Source=(local);Initial Catalog=pubs;User ID=sa;pwd=;");
     OleDbDataAdapter oCmd = new OleDbDataAdapter("SELECT * FROM Stores WHERE
[stor_id]=?", oConn);
     OleDbParameter oParam = new OleDbParameter("stor_id", OleDbType.Integer);
     oParam.Value = stor_id;
     oCmd.SelectCommand.Parameters.Add(oParam);
     DataSet oDS = new DataSet();
     oCmd.Fill(oDS, "stores");
     return oDS;
}
```

Displaying a Table from a Database

How you did it with VBScript in ASP

```
<%@ LANGUAGE="VBScript" %>
<%
Dim oRS
Function CreateTable(stor_id)
     Set oRS = GetStores(stor_id)
     Do While Not oRS.EOF
          Response.Write("<TABLE>")
          Response.Write("<TR>")
          For Each oField in oRS.Fields
               Response.Write("<TD Align = Center>")
               If isNull(oField) Then
                    Response.Write(" ")
               Else
                    Response.Write(oField.value)
               End If
               Response.Write("</TD>")
          Next
          oRS.moveNext
          Response.Write("</TR>")
     Loop
     Response.Write("</TABLE>")
     ORS.close
     Set oRS = Nothing
End Function

Function GetStores(stor_id)
     Dim oRS, oConn, oCmd, oParam
     OConn = "provider=sqloledb;Data Source=(local);Initial Catalog=pubs;User
ID=sa;pwd=;"
     Set oCmd = Server.CreateObject("ADODB.Command")
     OCmd.CommandText = "SELECT * FROM Stores WHERE [stor_id]=?"
     OCmd.ActiveConnection = oConn
```

```
        Set oParam = oCmd.CreateParameter("stor_id",3,1,,stor_id)
        OCmd.Parameters.Append oParam
        Set oRS = Server.CreateObject("ADODB.Recordset")
        ORS.Open oCmd
        Set GetStores = oRS
End Function
%>
<html>
<body>
<%
CreateTable("7066")
%>
```

How you do it with VB .NET in ASP.NET

```
<%@ Import Namespace="System.Data" %>
<%@ Import Namespace="System.Data.OleDB"%>
<%@ Page Language="VB" Debug="False" Trace="False" %>
<HTML>
    <HEAD>
        <SCRIPT LANGUAGE="vb" RUNAT="server">
        Sub Page_Load(sender as object, e as eventargs)
            CreateTable(7066)
        End Sub
        Function GetStores(stor_id As Integer) As DataSet
            Dim oConn as New OLEDBConnection("provider=sqloledb;Data
Source=(local);Initial Catalog=pubs;User ID=sa;pwd=;")
            Dim oCmd as New OLEDBDataAdapter("SELECT * FROM Stores WHERE [stor_id]=?",
oConn)
            Dim oParam as New OLEDBParameter("stor_id",OLEDBType.Integer)
            oParam.Value = stor_id
            oCmd.SelectCommand.Parameters.Add(oParam)
            Dim oDS As New DataSet()
            oCmd.Fill(oDS, "stores")
            Return oDS
        End Function

        Sub CreateTable(stor_id as Integer)
            Dim oDS As DataSet = GetStores(stor_id)
            grid1.DataSource = oDS.Tables(0).DefaultView
            grid1.DataBind()
        End Sub


        </SCRIPT>
    </HEAD>
    <BODY>
        <FORM RUNAT="server" ID="Form1">
            <ASP:DATAGRID ID="grid1" RUNAT="server" />
        </FORM>
    </BODY>
</HTML>
```

How you do it with C# in ASP.NET

```
<%@ Import Namespace="System.Data.OleDb"%>
<%@ Import Namespace="System.Data"%>
<%@ Page Language="C#" Debug="False" Trace="False" %>
<HTML>
    <HEAD>
        <SCRIPT LANGUAGE="C#" RUNAT="server">
        protected void Page_Load(Object sender, EventArgs E)
        {
            CreateTable(7066);
        }

        void CreateTable(int stor_id)
        {
            DataSet oDS = GetStores(stor_id);
            grid1.DataSource = oDS.Tables[0].DefaultView;
            grid1.DataBind();
        }
        DataSet GetStores(int stor_id) {
            OleDbConnection oConn = new OleDbConnection("provider=sqloledb;Data
Source=(local);Initial Catalog=pubs;User ID=sa;pwd=;");
            OleDbDataAdapter oCmd = new OleDbDataAdapter("SELECT * FROM Stores WHERE
[stor_id]=?", oConn);
            OleDbParameter oParam = new OleDbParameter("stor_id", OleDbType.Integer);
            oParam.Value = stor_id;
            oCmd.SelectCommand.Parameters.Add(oParam);
            DataSet oDS = new DataSet();
            oCmd.Fill(oDS, "stores");
            return oDS;
        }

        </SCRIPT>
    </HEAD>
    <BODY>
        <FORM RUNAT="server" ID="Form1">
            <ASP:DATAGRID ID="grid1" RUNAT="server" />
        </FORM>
    </BODY>
</HTML>
```

Variable Declarations

How you did it with VBScript in ASP

```
Dim x
Dim s
Dim s1,s2
Dim o
Set o = Server.CreateObject("ADODB.Command")
```

How you do it with VB .NET in ASP.NET

```
Dim i As Integer
Dim s As String
Dim s1, s2 As String
Dim o as new OleDbDataAdapter()
```

How you do it with C# in ASP.NET

```
int i;
String s;
String s1, s2;
OleDbDataAdapter o = new OleDbDataAdapter();
```

Statements

How you did it with VBScript in ASP

```
Response.Write("SomeText")
```

How you do it with VB .NET in ASP.NET

```
Response.Write("SomeText")
```

How you do it with C# in ASP.NET

```
Response.Write("SomeText");
```

Comments

How you did it with VBScript in ASP

```
' A One Liner

' Multi-line
' Comment
```

How you do it with VB .NET in ASP.NET

```
' A One Liner

' Multi-line
' Comment
```

How you do it with C# in ASP.NET

```
// A One Liner

/*
Multi-line
Comment
*/
```

Indexed Property Access

How you did it with VBScript in ASP

```
Dim s
Dim s1
s = Request.QueryString("Name")
s1 = Request.Cookies("Key")
```

How you do it with VB .NET in ASP.NET

```
Dim s As String
Dim s1 As String
s = Request.QueryString("Name")
s1 = Request.Cookies("Key").Value
```

How you do it with C# in ASP.NET

```
s= Request.QueryString["Name"];
s1 = Request.Cookies["Name"].Value;
```

Using Arrays

How you did it with VBScript in ASP

```
' One Dimensional Array with 3 elements
Dim x(3)
x(0) = "SomeText1"
```

```
x(1) = "SomeText2"
x(2) = "SomeText3"

' Two Dimensional Array with 3 elements
Dim y(3,3)
y(0,0) = "SomeText1"
y(1,0) = "SomeText2"
y(2,0) = "SomeText3"
```

How you do it with VB .NET in ASP.NET

```
' One Dimensional Array with 3 elements
Dim x(3) As String
x(0) = "SomeText1"
x(1) = "SomeText2"
x(2) = "SomeText3"

' Two Dimensional Array
Dim y(3,3) As String
y(0,0) = "SomeText1"
y(1,0) = "SomeText2"
y(2,0) = "SomeText3"
```

How you do it with C# in ASP.NET

```
// A One Dimensional Array with 3 elements
String[] x = new String[3];
x[0] = "SomeText1";
x[1] = "SomeText2";
x[2] = "SomeText3";

// A Two Dimensional Array with 3 elements
String[,] y = new String[3,3];
y[0,0] = "SomeText1";
y[1,0] = "SomeText2";
y[2,0] = "SomeText3";
```

Initializing Variables

How you did it with VBScript in ASP

```
Dim s
Dim i
Dim a(3)
s = "Hello World"
```

```
i = 1
a(0) = 3.00
a(1) = 4.00
a(2) = 5.00
How you do it with VB.NET in ASP.NET
Dim s As String = "Hello World"
Dim i As Integer = 1
Dim a() As Double = { 3.00, 4.00, 5.00 }
```

How you do it with C# in ASP.NET

```
string s = "Hello World";
int i = 1;
Double[] a ={ 3.00, 4.00, 5.00 };
```

If Statements

How you did it with VBScript in ASP

```
If i = 0 Then
     Response.Write i
elseIf i = 1 Then
     Response.Write i
Else
     Response.Write i
End If
```

How you do it with VB .NET in ASP.NET

```
If i = 0 Then
     Response.Write(i)
elseIf i = 1 Then
     Response.Write(i)
Else
     Response.Write(i)
End If
```

How you do it with C# in ASP.NET

```
if (i==0)
     Response.Write(i);
if (i==1)
     Response.Write(i);
else
     Response.Write(i);
```

Case Statements

How you did it with VBScript in ASP

```
Select Case sStockSymbol
case "MSFT"
    Response.Write("Buy")

case "ORCL"
    Response.Write("Sell")

case else
    Response.Write("Hold")
End Select
```

How you do it with VB .NET in ASP.NET

```
Select (sStockSymbol)
case "MSFT" :
    Response.Write("Buy")

case "ORCL" :
    Response.Write("Sell")

case else :
    Response.Write("Hold")
End Select
```

How you do it with C# in ASP.NET

```
switch (sStockSymbol) {
case "MSFT" :
    Response.Write("Buy");
    break;

case "ORCL" :
    Response.Write("Sell");
    break;

default :
    Response.Write("Hold");
    break;
}
```

For Loops

How you did it with VBScript in ASP

```
Dim i
For i = 0 To 10
     Response.Write "NewValue " & i
Next
```

How you do it with VB .NET in ASP.NET

```
Dim i As Integer
For i = 0 To 10
     Response.Write("NewValue " & i.ToString())
Next
```

How you do it with C# in ASP.NET

```
for (int i=0; i < 10; i++) {
     Response.Write("New Value" + i.ToString());
}
```

While Loops

How you did it with VBScript in ASP

```
Dim i
i = 0
Do While i < 1
     Response.Write(i)
     i = i + 1
Loop
```

How you do it with VB .NET in ASP.NET

```
Dim i As Integer = 0

Do While i < 10
     Response.Write(i.ToString())
     i = i + 1
Loop
```

How you do it with C# in ASP.NET

```
int i = 0;

while (i < 10) {   Response.Write(i.ToString());
     i++;
}
```

String Concatenation

How you did it with VBScript in ASP

```
Dim s1, s2
s2 = "hello"
s2 = s2 & " world"
s1 = s2 & " !!!"
```

How you do it with VB .NET in ASP.NET

```
Dim s1, s2 As String
s2 = "hello"
s2 &= " world"
s1 = s2 & " !!!"
```

How you do it with C# in ASP.NET

```
string s1;
string s2 = "hello";
s2 += " world";
s1 = s2 + " !!!";
```

Error Handling

How you did it with VBScript in ASP

```
Function WriteFile()
    On Error Resume Next
    'Do Something
    'Raise a Fake Error
    Err.Raise(1000)
    if Err.Number=0 Then
        WriteFile="No Errors"
    Else
        WriteFile= Err.Number & " was raised."
    End If
End Function
```

How you do it with VB .NET in ASP.NET

```
Function WriteFile()
    Try
            'Do Something
            'Raise a Fake Error
            Err.Raise(1000)
    Catch
            Return "Error Number " & Err.Number &" was raised."
    End Try
End Function
```

How you do it with C# in ASP.NET

```
public static string WriteFile(){
try{
    /* Do Something to
    Raise Error */
    throw new Exception("1000");
}
catch(Exception e){
    return("Error Number " + e.Message + " was raised");
 }
}
```

Conversion of Variable Types

How you did it with VBScript in ASP

```
Dim i
Dim s
Dim d

i = 3
s = CStr(i)
d = CDbl(s)
```

How you do it with VB .NET in ASP.NET

```
Dim i As Integer
Dim s As String
Dim d As Double

i = 3
s = i.ToString()
d = CDbl(s)
```

How you do it with C# in ASP.NET

```
int i = 10;
string s = i.ToString();
double d = double.Parse(s);
```

Get Up to Speed
in a Weekend!

Index

Continued

Hungry Minds, Inc.
End-User License Agreement

READ THIS. You should carefully read these terms and conditions before opening the software packet(s) included with this book ("Book"). This is a license agreement ("Agreement") between you and Hungry Minds, Inc. ("HMI"). By opening the accompanying software packet(s), you acknowledge that you have read and accept the following terms and conditions. If you do not agree and do not want to be bound by such terms and conditions, promptly return the Book and the unopened software packet(s) to the place you obtained them for a full refund.

1. **License Grant.** HMI grants to you (either an individual or entity) a nonexclusive license to use one copy of the enclosed software program(s) (collectively, the "Software") solely for your own personal or business purposes on a single computer (whether a standard computer or a workstation component of a multi-user network). The Software is in use on a computer when it is loaded into temporary memory (RAM) or installed into permanent memory (hard disk, CD-ROM, or other storage device). HMI reserves all rights not expressly granted herein.

2. **Ownership.** HMI is the owner of all right, title, and interest, including copyright, in and to the compilation of the Software recorded on the disk(s) or CD-ROM ("Software Media"). Copyright to the individual programs recorded on the Software Media is owned by the author or other authorized copyright owner of each program. Ownership of the Software and all proprietary rights relating thereto remain with HMI and its licensers.

3. **Restrictions On Use and Transfer.**

    (a) You may only (i) make one copy of the Software for backup or archival purposes, or (ii) transfer the Software to a single hard disk, provided that you keep the original for backup or archival purposes. You may not (i) rent or lease the Software, (ii) copy or reproduce the Software through a LAN or other network system or through any computer subscriber system or bulletin-board system, or (iii) modify, adapt, or create derivative works based on the Software.

    (b) You may not reverse engineer, decompile, or disassemble the Software. You may transfer the Software and user documentation on a permanent basis, provided that the transferee agrees to accept the terms and conditions of this Agreement and you retain no copies. If the Software is an update or has been updated, any transfer must include the most recent update and all prior versions.

4. **Restrictions on Use of Individual Programs.** You must follow the individual requirements and restrictions detailed for each individual program in Appendix F of this Book. These limitations are also contained in the individual license agreements recorded on the Software Media. These limitations may include a requirement that after using the program for a specified period of time, the user must pay a registration fee or discontinue use. By opening the Software packet(s), you will be agreeing to abide by the licenses and restrictions for these individual programs that are detailed in Appendix F and on the Software Media. None of the material on this Software Media or listed in this Book may ever be redistributed, in original or modified form, for commercial purposes.

5. **Limited Warranty.**

   (a) HMI warrants that the Software and Software Media are free from defects in materials and workmanship under normal use for a period of sixty (60) days from the date of purchase of this Book. If HMI receives notification within the warranty period of defects in materials or workmanship, HMI will replace the defective Software Media.

   (b) **HMI AND THE AUTHOR OF THE BOOK DISCLAIM ALL OTHER WARRANTIES, EXPRESS OR IMPLIED, INCLUDING WITHOUT LIMITATION IMPLIED WARRANTIES OF MERCHANTABILITY AND FITNESS FOR A PARTICULAR PURPOSE, WITH RESPECT TO THE SOFTWARE, THE PROGRAMS, THE SOURCE CODE CONTAINED THEREIN, AND/OR THE TECHNIQUES DESCRIBED IN THIS BOOK. HMI DOES NOT WARRANT THAT THE FUNCTIONS CONTAINED IN THE SOFTWARE WILL MEET YOUR REQUIREMENTS OR THAT THE OPERATION OF THE SOFTWARE WILL BE ERROR FREE.**

   (c) This limited warranty gives you specific legal rights, and you may have other rights that vary from jurisdiction to jurisdiction.

6. **Remedies.**

   (a) HMI's entire liability and your exclusive remedy for defects in materials and workmanship shall be limited to replacement of the Software Media, which may be returned to HMI with a copy of your receipt at the following address: Software Media Fulfillment Department, Attn.: *ASP.NET Database Programming Weekend Crash Course*™, Hungry Minds, Inc., 10475 Crosspoint Blvd., Indianapolis, IN 46256, or call 1-800-762-2974. Please allow four to six weeks for delivery. This Limited Warranty is void if failure of the Software Media has resulted from accident, abuse, or misapplication. Any replacement Software Media will be warranted for the remainder of the original warranty period or thirty (30) days, whichever is longer.

   (b) In no event shall HMI or the author be liable for any damages whatsoever (including without limitation damages for loss of business profits, business interruption, loss of business information, or any other pecuniary loss) arising from the use of or inability to use the Book or the Software, even if HMI has been advised of the possibility of such damages.

   (c) Because some jurisdictions do not allow the exclusion or limitation of liability for consequential or incidental damages, the above limitation or exclusion may not apply to you.

7. **U.S. Government Restricted Rights.** Use, duplication, or disclosure of the Software for or on behalf of the United States of America, its agencies and/or instrumentalities (the "U.S. Government") is subject to restrictions as stated in paragraph (c)(1)(ii) of the Rights in Technical Data and Computer Software clause of DFARS 252.227-7013, or subparagraphs (c) (1) and (2) of the Commercial Computer Software - Restricted Rights clause at FAR 52.227-19, and in similar clauses in the NASA FAR supplement, as applicable.

8. **General.** This Agreement constitutes the entire understanding of the parties and revokes and supersedes all prior agreements, oral or written, between them and may not be modified or amended except in a writing signed by both parties hereto that specifically refers to this Agreement. This Agreement shall take precedence over any other documents that may be in conflict herewith. If any one or more provisions contained in this Agreement are held by any court or tribunal to be invalid, illegal, or otherwise unenforceable, each and every other provision shall remain in full force and effect.